Brief Psychotherapy in Medical and Health Practice

Albert Ellis, Ph.D., distinguished psychotherapist, marriage and family counselor, and exceptionally active writer and lecturer of international prominence, is the founder and executive director of the Institute for Rational-Emotive Therapy in New York City. His widely read contributions in the areas of rational-emotive therapy and sexual fulfillment have established his reputation in and outside professional circles, here and abroad. Dr. Ellis, whose doctorate from Columbia University is in clinical psychology, is the recipient of the Humanist of the Year Award (1973), the Distinguished Professional Psychologist Award of the American Psychological Association, Division of Psychotherapy (1975), and the Distinguished Sex Educator and Counselor Award (1976).

Eliot Abrahms, M.D., a Diplomate of the National Board of Medical Examiners, is a graduate of the University of Pennsylvania and the George Washington University School of Medicine. The first psychiatrist to give a course on rational-emotive therapy at any annual meeting of the American Psychiatric Association, he and Dr. Ellis have coauthored several series of professional tape cassettes.

BRIEF PSYCHOTHERAPY IN MEDICAL AND HEALTH PRACTICE

Albert Ellis, Ph.D.,
and Eliot Abrahms, M.D.

Springer Publishing Company
New York

Springer Publishing Company, Inc.
200 Park Avenue South
New York, N.Y. 10003

78 79 80 81 82 / 10 9 8 7 6 5 4 3 2 1

Library of Congress Cataloging in Publication Data

Ellis, Albert, 1913–
  Brief psychotherapy in medical and health practice.

  Bibliography: p.
  Includes index.
    1. Rational-emotive psychotherapy. 2. Family
medicine. I. Abrahms, Eliot, joint author. II. Title.
[DNLM: 1. Psychotherapy, Brief. WM420.3 E47h]
RC489.R3E43   616.8'914   78-12947
ISBN 0-8261-2640-5
ISBN 0-8261-2641-3 pbk.

Printed in the United States of America

CONTENTS

PREFACE

In reading this book, you will see that rational-emotive therapy (RET) is a comprehensive system of psychotherapy which, though in some ways thoroughgoing and complex, is nonetheless relatively easy to learn and apply. To introduce you to it, let me give an example of someone who has helped himself tremendously through RET methods.

When he was in elementary school, he wrote his school song. And the next year he composed his junior high school song, which is still being used more than twenty years later. When he went to high school, he took several leads in school plays and became a member of the All-State Chorus. He was on the student council throughout high school and assumed several leadership positions in that group. And, with all this, he led a good social life.

He became a tennis star, and State Champion. Later he was named to the regional Junior Davis Cup team and played in the United States Men's Doubles Championships.

Now why do I mention this case? Because this young man kept overgeneralizing—kept thinking to himself, "I'm a good person when I do a good thing." He retained this same philosophy when he went to an Ivy League college and was asked to join the glee club. And he retained it when he became a member of what was touted to be the best fraternity on campus. And also when, through tennis, he won a varsity letter.

He still had the same outlook on life: that when he did a good thing, he amounted to a good person. So, naturally, with this outstanding record of achievements, he felt fine about himself. But, alas, he also subscribed to the other side of the coin: that when he did a bad thing, he amounted to a bad person.

When, years later, some of the things in his life turned out very badly, he went into a period of intense personal distress. So he

went to a psychoanalytically-oriented therapist, who was competent, empathetic, and moderately helpful, and with whom he
mainly discussed his past, especially his mother. He still felt depressed and decided to look for a new therapeutic approach.

So he went to a rational-emotive therapist. During the very first
session he was shown that he had been making himself anxious
and depressed for years, mainly through devoutly believing, and
continuing to tell himself, "Not only do I *want* success in sports, in
music, in social relations, and practically everything else, but I *have
to* have it!" He perked up, realized that his psychoanalytic therapy
really wasn't very effective, and felt that his rational-emotive therapist was right on the nose.

In a remarkably short period of time—literally, a few weeks—
he came to believe in an almost entirely new philosophy of life: to
believe that, "Though it's unfortunate when I don't get what I *want*,
I don't really *need* to get it, and it's not *awful* if I don't—unless I
define it as *awful*."

His mood soon lifted. He came out of his depression and has
not been seriously distressed since that time. Things are still going
well for him and he is continuing to have many successes—as well
as hassles. But now he doesn't stupidly overgeneralize and label
himself a "good person" when he does a "good thing."

Now this is a true story, and I happen to be that man!

Now when I find myself getting somewhat anxious, self-downing, hostile, or depressed, I look for my own self-defeating ideas,
which invariably seem to underlie and create these feelings. And,
as you may soon learn to do with yourself and your patients as you
read this book, I say to myself, "Granted that it's unfortunate when
things go badly for me, why is it *awful*? Prove that I *can't stand* it.
Where is it written that I *must* do better; and why am I a *worm* if I
don't?" Doing this kind of self-questioning, I quickly realize that
there isn't any evidence to support my own irrational beliefs—and I
give them up and no longer feel anxious, hostile, or depressed.

In other words, now I know how to change my *in*appropriate
feelings for appropriate feelings quickly and forthrightly when
things go wrong in my life and I fail to do or get something I
strongly prefer. Instead of feeling *anxious*, I tend to make myself
concerned. Instead of feeling *angry*, I get myself to feel merely *irritated*. And rather than feeling *depressed*, I almost always make myself feel only *sorry* or *disappointed*.

This is the approach I now take with my patients, and with the
world in general. And I also take this approach with myself. And

one of the main reasons I have collaborated on the writing of this book is to try to help you, the reader, help your patients apply the RET approach to their distorted emotions—or even to help you decide that you may want to apply it to yourself and your own self-defeating emotions and behaviors.

While reading this you might incredulously ask yourself, "Is this guy really suggesting that at times I might want to apply rational-emotive therapy techniques to myself?"

My answer is, "Yes!"

Let me, in this connection, quote Dr. Matthew Ross of the University of California, who recently reported at an annual meeting of the American Psychiatric Association that forty-six percent of senior students at one medical school were found to be suffering from major neurotic handicaps. Dr. Ross also said that addiction to narcotics is estimated to be thirty to one hundred times more common among physicians than in the general population, and that about ten percent of physicians in the United States commit suicide! He further added that as many as twenty-three thousand American physicians are, or will become, alcoholics.

Do nurses, too, have similar emotional problems? Most definitely. Nurses, medical technicians, and other health professionals are often anxious, hostile, or depressed. In the atmosphere of the unusual moral, intellectual, physical, and emotional demands of patient care, most of us are quite vulnerable to mental turmoil.

I mainly collaborated on the writing of this book with the hope that it would help you, as a health professional, to deal effectively and efficiently with the psychological distress of your patients—and with the desire that you might exercise the option, as I still do, of using rational-emotive therapy techniques to reduce your *own* emotional upsets and, in that way too, make yourself a more creative, capable medical or health practitioner.

ELIOT ABRAHMS, M.D.
New York, New York

Is Dr. Abrahm's story, as reported above, extraordinary? In some ways, yes. For he not only received rational-emotive therapy when he went through a period of personal turmoil, but he also *worked very hard* at applying it to himself. He thereby, in accordance with RET theory, first largely *made himself* disturbed and then *made him-*

self better. But this kind of *working* at minimizing one's own emotional problems has also been done, as I have seen during the years of my RET practice, by many other individuals. And Dr. Abrahm's story is therefore one that is eminently repeated and repeatable.

Not that all RET patients do work; and not that all who work hard achieve fast or phenomenally good results. By no means! But, as noted in more detail later in this book, because RET is a relatively simple, easily understood, and quite feasible mode of psychotherapy, many determined individuals do work hard at it—and most of them do help themselves significantly. Often, moreover, within a few weeks or months!

Can patients *really* make a profound, elegant, philosophic and behavioral change in their disturbability within a short period of time? Yes, many can; and some do.

I created RET around the beginning of 1955 mainly for efficiency purposes—because the psychoanalytic methods I had been using up to that time were long-winded, tortuous, and only partially effective. Almost immediately, I began to get gratifying results from this new philosophical-behavioral method of relatively brief psychotherapy. At first, I was almost alone in using this kind of active-directive, no-nonsense-about-it approach.

How times have changed! RET is now at the center of the widespread and increasingly popular cognitive-behavior therapy movement. It has been joined or copied by several other schools— including transactional analysis, reality therapy, provocative therapy, personal mastery counseling, and direct decision therapy. Its popularization, in books like Dyer's *Your Erroneous Zones,* Hauck's *Overcoming Depression,* Powell's *Fully Human, Fully Alive,* and Ellis and Harper's *A New Guide to Rational Living,* has made it familiar to almost every reader of self-help books. Good!

Perhaps my greatest satisfaction, however, comes from seeing many people, such as Dr. Abrahms, use it on themselves, with amazingly good, quickly achieved results. And, of course, I take great pleasure in seeing them go one step further, especially when they are psychotherapists or health professionals, and use it effectively with others.

So, as Dr. Abrahms says above, may you decide to use RET. Try it. Try it with yourself and your patients. Both you and they may well get satisfying results. Try it and see!

ALBERT ELLIS, PH.D.
Institute for Rational-Emotive Therapy
New York, New York

Brief Psychotherapy in Medical and Health Practice

1

Introduction: Health Problems and Emotional Disturbance

A 29-year-old secretary came to her doctor complaining of headaches and fatigue. The headaches, which lasted through the day and went away after work each evening, had started three months before when she heard that all the secretaries in her firm would be evaluated for promotion during the next six months.

An obese 45-year-old housewife came to the doctor complaining of chronic thirst, excessive liquid intake, and frequent urination. After appropriate tests, she was given a diagnosis of diabetes. She became very upset, cried, and said she could not go on, since she could never live a normal life again.

A 58-year-old accountant became anxious and depressed following a mild heart attack. He blamed himself for having gone off his diet and for smoking too much. He told a nurse that he often thought he would be better off dead.

On and on it goes; estimates are that up to 50 percent of the patients seen by physicians have some emotional distress that

The authors wish to acknowledge Patrick Huyghe for editorial help in preparing this volume.

does not stem directly from any organic ailment. At the same time, many physical disorders, such as peptic ulcers, asthma, or hypertension, have a strong psychosomatic element, and would either not exist or be much less serious without correlated emotional upsetability.

According to some medical authorities, many of the complications and exacerbations of illness stem from emotional reactions to events that occur in the course of everyday living. According to this view, it is not a question of whether, but rather to what extent, a patient's illness is organic or functional. All sickness is a combination of both, in varying proportions.

When ill or injured, people simultaneously tend to experience psychological changes of different degrees of intensity. These changes are sometimes more crucial than the ailment itself, and frequently give patients the primary motivation to seek medical treatment. It is well known that many patients (And we do not only mean young children!) are more frightened than sick and that, when they are assured that their physical disorder is not serious, their emotional relief enables them to reduce their complaints to a minimum.

Most health professionals are quite aware that their training has not equipped them to treat emotional disorders with the same degree of competence with which they can deal with physical illness. Understandably many of them feel unprepared, even afraid, to approach their patients' problems even when these are only mildly psychiatric.

Also, most health professionals simply do not have the time they once had to sit and discuss their patients' personal problems. Auntie Sara can no longer wander unscheduled into her friendly family doctor's office and chat about the difficulties of her everyday life. And nurses' time is at a premium, these days, often limited by their many different responsibilities.

Many of today's physicians, nurses, and other health professionals believe that they had better be equipped to help alleviate their patients' anxieties. Many, in fact, believe that relieving anxiety and depression is almost their first order of business. Unfortunately, they also realize that they often can do little in this respect but place many of their patients on drugs that are potentially addicting.

If a 54-year-old man suffers a coronary when he hears that his property tax is about to be raised—?

If a 17-year-old male weeps over a flare-up of acne—?

If a 38-year-old woman shouts at her husband when she has a recurrence of back pain—?

If a 66-year-old female on Hydrodiuril becomes dizzy when her social security check is delayed—?

What can you, as a health care professional, do in cases like these, where an emotional disturbance is linked to a health problem? The answer we shall give in this book is: You can learn to use rational-emotive therapy (RET) or cognitive-behavior therapy (CBT). For RET is a direct, clear-cut, relatively brief form of psychological treatment that practically every physician, nurse, or other health professional can master with a moderate amount of additional training and that can be used effectively in the vast majority of emotional disorders. Specifically, it is designed to be a form of psychological intervention that is a treatment of choice for intense and deep-seated feelings of anxiety, depression, inadequacy, hostility, and low frustration tolerance. It will not cure every known psychiatric illness, certainly not such serious disorders as schizophrenia and manic-depressive illness. But it can help appreciably even patients who have these most severe kinds of disturbances; it can help immensely with individuals with less serious disorders.

Your patients, we are sure, frequently upset themselves about such health conditions as heart problems, strokes, arthritis, backaches, skin disorders, gynecologic ailments, surgical problems, and malignancies. They also tend to disturb themselves about ophthalmologic conditions, hematologic disorders, nutritional deficiencies, and a wide range of other pathologies. But although these diseases and ailments cover a broad spectrum of physical malfunctioning, we have found that using the insights of rational-emotive therapy accompanying emotional difficulties are often remarkably similar, can be fundamentally understood in an amazingly short period of time, and can be effectively minimized by RET-oriented practitioners.

RET

RET can be used to help patients overcome their inappropriate feelings and behaviors in a reasonably brief time because it is an approach which, on the one hand, is comprehensive and multimodal; that is, it employs several cognitive, emotive, and behavioral methods in an integrative way. But it is also, on the other hand, a philosophic, theory-based therapy that seeks out people's fundamental disturbance-creating beliefs that seem to underlie their self-defeating actions; and it forthrightly shows these people how to zero in on their self-sabotaging philosophies and how to quickly begin to uproot them. It is a hard-headed, no cop-out, active-directive therapy. And its basic theory and practice can be learned by most professionals by reading, by listening to tapes of actual sessions, and by taking workshops and courses sponsored in various parts of the world by the Institute for Rational-Emotive Therapy, which has its main training institute and clinic in New York City.

There is no mystique in the rational-emotive approach to psychiatric disorders. Its language is simple—only everyday terms are used. It is often called a "common sense" method. Its techniques are easily applied by family practitioners, pediatricians, medical or surgical specialists, nurses, and other health professionals.

You may ask, of course: "Why RET, instead of one of the other more conventional modes of psychotherapy?" We would answer: "Because RET is especially designed for therapeutic efficiency, and because it particularly encourages relatively short-term therapy. It does so, as will be seen in the various chapters of this book, by stressing directness, a high degree of activity by the therapist, bibliotherapy, and specific homework assignments for patients to perform in between the RET sessions.

Rational-emotive therapy or cognitive-behavior therapy also—as indicated in detail in the *Handbook of Rational-Emotive Therapy* (Springer Publishing Co., 1977) edited by Albert Ellis and Russell Grieger—has not only demonstrated considerable clinical effectiveness, but is backed by a vast amount of experimental research. It is fast becoming an important part of modern scientific psychotherapy. We therefore think that the time has arrived for a presentation of its main principles and practices to those who usually are the first to see the great majority of people with emotional problems, namely, the physicians, nurses, and other health specialists to whom patients originally reveal their emotional problems.

Here, then, is an exposition of the main theories and procedures of RET, which we hope you can use to understand yourself, your patients, and others with whom you associate. As a health professional, you will inevitably be called upon to do some psychotherapy. We hope that the material in this book helps you do so with a considerable degree of clarity and effectiveness.

2
Self-acceptance and Illness

One of the most valuable of all human traits for the healthy, ill, or physically handicapped individual is full self-acceptance. But even the healthy person rarely knows what this kind of self-acceptance is, or how he or she can achieve it.

This is hardly strange, for few psychotherapists clearly define self-acceptance. They confuse and confound it with such terms as "self-confidence," "self-esteem," "self-approval," "self-love," and other traits that in some respects are almost the opposite of true self-acceptance.

Unconditional self-acceptance—or what Carl Rogers calls unconditional positive regard—means that you fully accept *yourself*, your *existence*, your *aliveness*, without any requirements or conditions whatever. But what we usually call "self-confidence" or "self-esteem" is a highly *conditional* form of acceptance. You have confidence in yourself or esteem yourself, because you have a specific reason for doing so, because you do something *well* or *outstandingly*. And if you esteem yourself for this kind of reason, you lose your confidence or esteem just as soon as you begin to function poorly.

RET, almost from its beginnings, has distinguished work-confidence (or achievement-confidence) and love-confidence, on the one hand, from self-confidence, on the other. Work-confidence exists when you tell yourself, "I have succeeded at this task before—and therefore am confident that I can succeed at it again." Love-confidence stems from convincing yourself, "I have won people's approval before, and I am pretty sure that I can win more approval again." Neither work-confidence nor love-confidence, however, give you *self*-confidence, since you still can wind up with the underlying irrational Belief, "If I lose the ability to work well or am no longer able to win people's approval, I fall back to being a pretty worthless individual. For only by *achieving* and by *winning* love do I continue to be of real value." Self-confidence, however, means, "I am determined *always* to accept myself, *whether or not* I do well or win people's approval."

You achieve self-confidence *not* by accomplishing anything or succeeding at love but by *pure choice.* You accept yourself merely by *choosing* to accept yourself; you do not require any special *reason* to do so. In recent years, many RET-oriented professionals have dropped the term "self-confidence" (along with "self-esteem," "self-love," and "self-approval") because they all imply that you must rate or measure your*self* by some kind of *performance.* And if you fail to perform well later, you will tend to hate yourself.

Rational-emotive therapists, therefore, now talk about self-acceptance or self-choosing because these terms do not stand for any self-rating or self-judgment. For humans are infinitely complex; their lives are an ongoing process that consists of thousands (perhaps millions) of acts, deeds, and performances. It is therefore virtually impossible to give a person a rating that says you *are* "good," "bad," or "indifferent." Your health, tennis game, appearance, or almost any other trait may be justifiably rated or assessed. But even if we knew what the ratings of all these traits were—and what they would continue to be in the future, how could we possibly get a single rating of *you, yourself,* or your *being?*

To make things worse, self-ratings lead to deification and devil-ification: because the main reason you want to say, "I am good because I have done this and that good thing," is to prove that you are a better person than someone else, and, in fact, better than *anyone.* And the real reason that you keep saying, "I am bad because I have these and those poor traits," is that you believe that you *should* and *must* do well and if you do not do what you *must,* you are worse than others, and perhaps worse than everyone else.

In the first edition of *A Guide to Rational Living,* I [A.E.] and Robert A. Harper gave an inelegant solution to the problem of ego or human worth. We said that you could help your patients rate their traits, deeds, and performances but not *themselves*. And if they insisted on giving themselves, their totality, any "worth" or "value," they could philosophize: "I am good not because I do well or am loved by others, but merely because I am alive. My goodness is my aliveness. Period."

This is a highly practical solution to the problem of human worth, because it sets up a simple standard of human "value" that is not dependent on anything your patients do or on anyone's opinion of their traits. Since they will only have value or worth while they are alive, and since they will not ask themselves, once they are dead, anything at all about their worth, they will always, by this practical standard, be "good," "valuable," or "worthy." A truly safe standard of self-judgment!

More recent RET writings—especially, *Humanistic Psychotherapy: the Rational-Emotive Approach, How to Live With—and Without—Anger*, and the *Handbook of Rational-Emotive Therapy*—have brought forth a more elegant solution to the problem of human worth. For philosophically, it is illegitimate to say, "I am good because I am alive," or "I am a worthy person because I exist." Why? Because this is a tautological and definitional statement and can never be proven or disproven. In terms of its "validity," you could just as well say, "I am bad because I am alive," and that would also be definitional and unprovable. Consequently, if you want a more elegant solution, you had better refrain from rating your *self* at all and *only* evaluate your traits, deeds, characteristics, and performances.

Thus, if your patients doubt their essential value or worth as humans, you could teach them justifiably to say to themselves: "First, I am alive. That is fairly evident and observable. Second, I choose to stay alive. Why? Simply because I choose to do so. Third, I desire, while alive, to live fairly happily, with relatively little pain and much pleasure. Because that seems conducive to my staying alive—and because I simply like being happy rather than miserable. Fourth, let me see how I can manage to decrease my pain and increase my short-range and long-range pleasure."

With this kind of view, your patients can then rate their traits in regard to how well they help them to obtain aliveness and happiness. They would never have to rate *themselves*, their *being*, at all! Or, putting it another way, you can help them always accept themselves, their aliveness, their existence, and be determined to get as much joy as feasible, no matter how "good" or "bad" are their traits. They can, of course, *prefer* to have certain highly rated or "good" abilities because such characteristics would often bring them increased pleasure. But they would not *need* to have these "good" abilities in order to feel "worthwhile."

RET and cognitive-behavior therapists tend to view this kind of full acceptance of life and the firm determination to enjoy it in the here and now as well as in the future as self-acceptance or self-choosing. These are more neutral terms than self-esteem or self-love because they do not imply any ego-rating. Although terms such as "I like myself" and "I have great ego-strength" seem fine on the surface, they are actually dangerous. For if your patients have a "good ego," this really means that they are rating themselves, not merely their traits and performances. In time, they may well wind up with a "poor ego," or rate themselves poorly. Whenever they invent mythical ego-heavens, they almost invariably also invent mythical ego-hells. It would be better if they merely accepted themselves and did not rate their being or essence at all.

We believe that even the phrases "accept yourself" and "self-acceptance" are limited and inaccurate because people's "self" or "ego" are not easily definable, any more than their "soul" or "spirit." To help your patients, therefore, you encourage them to neither accept nor condemn their "selves." Instead, try to help them accept the fact that they exist and have various traits, and that they can accept their existence, even when their traits are "poor" or "undesirable."

When your patients engage in this kind of "self-acceptance" they will more easily admit the undesirability of many of their traits and attempt to change these for the "better." And they can still accept their existence or aliveness, in spite of some of their deplorable behavior. Physically handicapped or ill people had better especially accept themselves in this sense, since they usually have traits and behaviors that they do *not* want to accept, such as mangled limbs, malfunctioning digestive tracts, high blood pressure, etc. Consequently, they had better work hard at minimizing or eliminating some of these ailments, but are unlikely to do this if they waste time and energy berating them*selves* for having them. If someone *is* a worm for doing a wrong, self-defeating act, how can a worm act unwormily and undefeatingly in the future?

Attempts at ego inflation may also sabotage good health. Sick or handicapped individuals had better follow hygienic and medical disciplines for practical reasons, and not because they will pat themselves on the back and consider themselves "good persons" if they become disciplined. If they have dire needs for others' approval, that could also tend to interfere with their own health regimens. They will foolishly drink, overeat, smoke, take drugs, or do other self-sabotaging acts because others urge them to do so.

Does not a powerful ego drive serve as one of the chief motivations to good health? Not exactly; although many people exercise, lose weight, or have operations for egoistic reasons, just as many or more neglect health-preserving actions because they are too perfectionistic, too anxious, or too depressed to take proper care of themselves. Look, for example, at the large number of self-lambasting, anxious individuals who avoid dental appointments, eat improper foods, and refuse to exercise.

How can you help your patients to be more self-accepting and much less self-damning? Mainly, as we shall keep showing in this book, by teaching them how to surrender their inordinate needs to do well and to win the approval of others. Not to surrender their desires to achieve and to lovingly relate; but to stop escalating these desires into overwhelming demands, commands, and insistences. To want to do well and to want to get along beautifully with others enables humans to live and to enjoy. But to absolutely *need* these desiderata—that is quite another thing!

To be more specific, here is a case in point. A 29-year-old chronic schizophrenic, whom I [E.A.] shall call Ray, felt ashamed and depressed about his severe disorder. He had good insight, realized that he had to take medication to stay out of the hospital, and took his prescribed pills regularly. But he was very depressed about taking medication. He felt depressed about being "different," and kept putting himself down.

"Why do I have to take those crummy pills?" he complained. "I can see that the doctors are right. I know that the drugs stop me from hearing voices. And I'm sure I'd be back in the hospital if I stopped taking my medicine. So I take the pills. But I think *it's terrible* to take them!"

"Why is it terrible to take medication?" I asked him.

"Because I have to remember to take it, and I have to take time to see you for appointments—and sometimes I get side effects from the medicine."

"And that's why it's *inconvenient* for you to take the pills. That's a rational Belief—'I don't like to take the pills because I find some of their effects unpleasant.' If you stayed only with that rational Belief—that taking medication is *inconvenient* or *unfortunate*—how would you feel?"

"I'd feel less depressed."

"Yes. You'd probably, if you only stressed the inconvenience or unfortunateness of taking the pills, feel sorry, or sad, or regretful about taking them. And that would be okay, or what we call 'appropriate' in RET. For if you find something inconvenient, you certainly don't want to feel *good* about it! So when you feel depressed, you really have *two* feelings: first the appropriate feeling of sorrow or regret, because you don't *like* to take the pills and yet you know that you'd better take them; and second, the inappropriate feeling of depression. And this second feeling, your inappropriate feeling, doesn't come from the rational Belief, 'I don't like to take the pills because I find some of their effects unpleasant.' It comes, instead, from a second belief, or what we call an irrational Belief in RET. What do you think your irrational Belief is?"

I was tempted to give Ray the answer right away. For in RET, the therapist usually knows or can easily figure out what the patient's irrational Beliefs are, and can easily make the patient aware of them. But I thought that if Ray could figure this out for himself, in the modified Socratic dialogue he was having with me, he would be better equipped, when I wasn't around to help him, to understand his irrational Beliefs and to learn to question and dispute them on his own. My leading him to question himself in this manner, however, is by no means the only way I could have helped him: since many health professionals have found that giving patients RET-oriented readings or giving them a "mini-lecture" during the initial therapy sessions also effectively helps them to understand what they are telling themselves and how to Dispute their irrationalities.

After about a half a minute of my remaining quiet, Ray answered: "The irrational Belief that causes me to be depressed? I guess, '*It's terrible* to take the pills!' "

"That's exactly right," I responded. "When you say to yourself, irrationally, 'It's *awful, horrible,* or *terrible*' to do anything, such as take pills, you're really creating your own depression."

"Then what do I do to feel better about myself?" he asked.

"First, understand exactly what you are telling yourself irrationally, in the manner that we're now going over it; and then give up these irrational ideas."

Whereupon I explained more fully to him the A-B-C-D-E's of RET. At point A, an Activating Experience, he was observing that he had schizophrenic reactions and that it was good for him to take pills to rid himself, at least temporarily, of some of his symptoms.

At point rB, he had a rational Belief, "I don't like to take the pills because I find some of their effects unpleasant." At point C, his emotional Consequence, he first had an appropriate set of emotions or feelings, which consisted of sadness, sorrow, or regret.

In addition, however, he had another set of irrational Beliefs (iB's) at point B: "I *must* not have to take pills and experience their side effects in order to feel good. It's *terrible* to have to take them. I *can't stand* being inconvenienced in this way! I think I'm a pretty *rotten person* if I have to take pills like this when others do not have to take them!" These irrational Beliefs were really causing his depression. And if he would Dispute them, at point D, and ask himself such questions as: "Where is the evidence that I *must* not take pills and experience their side effects in order to feel good? Why is it *terrible* to have to take them? Can I truly not *stand* this inconvenience? How does it make me a *rotten person* if I have to take pills like this when others do not have to take them?" he would then tend to give up these irrational Beliefs, stop making himself feel inappropriately depressed, and go back to merely feeling appropriately sorry and sad about his mental disturbance and the inconveniences of dealing with it.

So I showed Ray how he was strongly indoctrinating himself with irrational (as well as rational) Beliefs about his schizophrenic condition, and how he could Dispute them and change them. "First," I said, "you can teach yourself to accept yourself unconditionally, *with* your imperfections—including the imperfection of having an emotional disturbance and of requiring medication to keep it under control. Then you can work on that emotional disturbance itself, and quite probably reduce it. But if you don't accept yourself *with* your difficulties, you will only depress yourself, as you are now doing, and thereby significantly *add* to these difficulties."

In spite of his severe problems, Ray was able to see this and to stop downing himself for having schizophrenic reactions and for taking pills to cope with these reactions. He also was able to work to some degree in overcoming his secondary symptoms of castigating himself about his depression. For, like many disturbed people, he first had a symptom—chronic schizophrenia—and severely condemned himself for having it and made himself depressed about it. He then had a secondary symptom (depression), and, very typically, he put himself down for that symptom, too, and wound up with still another symptom: depression about his depression. I showed him, therefore, how he could first accept himself with his schizophrenia and his pill-taking; then accept himself with his secondary symptom, depression, and not condemn himself for bringing on that feeling, and, finally, accept himself with his depression about his depression, if he continued to make himself depressed about feeling depressed. On all three of these levels, he learned to see that his symptom, trait, or characteristic was inconvenient or disadvantageous, but that *he* was not a worthless individual for having such a trait.

"You mean," he said to me at one point, "I had better *just* accept my depression?"

"On the contrary," I replied. "What you had better do is to accept yourself fully *with* your self-defeating symptoms, such as your depression. But once you accept *you* with *it*, it would be far better if you work like hell to minimize or eliminate *it*. When you are castigating yourself for *being* depressed, you are mainly into your own navel and do not have much time and energy to do anything about the depression. But once you stop putting yourself down for your symptom, we hope, in RET, that you will then work very hard to remove the symptom—the depression."

"You think that my overgeneralization about myself stops me from working against my depressed symptom?"

"Yes. When you think of yourself as a 'depressed person' or as a 'rotten person for having a depression,' you are seriously overgeneralizing. Actually, you're a *person* with a *trait* of depression. And when you accept you, your total personhood, with your undesirable traits or aspects, such as your depression, you will be quite able to acknowledge the undesirable nature of these traits or aspects and to work hard at changing them."

Ray had been recording our sessions on a cassette recorder, and he kept playing them back to himself a number of times during the next few weeks. Apparently with good results. I saw him several times during the next year, and he seemed much more self-accepting than before. While he continued to strongly dislike his schizophrenia and its associated problems, he was much more able to accept *himself* with this disorder, to minimize his self-downing about it, and to enjoy himself to some degree in spite of his limitations.

3
The A-B-C Theory of RET and Health-related Problems

There are two kinds of psychotherapy: scientific and nonscientific. In the latter kind, therapists set up hypotheses about the way people act and how some of their dysfunctional acts can be changed; and they become quite convinced that a certain method of change, called a therapeutic system, works effectively. But only in scientific therapy do they really check their hypotheses, do controlled experiments to show whether or not people who undertake their form of therapy actually improve, and if they improve more than people who undergo another form of treatment. They keep checking these hypotheses, to see whether further evidence supports or denies them.

Rational-emotive therapy not only attempts to be scientific in the sense just described and to put its theories on the line for empirical confirmation or disconfirmation, but it also teaches patients to do the same thing about their theories about themselves and others; to question their own ideas, to discover which lead to "good" or self-helping results, and to discard those that lead to "bad" or self-defeating consequences. One of the main essences of RET, therefore, consists of establishing what peoples' irrational Beliefs (or hypotheses) about themselves and others are, and then

Disputing these hypotheses if they seem to be producing poor emotional and behavioral Consequences.

At the same time that it heavily emphasizes cognitive and philosophic analysis, RET also constitutes a comprehensive approach to psychological treatment, in that it specifically and heavily employs emotive and behavioral methods that help people see their irrational Beliefs and that aid them in Disputing and surrendering these ideas. For it assumes that people make themselves disturbed in complex (i.e., cognitive, emotive, and behavioral) ways; therefore no simple way exists in which they can help themselves to become less disturbed. What we call their psychological problems mainly arise from misperceptions and misconceptions about what happens to them at point A (Activating Events or Activating Experiences). But these problems also consist of emotional underreactions or overreactions to these Activating Experiences; they also comprise habitually dysfunctional behavior patterns, such as their addictions to health-destroying acts (e.g., overeating and smoking) and their avoidance of health-abetting acts (e.g., cleaning their teeth and going for regular dental and medical examinations). Because "disturbance" includes cognitive, emotive, and behavioral elements, RET provides a multifaceted analysis and attack on these elements, and is almost invariably a CEB (cognitive-emotive-behavioral) approach to therapy.

From a cognitive or philosophic standpoint, RET starts with the assumption or hypothesis that what we call our emotional Consequences (point C) or reactions stem mainly from our conscious and unconscious Beliefs (point B), or from our evaluations, interpretations, and philosophies about what happens to us at point A (Activating Experiences). This is the A-B-C system of personality formation and change which RET has now made somewhat famous. When, at point A, we fall ill, fail at a major task, or are rejected by some person whom we consider significant, and we feel anxious or depressed at point C (Consequence), A may seem directly to cause or lead to C. Actually, however, it is B (our Belief System) that directly makes us anxious or depressed, though A may have also contributed. B consists of, first, a set of rational Beliefs (rB's), such as "How annoying to be ill! I wish that I were really healthy and find it highly unpleasant to be plagued with this illness!" and, more importantly, a set of irrational Beliefs (iB's), such as, "I *must* not be ill, and *have to* get my health back easily and quickly! It's *terrible* and *catastrophic* if I do not!"

Dynamics of RET

RET stems from the stoical schools of philosophy, which seem to have originated some 2500 years ago: especially the Buddhist schools of the East and Stoic schools of the Greeks and Romans in the West. Perhaps even stronger than these schools, RET holds that there are virtually no "legitimate" reasons for people, including your health-care patients, to make themselves emotionally upset, hysterical, or seriously disturbed, no matter what kind of unpleasant stimuli are impinging on them at point A. Unlike some of the Eastern and Stoic schools, however, RET encourages people to feel strong appropriate emotions such as sorrow, regret, displeasure, annoyance, rebellion, and determination to change—when they experience poor health or other unpleasant Activating Experiences. But it contends that when they experience certain dysfunctional or self-defeating emotions at point C (Consequence) such as guilt, depression, worthlessness, or rage, they are acting and feeling inappropriately; these inappropriate emotions stem largely from anti-empirical and unverifiable hypotheses, that things *must* or *ought to* be different from the way they indubitably are.

You can employ RET with almost any type of person that, as a doctor, nurse, or other health care professional, you are likely to see, including those who are mildly disturbed (are "neurotic" or have "behavior problems") and those who are more seriously disturbed (are diagnosed as "schizophrenic," "borderline psychotic," having a "character disorder," or as moderately "mentally deficient"). By using rational-emotive therapy, you are provided with a structured and workable theory, and you can quickly see the few central irrational Beliefs (iB's) with which your patients foolishly upset themselves; can show these patients how they are mainly causing their own emotional problems and symptoms; demonstrate precisely how they can Dispute (at point D) their own irrational Beliefs; and can often induce them to surrender these ideas and replace them with more scientifically testable hypotheses about themselves and the world that are much less likely to get them into emotional difficulties in the present and future.

We may summarize the cognitive part of the theory and practice of RET as follows: At point A, your patients have an Activating Experience (or Agent or Action) about which they become disturbed (at point C). Example: A woman goes for her yearly physical examination and, after appropriate tests are made, is told by her physician that she may possibly have early cancer of the cervix. At point B (Belief System), she first has a set of rational Beliefs (rB's) about this Activating Experience (A). Example: she believes or tells herself, "It would be unfortunate if I do have cervical cancer. I certainly wouldn't like that!" This Belief is rational because your patient comes to A, her Activating Experience, with distinct goals and values, including the strong desire or wish to remain alive and to be happy and avoid needless pain. She therefore would hardly be rational or realistic if she thought, "How great it would be to discover that I have cancer of the cervix or am otherwise unhealthy!"

But your patient also has another set of irrational Beliefs (iB's) at point B, such as: "I *must* not have a serious ailment, such as cervical cancer! How *awful* this would be! I *could not stand* such an eventuality!" These Beliefs are irrational because: (1) There is no reason why she *must not, should not* have cancer, though there are several reasons why this would be highly unfortunate and against her basic goals and values. (2) It would not be utterly *awful* if she did have cancer, since "awful" normally means *totally* inconvenient or *more than* unfortunate. And even if she did have this kind of serious ailment, she could still cope with it, and could still have some distinct amount of happiness in her remaining life (which actually might be a fairly long one). (3) She certainly could *stand,* though she hardly would *like,* an undesirable state like cervical cancer. But she could cope with it and probably conquer it. And even if, at the very worst, she finally died of this kind of condition (which today is highly unlikely but still within the realm of probability), she could *stand* dying.

In having these irrational Beliefs (iB's), moreover, this patient is *demanding* or *commanding,* rather than strongly *wishing* or *prefering,* that she be in good health. And her demands or commands, rather than help her cope with the possibility of ill health, will help make her seriously disturbed, or "sicker" than she need be.

If your patient stayed with her rational Beliefs (rB's) that she be healthy, she would wind up with rational Consequences (rC's) such as legitimate *concern* that she remain healthy and without cancer. Thus, she would believe, "It would be unfortunate if I were ill," and she would feel determined to try to keep healthy. If by chance her medical examination and diagnostic tests indicated actual cervical cancer, she would feel exceptionally disappointed, displeased, and regretful about these tests; and her feelings and actions would be highly appropriate to her goals of remaining alive and happy about her situation that is occuring at point A (Activating Experiences). These appropriate feelings would help her cope with whatever happens to her at A.

She would not, instead, experience inappropriate Consequences (iC's), such as anxiety, self-pity, depression, or rage; and she would not tend to develop dysfunctional psychosomatic reactions, such as high blood pressure or ulcers. She would also not tend to feel defensive, fail to see her own health care mistakes (such as avoiding a medical examination for a long period of time). Nor would she become preoccupied with the "hopelessness" of having cancer and refuse to go through with the appropriate actions of doing something about it.

She would not, in other words, have what we call disturbed, neurotic, or overreactive symptoms or inappropriate Consequences (iC's)—inappropriate because they would not help her cope with her Activating Experiences at point A but would have appropriate Consequences (aC's) that would help her cope with cervical cancer, if she actually had it. Her rational Beliefs (rB's), "It is highly unfortunate, but *only* unfortunate, that I am ill," tend to help her meet her basic values or goals—those of staying alive and of being as happy as she can feasibly be while she is alive.

If you, as this woman's physician, nurse, or other health care professional, clearly see her A-B-C's and actively encourage her to look for her irrational Beliefs at B, you can then show her (and your other patients) how to continue to work with her D-E's, and really help herself in the process.

In this particular case, the patient's D-E's would be as follows: At point D, which stands for Disputing, you show her how to discover, debate, and discriminate among her iB's (irrational Beliefs). In this respect, you teach her the scientific method, for in science we set up a hypothesis, and then we ask questions about it: "Where is the evidence that it is true (or not true)? Prove that it is so. Where is it written that things would work out the way that the hypothesis says? Why is it true or false?" In RET, you teach people to ask about their own irrational Beliefs (iB's), pretty much the same scientifically oriented or empirically and logically oriented questions. Thus, this woman is irrationally believing: "I *must* not have a serious ailment, such as cervical cancer! How awful this would be! I *could not stand* such an eventuality."

You therefore can help her to Dispute these irrational Beliefs as follows: "Where is the evidence that you *must* not have a serious ailment, such as cervical cancer?" "If you did have cancer, why would that be *awful?* Where is it written that you *could not stand* such an eventuality, if it occurred?"

At point E, or new Effect of Disputing her irrational Beliefs (iB's), this patient is likely to have, first, a philosophic or cognitive Effect (cE): "There is of course no evidence that I *must* not have a serious ailment, such as cancer. There is much evidence, considering the nature of cancer and considering that I would very much prefer to live and be without pain, that my having such an ailment would be highly unfortunate and disadvantageous. But if I have it, then I *must* have it; and there is no law of the universe that says that I *must* not suffer hardship just because I do not *want* to have it."

Further: "It wouldn't be *awful* if I had cervical cancer. For *awful* really means more *than bad* or *worse than* extremely inconvenient; and nothing can be in that extra-bad category. I definitely would find it quite disadvantageous to have cancer. But with it, I could still lead a reasonably happy life—and probably even conquer it completely, given the proper gynecological care. At the very worst, however, I could not conquer it and would die. And even *that* would only be very unfortunate, but hardly *more than* that!"

And still further: "I *can* stand having cervical cancer (or some other kind of serious ailment)! Hearing that I have it certainly won't destroy me—though I could foolishly destroy myself if I keep telling myself nonsense about it. Poor health of this kind probably won't kill me; and even if it does, I could *stand* dying. Obviously, I can *stand* virtually anything that happens to me, even though I clearly won't *like* it. And if I decide to stand it, then I can again lead a reasonably good life, though not *as* good as I would lead if I had perfectly good health."

In this manner, you can help your patient with a fear of cervical cancer to Dispute (at point D) her irrational Beliefs (iB's) until she replaces them with a new cognitive Effect (cE) that harks back to her original rational Beliefs (rB's) and even goes beyond them. For, ideally, her new philosophy can be a more general and future-oriented view along these lines: "Yes, it really would be quite unfortunate if I got cancer, and certainly if I died of it. But since I am a mortal human who will always be heir to various kinds of weaknesses, I damned well could be afflicted with a serious illness like this. The chances are that I won't be; and that even if I am, I will recover. But if I am, I am! There are no *guarantees* that I will never be struck with a serious disease like cervical cancer. And I do not need such guarantees to lead a happy life. Whatever occurs, I shall do my best to meet and conquer. So let me, therefore, do what I can to find out whether I have this ailment and to see what I can do about it in case I do have it."

In this manner, you can help your patient Dispute her irrational beliefs until she not only temporarily conquers them, and gets rid of her current symptoms of anxiety, depression, or self-pity but also has considerably less of a tendency to recreate them in the future when she is again beset by some possible or actual physical ailment. For the more vigorous and persistent Disputing that she does, at point D, the more she will prepare herself to rationally meet future negative contingencies that arise in her life.

You can also, at the same time, help her dispute her irrational self-downing philosophies. In the illustration we gave, there was at first little or none of this since most people do not condemn themselves when they are afflicted with cancer or any serious ailment that they do not specifically bring on themselves (such as, for example, cirrhosis of the liver, which they can bring on by excessive drinking). So this patient would not be prone to put herself down for her possible affliction.

However, if she worried about having cervical cancer, knew that she was being foolish in worrying that much about it, and then continued to worry, she would create for herself a new Activating Experience at point A—her worry or anxiety itself. Then, at point B, she would rationally tell herself, "I don't like my worrying this much. I wish I didn't!" but she could also irrationally tell herself, "I *must* not worry this much. It's *terrible* that I do! What a stupid and rotten person I am for behaving so foolishly!" If so, her emotional Consequence, at point C, would be anxiety *about* anxiety; and it would also consist of self-downing or guilt or depression. In which case you could again encourage her to Dispute, at point D, her irrational Beliefs (iB's) and to come up with new cognitive Effects (cE's) at point E. Her main Disputing and its answers would be something like this:

Disputing: "Why *must* I not worry this much? Where is the evidence that it's *terrible* that I do? How does my acting stupidly in this respect make me a stupid or rotten *person?*"

Answer: "There is no good reason why I *must* not worry this much, though there are several good reasons why I'd *better* not: since my anxiety will do me little good, and making myself anxious about that anxiety will do me less good! It's not *terrible* if I do make myself overly concerned about getting cancer—only an uncomfortable pain in the neck! I probably won't die of this anxiety; but it will make my life much more inconvenient. I am *not* a rotten person when I act stupidly and make myself needlessly anxious, since a rotten person would have a soul of rottenness, would only and always act stupidly and rottenly, would be doomed to continue to do so for the rest of her life, and would be entirely damnable for doing so. No one is ever really a thoroughly rotten person, including me. Humans are human, and that means fallible, screwed-up humans! I shall always act stupidly in some respects for the rest of my life; that is my basic nature, and though I cannot say that I like having this kind of nature, I know that I can fully accept myself with it, and then work at changing it somewhat, so that I try to act at least a little less foolishly in the future."

In this manner, you can help your patient Dispute her irrational Beliefs on two levels: first, regarding the "horror" of contracting cervical cancer and second, regarding the "terribleness" of making herself unduly anxious about this possibility. When you help her to give up her anxiety and her anxiety about her anxiety, she will then normally proceed onward to Point eE, her emotional Effect of Disputing her irrational Beliefs. Thus, she will tend to feel much less anxious, self-pitying, and depressed. And she will also, often, tend to become much less defensive, less preoccupied with the possibility that her medical examination may show abnormalities, and tend to experience less physiological reactions (such as rapid heartbeating or gastrointestinal spasms) that may later lead to psychosomatic symptoms (such as cardiac complications or ulcers).

Finally, at bE (behavioral Effect), she will tend to *act* on the basis of her new cognitions and feelings. She will submit to diagnostic tests with little hesitation, since she will now be *determined* to do everything she can to help herself, no matter how uncomfortable she feels in the process. She will arrange for an operation, if that is what her doctor advises. She will take required medicines or exercises uncomplainingly. She will do what seems best to prevent any recurrence of her gynecological disorder or any instigation of a new kind of physical ailment.

If RET is used successfully this patient will undergo a profound, comprehensive change in her philosophy, emotions, and behaviors. All that you, as her physician, nurse, or other health care professional may do is to get her to go through the cognitive A-B-C-D-E's of RET as well as fully explaining any diagnostic or therapeutic procedures to her; but you will do so with the aim of helping her in a variety of ways. And, as shown later in this book, you will also probably use several more specifically emotive and behavioral methods of personality change with her. But if you teach her and encourage her to keep using the main cognitive procedures of RET, she may change remarkably in her attitudes toward herself and her health, and may do so within a few weeks' or few months' time.

Cognitively, then, RET employs direct philosophic confrontation, shows patients how they upset *themselves*, and do not *get* disturbed by others. You actively and directively teach them that just about every time they experience a self-defeating emotion or behavior at point C (Consequence), this only stems *in*directly from some Activating Experience, Activity, or Agent at point A. Much more concretely and importantly, it arises from their interpretations, philosophies, attitudes, or Beliefs at point B. You then show your patients how to scientifically and logically Dispute their own irrational Beliefs (iB's), and to persist at this until they consistently arrive at a sensible set of cognitive Effects (cE's), and then finally at appropriate emotional Effects (eE's) and more effective behavioral Effects (bE's).

Is RET almost primarily "rational" or "intellectual" rather than, like many of the other modern therapies are, "emotional" and "behavioral." No, as we shall show in succeeding chapters, it is also exceptionally emotive and action-oriented. On the emotive side, it especially is confrontational and evocative, in the sense that RET practitioners take a no-nonsense approach to their patients' problems, persuade their patients to express themselves openly and to bring out their real feelings, no matter how "painful" these may seem to be. As noted above, rational-emotive therapists may quickly evoke and attack their patients' defense-creating ideas while showing them how they can unconditionally accept themselves *with* their poor or stupid behavior.

Along these lines, if you use RET with your patients, you often will not hesitate to reveal your own feelings and to answer their questions honestly and fully, even when they involve you personally. For by practicing RET, you will tend to see that you and your own behavior are not sacred, and that you can face yourself no matter what comes up in the therapy sessions. You, like the people you treat, are not to be condemned or damned for anything you do, including, at times, for making therapeutic errors! You can therefore afford to open *yourself* up in the course of your sessions with others and model for them your lack of shame and embarrassment. In doing so, you will usually help them to be much more open in their own right, both inside and outside of the sessions.

As we shall show later in more detail, a central point of RET is that people do not need any outstanding traits, characteristics, achievements, purposes, or great social approval in order to accept themselves. In fact, although they had better rate and measure their acts and traits, in order to improve their behavior and make themselves happier, they really do not need any *self*-measurement or *self*-concept at all. For them to have a *self*-image (or picture of their total "goodness" or "badness") may be distinctly harmful. Because if they have *self*-esteem or *ego*-strength, they are really giving themselves some kind of a global evaluation, and almost invariably doing so on the basis of their competence, talents, good health, or other traits. And since all these characteristics may easily change, and go from "good" to "bad" or vice versa, they will always be underlyingly or overtly anxious, meaning, in danger of rating themselves as "worms" again.

RET, by solidly teaching people to avoid any kind of global or self-rating and encouraging them, instead, to measure their characteristics and performances, in order to help correct their behavior and to increase their enjoyment, gets to the deepest level of personality change. By using it, you offer your patients no panacea to end all their unhappiness, sorrow, frustration, and annoyance. But you do indicate, in a down-to-earth and easily understandable way, how to reveal, to combat, and to radically uproot the major sources of their needless self-destructive thoughts, emotions, and behaviors.

4
The Rational-Emotive
Approach to Interpretation

A great many schools of therapy seriously caution their practitioners against taking a direct approach to interpretation; yet, in actual practice, therapists of these schools do a great deal of interpreting, as Victor Raimy, for one, has clearly pointed out. In RET, we take a very forthright stand on interpreting patients' verbalizations and behaviors, so that they gain insight into their thoughts and actions and are able to use them to make fundamental changes in some important aspects of their functioning and malfunctioning. The RET view of interpretation is outlined in *Humanistic Psychotherapy: the Rational-Emotive Approach*. We shall now specifically apply it so that you can effectively interpret the causes and consequences of the disturbances shown by the patients which you, as a health-care professional, continually see.

In using RET, many interpretations are made which are somewhat similar to those made by therapists of other schools, including psychoanalytic and neopsychoanalytic practitioners. At the same time, if you employ RET you will tend to avoid making a good many interpretations that other therapists continually make.

Interpreting Past Influences

Particularly, in this connection, you will refrain from making long-winded "connections" between your patients' early history and their present emotional upsets. For one of the main premises of RET is that people are not made "neurotic" or (especially) "psychotic" by their past experiences but largely by their own unrealistic and overdemanding attitudes toward or interpretations of these experiences. In using RET, therefore, you would spend little time digging up and interpreting past events in your patients' lives. Rather, you would *interpret their interpretations* of these events.

Thus, instead of showing one of your male patients that he feels angry at dominating female nurses today because his mother presumably dominated him during his early childhood, you would show him that he childishly and irrationally *thought,* when he was a youngster, that his mother *must* not act domineeringly. He would be shown he foolishly *demanded* (and not merely *wished*) that she behave otherwise; and that now, in the present, he still self-defeatingly commands that most or all women, including nurses, be passive and warm rather than ruling and cold when he has contact with them. And you would try to get him to give up this crazy idea, which, ironically, is similar to the one that his mother presumably had toward him when he was young when she acted domineeringly.

With RET, then, you would keep interpreting your patient's *response* or *reaction* to his early history and to the similar things that are happening to him today. You would not make the huge error, which he easily tends to make himself, of saying that his previous experiences *caused* his present disturbed reactions. Rather, his cognitive style or crooked thinking, part of which may be innate, "caused" him *first* to overreact to his mother's domineeringness and *now* to overreact to that of other women.

Interpreting Unconscious Material

If you practice psychoanalysis or psychoanalytically-oriented therapy, you will tend to spend considerable time interpreting the deeply "unconscious" or "repressed" material of your patients. In RET and cognitive-behavior therapy, you do little of that because RET holds that *the* unconscious and *the* id are abstractions which have little real existence; that while people have thoughts, feelings, and actions of which they are sometimes unaware, and that may well underlie their disturbed behavior, most of their "unconscious" attitudes are not deeply hidden or deliberately kept out of consciousness because they are too ashamed to acknowledge them. Instead, their unaware thoughts and feelings are usually just below the level of consciousness, or, in Freud's original formulations, are in their "preconscious" minds; and these "preconscious" thoughts are seen and accepted by them with relative ease if you, as a health-care professional, will persistently, forcefully, and persuasively keep looking for them and showing them to your patients. Practicing RET, therefore, you will probably do more interpreting of "unconscious" material than do most other therapists. But you will do so quickly and directly, with no mysticism or mumbo-jumbo, and with no pretense that this material is exceptionally hard for disturbed people to discover and face.

Interpreting the Transference Relationship

Therapists of several different schools of thought, including psychoanalysis, often exaggerate the significance of the "transference" relationship between themselves and their patients. They spend a great deal of time interpreting to the patient that he or she has a deep-seated emotional involvement with the therapist and with therapist-surrogate figures. In RET, however, relatively little of this sort of thing is done. Instead, assume that your patients' relations with other significant people in their lives are more important than their relationships with you. If they have a dire need for *everyone's* approval this may, of course, include even you, and therefore their loving or hating you may be an illustration of this underlying need. If so, you would show them their underlying irrational Beliefs (iB's) that create this "transference" situation, namely, "I *must* have every significant person's love, including that of my therapist. How awful if my therapist didn't like me. That would make me a bad person!" In this manner, instead of interminably revealing and analyzing their "transference" reactions, you would largely reveal and help uproot their necessity-creating philosophy with which they create overinvolved reactions with you, and, of course, with others. At the same time, you might focus on teaching them how to employ skill training in relating to others more successfully, so that they would thereby have less need for an overinvolvement with you.

Interpreting Defenses and Resistances

Therapists who do a considerable amount of interpretation, especially those who are analytically oriented, frequently concentrate on
interpreting their patients' defenses and resistances, on showing
them how they rationalize, project, repress, compensate, and resist
therapy itself. If you practice RET, you are likely to overlap with
psychoanalytic therapists more in this than in other respects, since
showing your patients their rationalizing, their defensiveness, and
their inconsistent thinking is part of showing them their irrational
Beliefs (iB's) and how to Dispute these Beliefs. In RET, however,
you tend to show your patients quite directly and often quickly
their basic and specific irrationalities, and to teach and encourage
them to *attack* their rationalizing and evasive thought processes,
and to force themselves by emotive and activity homework assignments to do things that make it easier and easier for them to give
up their self-defeating defense mechanisms.

For example, I [A.E.] worked with a very stubborn patient,
who kept resisting a prostate operation, even though three well-
known urologists strongly advised him to have it done, and warned
him that there was a reasonably good chance of his winding up
with terminal cancer of the prostate if he did not go through with it.
He came in to see me week after week, with a new rationalization
for not having the operation done. Either he had too much work to
do at his business, where he insisted he was indispensable, or he
could not be away from his difficult family situation (one of his
sons was psychotic and living at home), or he was sure that there
would be a strike of the hospital attendants if he went to the hospital, etc. I kept knocking down these rationalizations, and kept
showing him that his basic irrational Belief (iB) was: "My life must
proceed in an exceptionally well-ordered fashion, with none of my
usual routines interrupted. Therefore, it is not only hard to have
this operation, but much *too* hard. I *can't stand* this amount of
disruption of my regular schedule. It's not worth it—even if I have
to take the risk of dying of cancer!"

I showed this patient—who, incidentally, was a very successful
and competent executive of a large business—that he was demanding that things *easily* go well and that the routines of his life *must* be
in almost perfect order, and helped him work to give up his de-
mandingness. But I also, very concretely, gave him several homework assignments of deliberately disrupting some of his routines

by coming late to work at times, by canceling appointments with some of his friends, and by ignoring some of the demands of his psychotic son, until he got used to the fact that he *could* arrange his life in a somewhat disordered fashion and still live happily and successfully. When he began to see this, he dropped his rationalizations, quickly made an appointment to have a prostatectomy, and nicely went through the so-called horrors of hospitalization and of being away from his regular business and family routines for a few weeks.

Interpreting Dreams

Dream interpretation has always proved popular in psychotherapy, as it has been popular for centuries before Freud, and has been happily endorsed and indulged in by psychoanalysts, Jungians, Gestalt therapists, and almost every other kind of therapist. In RET, we do not completely avoid dream interpretation, but are most skeptical that it provides the "royal road to the unconscious" or that it usually gives very important aspects of patients' thoughts and wishes that are not easily available from dealing with their waking thoughts and fantasies.

Using RET, therefore, you will usually spend little time on dream analysis and will choose, instead, to examine your patients' current nondreaming thoughts and behaviors. These almost always reveal what is actually going on in their lives and what their underlying irrational philosophies and self-defeating attitudes toward themselves and others are, and reveal this more clearly and accurately than do their dreams. By the same token, in RET you will usually choose to avoid spending too much time interpreting your patients' obscure symbolisms, whether these occur in waking or sleeping life, because there are too many allowable interpretations to such symbolic processes, and it is often impossible to define exactly what a given symbol means. You can more precisely determine your patients' basic postulates and what you can do to help them change their irrationalities by sticking fairly closely to the actual data of their nondreaming lives. No matter how much you *enjoy* dream analysis, do not be fooled into thinking that it is necessarily a highly useful procedure. When you do engage in it, look for the irrational *shoulds, oughts,* and *musts* that occur in dreams, just as they occur in nondream states.

The Use of Nonverbal Material

Many therapists, particularly those of the experiential schools, make much of their patients' nonverbal material: gestures, postures, tones of speech, etc. As an RET practitioner, you can do this to some extent, but watch how easy it is for you (and the patients themselves) to read meanings into nonverbal material that are not really there. The correlation between whether people cross their legs or keep them apart while sitting and their interest in going to bed with those to whom they are talking is rather low. Most of the material that claims that it is very high is of dubious validity.

As usual, as an RET-oriented therapist you will mainly be interested in discovering the ideas, especially the irrational ideas, behind your patients' nonverbal expressions, rather than in merely demonstrating the "important" existence of these expressions. Thus, if you notice that one of your female patients is holding herself back physically or is speaking in a stilted manner, you can point this out and see if (not assume that!) this means something about her basic inhibition. If it seems that it does mean that she is overly inhibited, then you would not merely point this out to her, but look for her underlying irrational Beliefs (iB's) that make her create this inhibition. Thus, she might well believe, "If I let myself go and revealed myself in a relaxed and unstilted manner, the people I associate with would find out what I really am like and would hate me. That must not be! Therefore, I cannot let myself go." Using RET, you can reveal this set of beliefs behind her nonverbal behavior and help her attack and give up these beliefs, rather than merely emphasize her posture itself, or rather than mainly help her to use her body in a more relaxed manner.

Getting at "Unconscious" Material

Many therapists, particularly those influenced by psychoanalysis, tend to interpret almost all their patients' expressions, fantasies, and behaviors, and to assume that these significantly cover up unconscious meanings that motivate these patients to be disturbed. Thus, they will overemphasize when patients are late to appointments, or display slips of the tongue, or express their liking or disliking for others with whom they come into contact.

Using RET, you will only interpret your patients' "unconscious" motivations in a selective, highly tentative manner. You

will take important self-defeating behaviors, such as their habitually coming late to work or to appointments with friends (or to
therapy sessions!) and will look for the conscious or unconscious
meanings behind *these* acts. But you will not do it in an obsessive
and compulsive manner, or because it is something of a hobby for
you to look at the meanings behind their simple everyday occurrences and encourage them to believe that these meanings are exceptionally important or disturbance-producing.

Rational-Emotive Interpreting

When you do use interpretation in RET, try to make it philosophic
rather than merely expository or explanatory. If one of your male
patients has psoriasis, for example, and is unaware that he is overly
dependent on others, you may not only reveal his dependency to
him but also show him that it results from specific ideas, beliefs, or
values. Especially the beliefs that he *must* have others' approval and
help, that he *cannot* take care of himself, and that he is pretty
worthless as a person if others do not like him and he has to depend
on himself. You then may urge him to question and challenge these
hypotheses, to show himself how invalid they are, and to replace
them with other ideas, e.g., that it is great to have others' approval
but that he can fend for himself and accept himself *whether or not*
they like him.

The main general philosophies that your patient with psoriasis
probably has, and that may cause him to have dysfunctional feelings, behaviors, and psychosomatic symptoms, include such ideas
as: (1) He *must* not act badly or imperfectly and *must* condemn
himself totally when he does. (2) He *must* attain a high degree of
perfection in his own and in others' eyes. (3) He *must* feel absolutely certain that important desirable events will occur and that
other undesirable events will not. (4) He (and others) must follow a
"heroic" line and turn out to be complete heroes when they do act
properly and total villains when they do not. If you help this patient
to look for, discover, and uproot these kinds of ideas he will finally
begin to see that he frequently acts bigotedly, moralistically, perfec-
tionistically, and dogmatically; and that by accepting reality, uncertainty, and tolerance of himself and others he will likely surrender
his "emotional" disturbances.

If you take a cognitive-behavioral approach to interpretation,
you can also show your patients that their irrational premises bring

about poor consequences. If they believe that others *must* approve of them, they probably *will* make themselves anxious and depressed. If they intolerantly condemn people for their mistakes and failings, they very likely *will* make themselves quite hostile. You will find it highly desirable, therefore, to show your patients, by the laws of logic and by empirical observation, that their unrealistic philosophies *do* result in such self-defeating symptoms as phobias, obsessions, and psychosomatic disorders, and that if they change these philosophies, they are likely to make significant improvements.

Interpreting the Past, Present, and Future

Psychoanalytically oriented therapists overemphasize the historical "causation" of people's present aberrations. In RET, instead, you can show your patients that *they*, and not their past experiences, are in the saddle seat; that they largely brought on their disturbances by overreacting (or underreacting) to their early environment; and that they continue these disturbances by persisting in their foolish ideas and by insisting on responding in the same basic manner as they did years ago. You can fully acknowledge that your patients' biological tendencies, as well as their sociological conditioning, make it very easy for them to acquire dysfunctional habits and to continue to behave in self-sabotaging ways. But you also can show them that because it is *difficult* for them to change, this does not mean that it is *impossible.* They can, with sufficient work and practice, modify their basic perceptions and conceptions, and they had *better* (not *have* to!) do so if they want to live with minimal anxiety, depression, and hostility.

In other words, by using RET you emphasize the *two*-sidedness that underlies your patients' past, present, and future behavior. You demonstrate, on the one side, how they are biosocially predisposed to indulge in neurotic thinking and behaving, and how, on the other side, they have a special faculty, which we call reasoning, and another unique faculty, which we call determined effort, that they can employ to overcome their "natural" oversuggestibility, short-range hedonism, and rigid thinking. You interpret to your patients not only how they got the way they are, but exactly what kinds of irrational Beliefs (iB's) they keep using to reindoctrinate themselves and to remain that ineffectual way. And you show them how they can logically pause, reflectively challenge, and strongly uproot their own unproductive Beliefs. Using RET in this manner, your interpretations actually go much "deeper" and make wider inroads against disturbed ideas, emotions, and actions than the pseudodeep interpretations of many other therapists.

Teaching and Interpretation

Interpretation, if we are honest about it, includes instruction or teaching. With the use of RET, you interpret by teaching your patients informally and in simple language the general principles of scientific method and logic. Thus, you show them that their disturbances largely stem from some of the false conclusions that they make about themselves and the world around them: "I'll *never* be able to get what I want in life," or "It's *terrible* that I failed at school (or a job or at a love relationship)!" These disordered conclusions follow from, first, setting up false premises and, then, making reasonably logical deductions from these premises. For example, if they start with the premise, "I *must* always do very well at school," they will "logically" conclude, "but since I have not, to date, done what I *must*, it's therefore *terrible*."

Second, they set up valid premises and then make illogical deductions from these premises. For example, they start with, "It's highly desirable or advantageous for me to do well at school," and then they conclude, "and since I have not yet done this desirable thing, I have no ability to do so, and my life will remain completely miserable forever!" You get them to challenge and dispute both their irrational premises and their illogical deductions from rational premises. You also show them that they really have a hidden *must* in one or more of their premises. For even in this example where patients start with a rational premise, the illogicality of their deduction usually includes a *must*. Thus, it is rational to start with "It's highly desirable or advantageous for me to do well at school," because one's goals in life include such things as getting along well in a profession or in industry, and to achieve these goals it is usually desirable to do well in school.

But the illogical conclusion, "and since I have not yet done this desirable thing, I have no ability to do so," has the hidden *must*: "I *must* do well in school easily and *all the time*; and since I have not done so yet, I *must* not have the ability to do so."

Generally speaking, people start with an underlying (and often unconsciously held) *must* and then make false deductions from it or as a result of it. Their main premise usually is, "I *must* do well almost all the time at important tasks and *must* thereby win the approval of others who are significant in my life." Once they devoutly believe this premise, they easily, and almost inevitably go on to three "logical" derivatives of this must: "Because I am not doing as well as I *must* do, and am not winning the approval of others as I *must* win it, then (1) It is *awful!* (2) I can't stand it! and (3) I am a rotten person!"

In other words, what we call awfulizing, I-can't-stand-it-itis, and self-downing in RET are "logical" derivatives of the highly irrational premises, "I *must* do well and be approved of by others for doing well." Without these fundamental, prior premises, your patients could get to awfulizing, claiming that they can't stand their imperfections, and severely putting themselves down. But they probably wouldn't! And you therefore had better show them that they do have these underlying premises and that they are making "logical" deductions from such irrational premises. Then you'd better also show them or teach them how to look for their basic premises and how to give them up. In this way, your interpretation of what they are doing, precisely why they are doing it, and how they can undo it becomes much more depth-centered and basically philosophic than the "depth-centered" methods of psychoanalysis and other psychodynamic therapies.

Other Interpretative Aspects of RET

In using RET you show your patients how to accept hypotheses *as* hypotheses or theories and not as "facts." You also show them how to experiment, as much as is feasible, with their own desires and actions—to discover what they truly would like to do in their lives. You serve as a cautious interpreter who teaches your patients how to model themselves after the teachings of science in general and scientific psychotherapy in particular, how to follow the hypothetical deductive method of scientific psychology, and how to apply it specifically to their own value systems and their own emotional problems. As Aubrey Yates, Hans Eysenck, Carl Thoresen and Thomas Coates, and other theorists of behavior therapy have shown, in cognitive-behavior therapy one sets up hypotheses with one's patients and one teaches them to be, in their own way, experimental and scientific. This is what you specifically do if you follow the principles of RET.

To summarize, as an RET-oriented therapist, you tend to interpret your patients' thoughts, emotions, and actions in the following ways:

1. You make your interpretations in an active-directive and not in a very circumlocuted, tortuous manner. You take an educated guess, right at the start of therapy, about how your patients are upsetting themselves by believing devoutly in some irrational idea(s). As soon as you pinpoint such notions, you tend to confront them with their irrationalities and forthrightly attempt to help them give up these irrationalities. Where most other therapists tend to be passive and nondirective in interpreting, as an RET-oriented practitioner you tend to help your patients make direct, concerted, and sustained attacks on their long-held and deep-seated irrational Beliefs (iB's).

2. Where many therapists tend to follow Lewis Wolberg's rule that "it is important to interpret to the patient only material of which he has at least some preconscious awareness," you will tend to try to show disturbed people, from the first session onward, material of which they tend to be unaware and that they may even have repressed. You will not feel intimidated by their possibly becoming temporarily more upset when confronted with some of their own covert thoughts and feelings, since you will know how to work on showing them how they are *creating* their own upsetness and how they can change.

3. Where most therapists only dare to make "deep" interpretations after they have spent a rather long period of time building a good relationship with their patients, you will be able, using RET, to make direct, depth-centered philosophic interpretations from the first session onward, whether or not you have achieved a warm or intense relationship with your patients. You will frequently be able to be didactic and explicatory, relying more on your patients' reasoning powers and growth potential than on their highly emotional attachments to you.

4. As we show in more detail later in this book, while not necessarily being warm, parental, or outrightly loving to your patients, you will be able to give them what Carl Rogers calls "unconditional positive regard," or what we call in RET full acceptance. This means that you can judge their "poor" or "bad" behavior, but accept them *with* their mistakes and immoralities. You will also be able to teach them to fully accept themselves (and other people) even when they (and these others) are indubitably "wrong" or "irresponsible." Following the basic philosophy of RET, you will show yourself and your patients that they do not have to globally evaluate

themselves (or others) as *persons* but can merely rate their own (and others') deeds, performances, and traits. You can then feel free to interpret undesirable aspects of their *behavior* while not rating *them* for such behaviors.

5. Because, again, you follow the RET theory and practice, of never attacking or condemning your patients but only endeavoring to get them to give up their self-condemnation (and their concomitant feelings of shame and guilt), you need not watch the timing of your interpretations too carefully, as psychoanalytic and other therapists often do. Nor need you wait very long to begin making RET-oriented interpretations. Most of the time, once you begin showing people that they need not condemn themselves for *anything* they do, you can quickly help your patients face their uncomfortable feelings and discover and extirpate the irrational Beliefs (iB's) with which they directly create these feelings.

6. You can directly give your patients mini-lectures about how they keep upsetting themselves and how they can refrain from doing this. But it is usually better if you first get them to see for themselves what they are saying to themselves. Thus, you can ask a man with duodenal ulcer complications, "What are you telling yourself to make yourself anxious about your ulcer problems?" And if he responds, "It would be terrible if I had to go for an operation!" you can then ask: "Why would that be terrible? What catastrophe do you think would occur if you had to have a major operation?" By these kinds of questions you can help your patients arrive at their own highly negative interpretations, and then can challenge and Dispute (at point D, in RET) their awfulizing attitudes.

7. You may find it desirable to make the same kind of interpretations repeatedly, before your patients acknowledge their truth or begin to act on them. You may show them, for example, that they keep demanding that they *must* not be greatly inconvenienced by various medical procedures and that it would be *horrible* if these inconveniences occurred. Even if they agree with your interpretations, however, that does not mean that they *really* agree, nor that they intend to *do* anything about changing their *must*-urbatory and *horribilizing* ideas. In these instances, you need not hesitate to repeat your interpretations, to get them to argue with such interpretations, and to show them several times why you made these constructions, and what the specific evidence is for their validity.

8. You may often find it highly advisable to be quite vigorous and vehement about some of your interpretations. Do not forget, in this connection, that people disturb themselves not only because

they think irrational Beliefs but because they keep powerfully in-doctrinating themselves with these Beliefs. If you merely show them, somewhat namby-pambily, that they do hold such ideas, or if you only Dispute them in a boy-scout or girl-scout manner (as various kinds of nondirective therapists do), you may not be very helpful or encouraging in getting your patients to surrender their irrationalities. So don't hesitate, at times, to *strongly* interpret what they are doing, thinking, and feeling, and how they'd better *do* something about changing these behaviors. I [E.A.] once said to one of my young male patients, "Look! If you keep convincing yourself that you *have to* do well on your job at all times, what else are you likely to be but constantly panicked when you go to work? And I mean panicked! Now what the hell are you going to *do* about that *have to* and the panic that stems from it?" Almost immediately this young man, who up to this time had very reluctantly looked at his *musts* and seldom done anything about them, began to make note of them on many occasions, and contradict them vigorously. Without my *powerfully* bringing this to his attention, I doubt whether he would have done anything about them for a long time to come—or even forever!

In many ways, then, both the content of your interpretations and the direct, often quickly delivered, and strong manner in which you make them can follow the common RET line. And that line, as usual, tells your patients: "*You*, and not the people and things around you, largely upset yourself! *You* had, therefore, better as-sume responsibility for doing so, and not cop out or defensively blame others. And *you* had better get to work to *stop* believing the nonsense you believe, and *stop* acting against your own interests." You can use RET, along these lines, as a "No-copout therapy," as an article in *Psychology Today* called it. For its interpretations di-rectly tell patients that they are largely responsible for originating and maintaining their own disturbed behavior and that they, and really only they, have the power to understand, review, and change it. Making these kinds of interpretations, you can often help your patients to improve considerably, and frequently to do so in a sur-prisingly short period of time. Their self-therapy, actually, will in many respects take them a lifetime to carry out. But you can teach them the main elements of RET in relatively few sessions.

5

The Theory and Practice of Rational-Emotive Therapy

Rational-emotive therapy (RET) consists of a theory of personality, a system of philosophy, and a technique of psychological treatment. We shall now briefly present its main aspects and then illustrate these with a case presentation.

Rational and Irrational Behaviors

In RET, we define rational thoughts, appropriate feelings, and effective behaviors as those that aid human survival and happiness. These are the goals that practically all humans select during their lives: to continue the existences given them at birth and to attempt to continue to live in a reasonably happy, relatively pain- or annoyance-free way. More specifically, when we say, in RET-oriented discourse, that a person is "rational," we usually mean that he or she has decided or chosen to live happily by (1) accepting what actually exists in the "real" world, (2) trying to live amicably in a social group, (3) relating intimately to a few members of this social group or community, (4) engaging in productive and enjoyable work, and (5) participating in selectively chosen recreational pursuits (ranging from sports to art and science). Irrationality or feeling and acting inappropriately consists of needlessly interfering with one's own life or needlessly harming oneself.

The Importance of Values

RET stresses the importance of human values. It holds that what we call personality largely consists of beliefs, constructs, or attitudes; that men and women tend to function healthfully when they have rational or empirically-based values; and that when they have absolutistic, perfectionistic goals and purposes they tend to feel "emotional" disturbance. A great deal of recent evidence by research psychologists tends to show that values significantly influence behavior and that modifying one's values directly "causes" personality change. (See in this regard a *Handbook of Rational-Emotive Therapy* by Ellis and Grieger.)

The A-B-C Theory of Human Disturbance

As noted previously in this book, RET holds that when people have emotional Consequences (C) after having an Activating Experience (A), A contributes to but does not directly cause C. Their Belief System (B) largely and more specifically leads to C. Thus, if they feel depressed at C after getting rejected by someone at A, their being rejected does not *make* them depressed, their Beliefs *about* this rejection directly lead to the depressed feelings.

At B, they first tend to have a set of rational Beliefs (rB's), that stem from their basic value system, their *wants*, and *preferences*. Since they *desire* to stay alive, feel happy, and gain acceptance from others, they will almost always find rejection *un*desirable, and, at point rB (rational Beliefs) they will conclude, "I don't like being rejected! How unfortunate!" They then will feel, at C (Consequence), sorry, displeased, or regretful.

At B, they also have a set of irrational Beliefs (iB's) such as, "I *must* be accepted by significant others; I *have to* get what I want! And if I am rejected, that's *awful*; I *can't stand* it! Rejection makes me a *rotten person!*" They then will feel, at C, depressed, self-downing, perhaps even suicidal. Their irrational Beliefs (iB's) almost invariably stem from escalating their rational desires and preferences into absolutistic demands or commands. With these

Beliefs, they no longer *want* to get what they want, but dogmatically think that they *must* get it.

According to RET, if you get rejected by a significant person at point A (Activating Experience), your rB's (rational beliefs) about this rejection will make you feel sorry and frustrated at point aC (appropriate Consequences); while if the same thing occurs at A, your iB's (irrational Beliefs) about it will make you feel depressed and self-downing at point iC (inappropriate Consequence).

Confronting and Attacking Irrational Beliefs

As will be consistently shown throughout this book, rational-emotive therapists confront and Dispute (at point D) their patients' disturbance-creation Beliefs far more actively and vigorously than therapists of most other schools. They clearly bring to the attention of these patients their irrational, self-defeating philosophies, explain how these create emotional upsets, and teach patients how to attack them on logical and empirical grounds and to give them up. RET therapists also help patients uproot their irrationalities by giving them emotive exercises and activity homework assignments that serve as disrupters of rigidly held ideas. But in the elegant form of RET, they especially emphasize cognitive restructuring or Disputing.

Homework Assignments

RET principles do not assume that people are trained by their parents or other early conditioners to be emotionally disturbed, but that they have their own innate tendencies to disturb themselves, and also strong tendencies to fall back to dysfunctional behaving once they have temporarily overcome it. It is therefore almost necessary to have them work to change themselves in between the therapy sessions, and to do so by following specific homework assignments. These may be cognitive (e.g., filling out the Self-Help Report Form published by the Institute for Rational-Emotive Therapy which is reproduced on pages 119–122 of this book); emotive (e.g., doing some of the famous RET shame-attacking exercises); or in vivo activity homework assignments (e.g., forcing themselves to ride in elevators or do other things that they are irrationally afraid to do).

In the course of giving homework assignments, RET practitioners frequently employ operant conditioning techniques, pioneered by B. F. Skinner and his followers, or self-management procedures, pioneered by Fred Kanfer and many behavior therapists. With these methods, patients are taught how to reinforce themselves with something they truly enjoy (e.g., eating or listening to music) after they do their homework; and sometimes to penalize themselves (e.g., by cleaning the toilet or burning a 20-dollar bill) if they fail to do their RET homework.

Group Therapy and Marathon Encounters

Because of its psychoeducational emphasis and its philosophic foundations, RET stresses group therapy and marathons, employing a cognitive-emotive-behavioral approach instead of the one-sided experiential and abreactive approach that many therapy groups use. In RET groups, a great deal of cognitive Disputing and problem solving is done, but the members also do risk-taking, shame-attacking, self-disclosing, role-playing, and other emotive-behavioral exercises to help them see that what they consider as "shameful" and "awful" is only really "unfortunate" and "inconvenient" behavior.

A Comprehensive Approach to Personality Change

In RET, human cognition, emotion, and behavior are viewed as being inextricably interrelated. When we think, we also feel and act; when we feel, we simultaneously think and behave; and when we behave, we concomitantly think and feel. Because humans are uniquely cognizing animals, and can think about their thinking (as well as think about thinking about their thinking!), as lower animals cannot, RET espouses cognitive-persuasive therapy or emotional education as one of its core methods. But it is never exclusively cognitive, and invariably uses several emotive and behavioral procedures, too.

Unlike many other psychotherapists, RET-oriented health professionals do not oppose the appropriate use of psychotropic medications. This is because controlled studies have demonstrated that drugs can often be quite effective for severe states of depression, overweening anxiety, and psychotic states. When these conditions exist, the rational use of psychoactive medication can help bring emotionally disturbed people to a point where they are receptive to psychotherapy. Effective psychotherapy (particularly RET!) as several studies have shown, remains the treatment of choice for long-term reduction and elimination of most self-defeating emotional and behavioral disorders.

Criteria for Therapeutic Change

RET acknowledges that no foolproof criteria exist for the measurement of therapeutic change, and that of scores of experimental studies showing the so-called effectiveness of cognitive-behavior therapy, none remains entirely unchallenged on methodological grounds. In measuring personality change, RET adopts a strict rule of thumb: that the goal of therapy is to help people *get* better and not merely to *feel* better. This means that they not only had better make significant symptom improvement, and see themselves as leading happier lives, but that they had also better make such a profound philosophic change in their attitudes toward themselves, others, and the world around them that if any new obnoxious conditions arise, they will have little likelihood of seriously upsetting themselves.

In the case of patients with severe hypochondriases, for example, RET would look upon these people as "cured" when (1) they strongly believe that having an illness or ailment is distinctly undesirable and unfortunate but hardly *awful* or *horrible*; (2) they can think about having a disease or can actually have one without experiencing extreme anxiety, depression, or obsessive rumination; (3) they deal with any medical problem, including a medical examination, instead of running away from it; and (4) they use the anti-awfulizing, risk-taking, and behavioral methods they learned in their therapy sessions to overcome similar phobias or obsessions that they may inflict on themselves in the future.

Case Presentation

To show how RET actually works, let me cite one of my [A.E.'s] previously published cases which I included in a chapter on rational-emotive therapy in *Modern Therapies* by Virginia Binder, Arnold Binder, and Bernard Rimland. My patient was a 27-year-old male who presented several symptoms: he felt shy and inhibited when trying to relate to women; he had very rapid ejaculation in intercourse; and he was hostile to authority figures, including his parents and his immediate supervisor at work. I first discussed his enormous fears of failure and his long-standing feelings of worthlessness. Our second session went as follows:

THERAPIST You seem to be terribly afraid that you will fail to make good initial contacts with a woman and also succeed sexually.

PATIENT Hell, yes! To say the least, I'm scared stiff on both counts.

THERAPIST Because if you fail in either area . . .

PATIENT If I fail, I'll be an utter slob!

THERAPIST Prove it!

PATIENT Isn't it obvious?

THERAPIST Not for me! It's fairly obvious that if a woman rejects you, socially or sexually, it'll hardly be a great thing. But how will that prove *you*, a total person, will be no good?

PATIENT I still think it's obvious. Would this same woman reject *anyone*?

THERAPIST No, probably not. Let's suppose that she accepts many men, but not you. Let's also suppose that she rejects you because she finds that, first, you're not terribly good at conversation and, second, you come quickly in intercourse. So she finds you doubly deficient. Now, how does that still prove that you're no good?

PATIENT It certainly proves that I'm no good for *her*.

THERAPIST Yes, in a way. You're no good for her conversationally and sexually. You have two rotten *traits*.

PATIENT And she doesn't want *me*, for having those traits.

THERAPIST Right. In the case we're assuming, she rejects *you* for having those two traits. But all we've proved is that one woman despises two of your characteristics; and that this woman therefore rejects you as a lover or a husband. Even she, mind you, might well accept you as a nonsexual friend. For you have, don't forget, many other traits—such as intelligence, artistic talent, reliability, etc.

PATIENT But not the traits she *most* wants!

THERAPIST Maybe. But how does this prove that *all* women, like her, would find you equally wanting? Some, actually, might like you *because* you are shy and *because* you come quickly sexually—when they don't happen to like intercourse, and therefore want to get it over rapidly!

PATIENT Fat chance!

THERAPIST Yes, statistically. For *most* women, presumably, will tend to reject you if you're shy or sexually inadequate, in their eyes. But a few, at least, will accept you for the very reasons that most refuse you; and many more, normally, will accept you in spite of your deficiencies, because they nonetheless become attached to you.

PATIENT   Who the devil wants *that!*

THERAPIST   Most of us do, actually, if we're sane. For, since we're all highly imperfect, we're happy that some people accept us *with* these imperfections. But let's even suppose the worst—just to show how crooked your thinking is. Let's suppose that, because of your shyness and fast ejaculation, *all* women reject you for *all* time. Would you still be a worthless slob?

PATIENT   I wouldn't exactly be a great guy!

THERAPIST   No, you wouldn't be Casanova! But many women, remember, wouldn't want you if you were. Most women, at least today, wouldn't want Casanova just *because* he was so sexy and promiscuous. Anyway, we're evading the question; *would* you be a total slob?

PATIENT   Well, uh, I—no, I guess not.

THERAPIST   Because?

PATIENT   Well, because I'd still have other, uh, good traits. Is that what you're getting at?

THERAPIST   Yes, partly. You'd still have other good traits. And *you*, if you were to rate yourself at all, would equal *all* your traits, not merely two of them.

Working along these cognitive lines, I revealed to the patient his underlying philosophic assumptions, how they led to his "emotional" problems (including his anxiety, fear of failure, and semi-impotence), and how he could change them. The A-B-C's of RET were used to attack his disturbance-creating Belief System. Starting with his emotional Consequence (C), which was his shyness and inhibition when approaching attractive women, we went on to his Activating experiences (A), usually his seeing an attractive woman at a social affair and wanting to approach her. Immediately after A occurred, he felt self-conscious and inept at C.

I showed him that instead of A causing C, his Belief system at B directly created it. First, at B, he had a rational Belief (rB): "I'd like to befriend this woman, but I may fail and get rejected; and I would find that unfortunate. How annoying to experience rejection!" If he stayed rigorously with this rational Belief, he would feel, at C, *appropriately* concerned and somewhat cautious. If he did try to make contact with the woman and actually got rejected, he would feel sorry, regretful, and frustrated.

But the real issue for the patient consisted of his irrational Beliefs (iB's): "How *awful* if she rejected me! I *couldn't* bear it! It would prove me an utter worm!" These irrational Beliefs made little sense for several reasons:

1. A woman's rejecting the patient would not make things *awful* because the term "awful" (when clearly defined) means: (a) extremely disadvantageous or noxious, in terms of the individual's basic goals of surviving and getting what he or she wants out of life; and (b) something so undesirable that it *should* not, *must* not exist, and therefore is *more than* bad or noxious. Although the patient could legitimately hold the first of these hypotheses, the second one includes magic and unverifiability.

2. While the patient might never *like* rejection by a woman, he clearly can *bear* this rejection. It won't kill him. He can go on to other rejections—and acceptances. And he can live fairly happily in spite of it. Only his foolish *Belief* that he cannot bear it would make it "unbearable."

3. How could a woman's rejection make him a *worm* or a *worthless individual?* It might indicate wormy behavior on his part or it might not (since he could get rejected because a woman liked a man with blue eyes rather than brown eyes). But even if he showed poor, inept, or inadequate behavior with the woman, that would only consist of a *part,* and never the *whole,* of his self.

No one could ever legitimately label him a worm as a *total person.* Actually, his entire personhood would remain too complex for any kind of overall rating. And he would always consist of a *process,* an *ongoingness,* and how can he or anyone validly rate an ever-changing, future oriented process?

When, in a few RET sessions, I showed the patient how he illegitimately rated *himself* rather than appropriately evaluating his *traits* and *performances,* he began to see how this kind of self-rating would almost inevitably lead to feelings of worthlessness, depression, and the false conviction that he could *never* find acceptance by a woman he found attractive. These feelings and convictions, in turn, caused him to experience shyness, withdrawal, and inept behavior with women.

As the patient saw the philosophic underpinnings of his inhibited behavior and his anxiety, he asked, "How can I get rid of my irrational beliefs? What can I do to change them?" Our dialogue about this question follows:

THERAPIST For ten minutes every day, take *any* irrational or nutty belief that you have, such as the one that it's terrible for you to be rejected by a woman you find attractive, and practice giving it up, even when you are not being rejected.

PATIENT   How?

THERAPIST By using the logical and empirical method of seeing whether your hypothesis is consistent with your other goals and hypotheses, and by asking for factual evidence to sustain or invalidate it.

PATIENT   Can you be more specific?

THERAPIST Yes, in my group therapy sessions, recently, I have been giving most of the members of the group Disputing assignments and also using operant conditioning—a self-management technique adapted from B.F. Skinner's theories—to help them carry out these ten-minute-a-day disputations.

PATIENT   What do you mean by operant conditioning?

THERAPIST I'll explain in a minute. But first, the point is for you to decide exactly what hypothesis or nutty idea you want to work on for at least ten minutes a day. And, in your case, it would be the idea, again, that it's terrible for you to get rejected by a woman you find attractive. You would take this idea, and ask yourself several basic questions, in order to challenge and dispute it.

PATIENT   What kind of questions?

THERAPIST Usually, four basic questions—though they have all kinds of variations. The first one is, "What am I telling myself?" or "What silly idea do I want to challenge?" And the answer, in your case, is, "It's terrible if a woman whom I find attractive rejects me." The second question is, "Is this, my hypothesis, true?" And the answer is . . .

PATIENT   Uh, well, no, it isn't.

THERAPIST Fine. If you had said this was true, the third question would have been, "Where is the evidence for its being true?" But since you said it isn't true, the third question is, "Where is the evidence that it's not true?" Well . . . ?

PATIENT   Well, uh, it's not true because, as we said before, it may be *inconvenient* if an attractive woman rejects me, but it's not *more* than that. It's *only* damned inconvenient!

THERAPIST Right. And there's other logical and empirical evidence that it isn't terrible. For one thing, because *this* woman rejects you hardly means that *all* will. For another, you obviously have survived even though you have been rejected. For still another, lots of other people in the world have been rejected by the woman they most love, and it has hardly been terrible for all of them, has it?

PATIENT   I see. There are several evidences that my being rejected isn't awful. And there is no reason, as we again noted before, why I *should* not get rejected. The world simply isn't a totally nonrejecting place!

THERAPIST   Yes. I think you're getting that well. Now, the fourth question is, "What is the worst thing that could happen to me, if an attractive woman rejects me?"

PATIENT   Very little, I guess. I was at first going to say that the worst thing that could happen to me was that I would be very depressed for a long time. But I now see that such a thing would not happen from any rejection but from my *view* of the horror of being rejected.

THERAPIST   Really, then, not so much could happen to you, if you got rejected. Is that right?

PATIENT   Yes. As a matter of fact, I would learn something about approaching an attractive female. And I might learn something valuable about myself.

THERAPIST   Right. Now, this method of asking yourself these four questions, and persisting until you get sensible answers to them, is something you can do at least ten minutes every single day, even when there is not much going on in your life and you are in no danger of being rejected. And you can combine it with operant conditioning, to increase the probability of your actually spending the ten minutes a day working at doing it.

PATIENT   Oh, I know now. That's Skinner's reinforcing technique.

THERAPIST   Yes, basically. You first discover what you really like to do and tend to enjoy—or would enjoy if you did it—every day. Like sex, eating, smoking, talking to your friends, whatever. What would you say was the thing you like best, along these lines?

PATIENT   How about eating ice cream?

THERAPIST   You really eat some, or try to eat some, every day?

PATIENT   Oh yes. I rarely eat less than a pint a day. I love it!

THERAPIST   Fine. Now, what do you intensely dislike doing, that you intend to avoid doing?

PATIENT   Uh, cleaning my apartment. I keep putting it off. I rarely do it.

THERAPIST   O.K. Then, let's say you agree with me—really with *yourself*—that if you work at least ten minutes a day at contradicting and disputing your nutty idea, "It's awful to be rejected by a woman I find attractive," you will then, and only then, allow yourself to have any ice cream that day. And if you fail to work at it, this idea, you will not only not have the reinforcement, the ice cream, but you will also take on the penalty of cleaning your apartment for at least an hour.

The patient agreed to this kind of antiawfulizing therapy combined with operant self-management, and within the next three weeks began to give up his idea that attractive women *had* to accept him. He did so well in this respect that he also started disputing his irrational Belief that he had to last a long time in intercourse; and as he began to surrender this notion, and to stop putting himself down for coming to orgasm quickly, his fast ejaculation slowed down considerably.

Other cognitive, emotive, and behavioral methods were used with the patient, in accordance with RET's comprehensive approach to treatment. Cognitively, I employed sensory imagery and rational-emotive imagery. With sensory imagery, the patient practiced seeing himself in bed with a woman, getting a fine erection, and enjoying copulation for five minutes or more of active intercourse. Using rational-emotive imagery, the patient vividly pictured himself failing to date a woman and failing, at times, to last long in intercourse. While imagining failure, he changed his "normal" feelings of panic and depression to those of sorrow and disappointment by concomitantly changing his awfulizing about failing.

Cognitively, I also explained to the patient some common myths and facts about sex and showed how he could easily satisfy most females noncoitally, in case he did not get an erection or last long enough in intercourse; and how he could employ the "sensate focus" made famous by Masters and Johnson in the 1970s but also taught in RET sex therapy in the 1950s. Emotively, the patient's therapy group used direct confrontation to help him face some of his basic problems and discuss them openly. The group members and I showed him, through feeling feedback, his attractiveness to females, and we provided him, at times, with direct support from a few people in group, who volunteered to go with him on some of his dating homework assignments and make sure that he actually approached some attractive woman.

Behaviorally, I used several active-directive homework or in vivo desensitizing assignments. I (and his group members) gave him graduated assignments to meet, talk with, try to date, and make sexual overtures to women. Also, while working on his hostility to authority figures, he was deliberately assigned to have more contacts with his parents, whom he normally avoided, so that (1) he could experience intense feelings of hatred and rebellion toward them, (2) observe exactly what he irrationally told himself to create these feelings, and (3) work at disputing his hostility-creating beliefs.

In the course of 14 sessions of individual and 37 sessions of group RET, this patient significantly improved in his presenting symptoms. He lost almost all his shyness about making contact with women and easily approached those he found personable. He usually lasted more than five minutes in active intercourse, and sometimes held off orgasm so long that he had to resort to intense sensory imagery to bring it on. He no longer felt hostile toward his parents, though he did not greatly desire to visit them. He lost his anxiety and anger toward his supervisor at work and, by his using RET educational methods with this person, the supervisor even felt considerably helped and somewhat dependent on the patient.

At the close of therapy, the patient reported, "I don't think I'll fall back into self-downing. I know that I shall continue to screw up, in various ways, for the rest of my life. I've come a long way during the last several months; but I still haven't been able to maintain a steady love relationship with one woman, which I really want to do. But I'm sure—well, I'm *practically* sure—that I'm just not going to put myself down any more, no matter how stupidly I behave. I am determined to accept myself in spite of my nutty, self-defeating behavior. At least, I'm going to try!"

As can be seen from this case, RET consists of a comprehensive form of treatment that heavily stresses the cognitive, philosophic, value-oriented aspects of human personality. It holds that people largely manufacture their own psychological symptoms and have the ability, with consistent work and effort at changing basic attitudes, to eliminate or minimize these symptoms and make themselves much less easily disturbed. It does not strive for symptom removal so much as for a profound philosophic solution to people's fundamental "emotional" problems. It constantly gains support through controlled clinical and experimental studies; and it thrives as an intrinsic and vital part of the rapidly developing field of cognitive-behavior therapy. Although not a panacea for all ills, RET provides an important part of today's psychotherapeutic methods.

6
Illness-related Anxiety and Depression

A 58-year-old woman whose mother had breast cancer became short of breath when she felt a breast mass.

A 47-year-old banker who had used antacids, anticholinergics, and sedative drugs for six years for his diagnosed duodenal ulcer developed marked pyloric obstruction. He screamed and became hysterical when his surgeon told him that an operation was necessary.

A 46-year-old school teacher, gravida four, para four, suffered from uncontrollable hemorrhaging. When her gynecologist suggested hysterectomy, she ran out of the hospital in her nightgown.

You, as a physician, nurse, or other health care professional, know only too well that even a remote prospect of surgery often precipitates extreme anxiety in your patients. Some of them think immediately of a radical procedure when their physician suggests consultation, and become utterly terrified. To these frightened individuals the surgery is often viewed as life-threatening. And similar feelings are frequently associated with radiological, medical, and other procedures.

Even before being confronted with a recommendation for diagnosis or treatment many patients are anxious and depressed about the illness that brought them to a doctor in the first place. These frightened people, in addition to their anxieties over pain and death, are often worried about medical costs. But, of course, not all sick people are like this. Psychological reactions to suggestions for surgery vary from rational concern to deep emotional disturbance.

Fortunately, you can help your patients to a large extent choose their own feelings about impending surgery and other "dangerous" health-related procedures. And you can help them choose appropriate feelings, such as sorrow, regret, and annoyance, instead of inappropriate feelings, such as panic and despair.

Here is a case illustration. Frank, a 48-year-old professional tennis player with a chronic cough became very upset when a surgeon recommended an operation for his hernia. I [E.A.] was called in for a consultation and saw Frank later that day. After I had spoken to him briefly, I showed him that he did not have to make himself greatly anxious and depressed about this potential operation.

"What do you mean?" he asked, bewildered.

"I mean," I answered, "that if I can help you see the A-B-C's of emotional disturbance, you will also see that you have a choice about what feelings you have, at point C. First, at point A, something happens in your life—the surgeon, for example, suggests a hernia repair. At point C, what we call your emotional Consequence in rational-emotive therapy, you feel very anxious and depressed. Mistakenly, then, you connect C directly with A, and think that A, an Activating Experience of an unpleasant nature, directly caused C, or that the surgeon's remark caused your anxiety. But in spite of what you and most people would think in this kind of circumstance, A really doesn't cause C."

"What does cause my anxiety, then?" Frank asked.

"B does," I replied. "And B consists of the Beliefs that you are telling yourself about A, your Activating Experiences. Thus, you could tell yourself something like, 'O.K., it's too bad that I require an operation. It's really unfortunate and frustrating, but it's hardly a horror.' In which case, would you feel anxious and depressed?"

"I might."

"Yes, you might; but I doubt whether you would. Instead, you'd tend to feel disappointed and concerned—but hardly depressed."

"Oh, I see. Yes, I guess you're right. I would feel concerned and disappointed if I thought it only unfortunate."

"Right. But, in order to make yourself feel anxious and depressed, you're telling yourself something much stronger, something more than 'It's too bad' or 'It's really unfortunate and frustrating.' Now what do you think that your stronger B-statement is?"

"Mmm. Let me see. Oh, yes: 'Oh, my god! How *terrible* that I have to have this operation! I *must* not have it! Wouldn't it be positively *awful* if something went wrong during the procedure!' "

"Right again! And by telling yourself these awfulizing sentences, instead of more rational ones, you make yourself anxious and depressed at point C. See what I mean?"

"Somewhat."

When I explained this to Frank, I was then able to help him Dispute (at point D) his *must*urbatory, awfulizing ideas at point B, and thus to face the fact that it might be highly *inconvenient* but hardly *horrible* to have an operation. He then began to feel appropriately concerned, at point C, but no longer panicked. And he quickly arranged to go through with the operation.

Frank's anxieties actually lessened as the date of the operation approached. And after his hernia repair he seemed less upsettable than he had ever been. I saw him several times on a follow-up basis, and he then began to speak about the several chronic emotional problems that he had had. He had for many years felt shy and weak in many business and social situations. So, along with working on the turmoil he had been feeling when confronted with surgery, he began to work on his shyness and weakness. After a few months of RET, he improved considerably. I have had contact with him since, and he has maintained his improvement for the last two years. His anxiety and depression about surgical procedures, as well as about other difficulties in his life, seem to be markedly decreased.

I [E.A.] have not forgotten what an experienced surgeon told me through his surgical mask as I assisted him on a thyroid operation on a 46-year-old woman, Mrs. Green. I was a third year medical student at George Washington University then, and hungry for a practical tip from a senior faculty member.

He said to me, "Dr. Abrahms [I remember it well, because nobody ever called me "Dr." before], Mrs. Green was much less anxious about her surgery than many other surgical patients are because I took ten minutes and talked to her about the operation. I told her why the procedure was needed. I described the operation in general terms with the help of a diagram. I let her know what she could expect, both before and after the operation.

"It's that old teaching principle, Dr. Abrahms," he continued, "tell them what you plan to tell them, tell them what you want them to know, and make sure they understand what you've told them."

Today I still appreciate this surgeon's advice. When a patient contemplates a procedure for diagnosis or treatment, and his or her doctor explains the reasons for it, and gives an adequate explanation of the procedure, he says something like this to himself or herself: "Now that I have a general idea of what's going to happen to me, I can see that it isn't really awful after all."

As a health practitioner you can help your patients even more by directly disputing at point D their irrational beliefs at point B that directly underly their anxiety and depression at point C.

When your patients have any overwhelming anxiety or feelings of depression about illness or physical handicaps, you can show them, using the principles of RET, that these feelings are unnecessary. Practically everyone has a tendency to be anxious and depressed over many things that occur in their lives—because they are human, they *do* worry much of the time. But they do not have to give in to—to *indulge themselves* in—their "natural" tendencies, any more than they have to overeat because they are born with a tendency to do so.

How can you help your patients feel appropriately concerned and disappointed when faced with "dangerous" medical and surgical procedures, rather than inappropriately panicked? First, by helping them to acknowledge that they are largely making and keeping *themselves* anxious by their own irrational thinking. Once you get them to see this thinking, they can stop, examine, and surrender it. They believe, for example, that almost any major ailment or medical procedure is *awful;* that it *must* not exist. What is behind this belief, and how can your patients uproot it?

Behind the belief that major health ailments are *awful* and *must* not exist are a few facts and many fictitious assumptions. The facts usually are that the ailment is distinctly inconvenient, since it will often prevent ailing people from getting some of their desires fulfilled; and that it may be dangerous and may lead to prolonged illness or even to death. The fictitious assumptions that they inextricably link to these facts include the following:

1. "My medical condition is not only quite inconvenient but will doubtless lead to all kinds of discomfort—nausea, vomiting, feelings of physical insecurity, numbness, etc.—that absolutely *should* not exist and that I *can't stand* if they do exist." This assumption is false, since obviously the discomfort that your patients pre-

dict may not actually occur. But even if it does, it *must* exist, because it *does*, it is not *awful* that it exists, because an inconvenience that is *awful* is one that tends to be (a) *totally* bad, (b) *more than* bad, (c) as bad as it possibly could be, and (d) more bad than it *should* be. But the inconveniences of illness or surgery are hardly *completely* or *totally* bad. They certainly can not be *more than* bad, or 101 percent bad! They could almost invariably be worse than they are. They *should be* just as bad as they are, since that is the way they are! Where, therefore, your patients' inconvenience when ill is usually based on facts, their awfulizing about illness is based on fictional distortions of what they think *has to* and *must not* be.

2. "If I act badly in the course of my illness or my operation and other people criticize me for acting foolishly or childishly, I *can't bear* their criticism and would have to consider myself a *worm* for incurring it." This is a nutty, and fictional, assumption, because if your patients do act badly in the course of their illness and are criticized by others for acting that way, they of course can *bear* (though not necessarily *like*) this criticism; and they don't have to consider themselves as *worms*, but merely as people who have acted childishly or foolishly.

3. "If I die in the course of my illness or any operation that I have in connection with it, that would be a *perfectly horrible* way to go! My premature death, in that fashion, *must* not come about!" This is another fiction, since if your patients did die from their illness or from surgical procedures, which they most probably will not, they again, at most, would be enormously deprived and would merely be *viewing* that deprivation as a *horror*. They have to die eventually, anyway, and their demise would merely occur sooner rather than later. To contend that they *must* not die, or die so soon, when they indeed will die and may go in the near rather than the far future, is arrant nonsense. Perhaps they'd *better not* die; but that never equals *must not!*

You can look for these irrational Beliefs or assumptions whenever your patients feel anxious or depressed about illness or about medical procedures; and you will almost always find them quite quickly and easily. Then you have a more difficult job: to convince these patients to acknowledge these irrational hypotheses *as* hypotheses, and not as facts; to get them to give them up, in order to make themselves feel much better; and to help them to continue to no longer believe in these highly irrational Beliefs in the future.

Don't forget Step One: Show your patients that they *do* have irrational Beliefs or assumptions whenever they feel anxious or depressed; and that they can, at first with your help and later without it, discover what are their irrational Beliefs, and forthrightly and effectively combat them and give them up. So don't let your patients cop out or claim that something *made them* disturbed or that they are panicked for *no reason*. Nonsense! Encourage them, instead, to say to themselves: "O.K.: so I feel panicked. Now there's no way I could get that feeling without some crazy idea. *What* idea? What am I *telling myself* to make myself have this feeling?"

Show your patients, moreover, that they rarely have twenty-thousand, or an infinite number of, ideas with which they disturb themselves. Or, if they do, these can all be subsumed under a few major subheadings. In regard to illness, for example, they will rarely assume that God is punishing them for wanting to be healthy or that if they have a pain in their toe a neurosurgeon will suddenly appear at their bedside and perform brain surgery.

It is much more likely that they are going to do the three major things that humans do in regard to almost any obnoxious condition: whine about (1) their own stupidity or weakness; (2) the unfair way in which they may be treated by others; and/or (3) the unpleasant conditions that exist in the world around them. These three forms of whining or demanding stem from three basic irrational Beliefs (iB's) which, in RET, we find exceptionally common among virtually all individuals:

1. The idea that it is a *dire necessity* for an individual to act competently and to be approved by others for this degree of competence, and that he or she *must* have success and approval to feel worthwhile.

2. The idea that significant people in an individual's life *must* act considerately and fairly to him or her; and that those who do not act in this manner *should* be severely punished and damned.

3. The idea that life *must* not have severe hassles, that it *has to* include ease and comfort, and that the world is a thoroughly rotten place if it is *too* difficult to live in comfortably.

If you keep these basic human irrationalities in mind, look for them in your patients when they feel emotionally upset, and help them find them for themselves, then you will be doing yourself and them a favor. The general principle, as has been noted in RET for over two decades now, is: "Cherchez le *should*, cherchez le *must!* Look for the *should*, look for the *must!*" Following this principle, you and your patients can fairly easily and quickly zero in on disturbance-creating ideas.

Helping Patients Look for Their Irrational Ideas

You can assume that just about every time your patients feel emotionally harrassed about any health problem, they are making some irrational assumptions, some *shoulds, oughts,* or *musts.* Suppose, for example, a 60-year-old woman is exceptionally afraid of illness, and looks for what she is telling herself in this connection. She soon discovers she is saying, "If I have blood vessel problems, I may have to go for vascular surgery, and that could easily result in painful or fatal complications." Her view in this respect seems a reality-centered observation, since if she does have, say, a femoral aneurysm or cardiac problems, she may well have to go for vascular surgery, which could result in painful or fatal complications.

If this woman is very anxious about the possibility of having a lower extremity aneurysm, however, you may guess that she is saying other things to herself about this possibility, which include some powerful *musts.* She may well be telling herself, for example, "I *must* not have blood vessel problems because I might have to have an operation, and I *must not* suffer greatly or die as a result of such an operation." Or, stated a little differently, her basic philosophic premise, which she brings to the possibility of her having cardiac problems, is: "I *have to* live a long and fairly painless life; and therefore I *must not* have any serious health difficulty, such as a femoral aneurysm, which might not give me what I *have to* have!"

Again, if you ask her what she is telling herself about possible vascular complications, she may reply: "It would be *horrible* if I had an aneurysm and I had to have a major graft operation!" You can then guess that she also believes: "I *must not* have an aneurysm and have to undergo a major operation; and *therefore* it is terrible if I have what I *must* not have!"

To help this patient, you again ask her what she is telling herself to make herself anxious. Whatever she answers, you try to show her that it includes an overt or covert absolutistic *should* or *must.* Get her to see what her *musts* specifically are, and then help her challenge them with scientifically-oriented questions, such as: "Where is the evidence that I *must* not have an aneurysm and undergo a leg operation? Prove that it is *terrible* if I do have cardiac problems and had better have an operation. *Why* do I *have to* live a long and fairly painless life?"

As usual, if you guide her along these lines, she will probably end up with a new cognitive Effect (cE): "There is no evidence that I *must* not have an aneurysm, for if I actually have such a condition, then I do! If I had better undergo a major operation, it surely will be highly inconvenient and possibly obnoxious; but I can't prove that such inconvenience would be *terrible*, because if it were it would have to be *totally* obnoxious or *more than* disadvantageous; and that isn't very provable! There is no reason why I *have to* live a long and fairly painless life, though it certainly will be fortunate if I do." Coming to these kinds of new, rational conclusions, she will quickly tend to lose her feelings of panic, to replace them with appropriate concern, and perhaps to arrange for a complete vascular examination and to cooperate with her surgeon.

If you keep working with your patients along the lines just outlined, you will help them conquer their anxiety and depression about sickness, about diagnostic procedures, and about operations or other medical measures that seem advisable in their particular cases. At the same time, you will be helping them to seek out and discover the basic assumptions behind all their other, non-health-related anxieties, obsessions, and phobias; to see clearly the *shoulds, oughts,* and *musts* with which they make themselves "emotionally" disturbed; and to actively and vigorously Dispute—at point D—these irrational Beliefs (iB's).

As Thomas Watson, of IBM, pointed out to his associates a good many years ago: "THINK!" Think about what your patients are doing to upset themselves needlessly about their health and other problems. And push them to think, too. This won't be a panacea for all their ills. But it certainly may help!

7
Sickness and Hostility

In RET, we have pioneered in the teaching of assertion training to people, especially in the course of their social and business relations; and, in this respect, we have always distinguished clearly between assertion and aggression. Assertion merely means that people know what they want or do not want when they associate with others, and that they clearly and forthrightly make their desires clear to others. It does *not* mean that they always *get* what they want, but merely that they express their desires, and *try* to have them fulfilled.

Aggression, on the other hand, really means anger, hostility, rage, or physical abuse displayed toward others. Aggression, unfortunately, often aids assertion: many people find it much easier to assert themselves by first enraging themselves at others for not easily perceiving what they want and immediately giving it to them. Because these people notice that they are considerably more assertive when they feel angry than when they are merely desirous, they falsely conclude that anger or aggression is necessary for assertion, that they are "strong" when they are aggressive, that aggression helps them correctly perceive reality and know what is going on in the world, and that a state of anger or aggression is a highly desirable, productive feeling.

How wrong these highly aggressive people are! They confuse healthy assertion with unhealthy, disturbed hostility. Assertion is usually—though not always!—healthy because it merely means, again, that we want something and make this clear to our associates, or that we do not want something else, and also make this clear to the people around us. It therefore often increases our chances of getting what we want and not getting what we do not want.

Hostility is vastly different! For example, one of your male patients hates his doctor for charging what he considers is far too much money. He loathes his nurse for not rushing immediately to his hospital bed when he rings. He bitterly resents other people in his business or social life who make more money or get more favors than he does. This man, as you can easily see, does not merely strive to get what he wants, but also puts down those who want something other than what he does or who do not immediately provide for all his wants. He insists that the universe *should* and *must* be run the way he wants it to; and when it does not, he upsets himself about this "horrible" state of affairs.

This man's hostility, you will note, seems to stem from his differences with others or from their not following the rules of living that he knows as "right." But it actually follows from his refusal to accept the fact that others see things differently and from his devout Belief that they *should* feel the same way that he does. He believes, underlyingly, that he runs the universe, and that others *have to* serve his wants—a rather false belief, to say the least!

It may appear on the surface, therefore, that this man's hostility flows from his differences with others or from their blocking his desires. Actually, he causes it by his refusal to accept these differences and frustrations and from his *dictating* that everything be the way he wants it to be. If he would keep striving to have his desires fulfilled but give up his dictatorial attitude, he would be assertive but not hostile.

"But isn't it good," you as a health practitioner may ask, "for people like this to feel honestly angry, and even to express their anger to others? Won't this save them from building up too much steam inside, and eventually winding up with ulcers, high blood pressure, and other psychosomatic reactions? Shouldn't I encourage him to express his anger more openly?"

Hell, no! As explained in detail in *How to Live With—and Without—Anger*, you had better not confuse people's *acknowledging* that they do feel angry or hostile with, first, their *continuing* to feel it and, second, with their *expressing* their feelings overtly. The *feeling* of anger, as we shall show below, is almost always a bad (self-defeating) thing, and it is quite different from the feeling of *displeasure* or *irritation*. If someone indubitably treats you unfairly, you will usually feel highly displeased and dissatisfied with this person's *acts;* but you do not have to feel angry, or damning, about the person who commits the acts. Annoyance or irritation at others' poor *behaviors* is often (though not always) justified, but hostility toward *them* for exhibiting these behaviors is not.

Second, even when your irritation at others for their execrable deeds and acts is almost indubitably justified, it is often foolish for you to *express* this annoyance (or anger) to them. With close friends, lovers, mates, or relatives, you can usually get away with overtly showing them your irritation, and perhaps inducing them to change their behavior. But with employers, supervisors, professors, traffic cops, or other authority figures, it is often best for you not to express your displeasure. Else, you risk their leveling real sanctions against you, and thereby defeating your own interests.

At most, therefore, you had better feel annoyed rather than angry; acknowledge that you really feel annoyed (or even angry) when you do; keep your feelings to yourself in some instances; and directly and honestly express them in other instances, where you are likely to help yourself get more of what you want or less of what you don't want by this expression. If you make these kinds of discriminations, you will get yourself into relatively little emotional and relationship trouble. If you don't make them, beware of the consequences of your own lack of discrimination!

What are some of the reasons why it would be far better for your patients to forego their feelings of anger and mainly stick with asserting themselves without aggression? Here are some of the main ones that you can bring to their attention:

1. Anger, when properly defined, almost always consists of a Jehovian command that people *have to* do what the angry individual *wants* them to do. But, of course, they don't! Consequently, it is a highly unrealistic, godlike demand that will continually be ignored or refused.

2. Anger leads to painful feelings in the angry person's guts. Although there is some evidence that feeling anger and squelching it may increase one's tendencies to acquire high blood pressure and other psychosomatic reactions, there is a great deal of evidence to show that feeling anger and expressing it will also frequently lead to the same unfortunate psychosomatic sequelae. For many years, for example, it has been known that people, in a fit of anger, can

easily bring on apoplexy, epileptic attacks, and other painful or fatal physiological reactions. Constant or strong feelings of anger rarely seem to do the human body any good, whether or not people inhibit or express these feelings.

3. When people make themselves greatly angry at others, they almost always tend to become preoccupied with these others and to think quite obsessively about them. You will actually tend to think steadily, sometimes constantly, of this hated individual and to waste enormous amounts of time and energy keeping this person in your head.

4. Feelings of anger often lead to vindictive plans and actions. In this case, you become even *more* preoccupied with the person you hate and you obsess yourself with the possibility of reprisals against this person. This is hardly a constructive policy.

5. Just as love begets love, hate usually begets hate. Although your anger presumably is aimed to correct the wrongs that others have done to you, it actually comes across so badly to most of these others that they tend to hate you back and to wrong you more! If you correct people assertively, you may be able to induce them to change their ways. But if you correct them angrily, they will often react so poorly to your tone of voice and your angry actions that they will deliberately, vindictively oppose you more and change their ways less.

6. Angry actions frequently incite a vicious circle of returned angry actions, which in their turn incite more hateful acts. Anger, on an individual or social basis, often leads to feuds, murder, wars, genocide, and some of the worst possible kinds of incessant combat. Perhaps most of the social and political atrocities that have ever existed in human affairs have been incited or escalated by intense feelings of anger.

7. Anger and even righteous indignation tend to spur you to abuse some of your subordinates, whom you see as acting badly, including powerless minors, employees, or subordinate citizens over whom you may have some control. Almost all the battered children who exist by the thousands in the United States and throughout the world have been abused by irate parents or parent-surrogates.

8. By making yourself extremely angry at others you often take on some of the very characteristics that you hate in them. William Irwin Thompson points out that "we become what we hate," which is not one hundred percent true but certainly has a great deal of truth in it.

9. By making yourself angry instead of merely assertive, you frequently stop upholding your own rights and actually tend to violate the rights of others. As Janet L. Wolfe points out, the difference between assertion and aggression is that the former consists of "the ability to express feelings or legitimate rights straightforwardly, without attacking others or violating their rights. Aggressive behavior, to the contrary, violates the rights of others, or puts them down." As she implies, anger includes an intrinsically fascist or elitist philosophy, for it denies the rights of others in favor of your own 'special' rights.

For many reasons, such as those just listed, you can see that people get real satisfaction out of their angry feelings and may direct them toward health care professionals who care for them. If, for example, one of your female patients is recovering from a spinal operation and dislikes her orderlies or one of the blood team technicians, she will either tend to communicate her feelings to these practitioners, which may not be very good for her, or else she will keep it to herself and produce painful psychosomatic reactions, which also won't be very good.

It would be better for this patient to accept the fact that these health practitioners are far from angelic; that they are error-prone in various important ways; that they may easily act carelessly; and that no matter what their errors are, she had better bring them to their attention tactfully. There is no reason for her to demand that everyone in the hospital, including the hematology team technicians, be completely competent or capable. Even when, because of their incompetence, they inadvertently jab her five times in the left antecubetal area while looking for a good vein, that's tough! But it isn't *awful* or *horrible*. That is the way the world is; and there is often nothing constructive, particularly during a short stay in the hospital, that your patient can do about it.

This is also true of many of the people with whom your patients work, live, or socialize. Many of them are often incompetent, and just about all of them behave incompetently at certain times, for almost all humans *easily* act slothfully, goofingly, side-trackingly, and ineffectually. Consequently, if your patients want to be effective in tending to their own illnesses or disabilities, and to avoid making themselves angry and upset, they had better face this reality. Occasionally, they will encounter blood technicians who almost never find a vein the first time, or pharmacists who constantly keep them waiting while filling a prescription. But much of the time they will meet with reasonably efficient technicians and pharmacists.

The point is that some humans are distinctly schlemielish but even those that are basically competent have their flaws and failings. You had better teach your patients, therefore, to *expect* others with whom they deal, including the doctors, nurses, and pharmacists who care for them, to be exceptionally fallible. Your patients had better accept this reality and stop making themselves angry about it.

Let us, for example, describe the case of Janet J., a 31-year-old mother of two, who had a diagnosis of endometriosis, and who was seen postoperatively after a total abdominal hysterectomy with removal of both tubes and ovaries. Being uncomfortable after the operation, Janet kept ringing the bell for her nurses to come to her bedside every five minutes. Since there were other patients also requiring attention, her nurse was not able to respond immediately each time Janet rang, so she became very angry at the nurse.

At point A, Janet's Activating Experience was obvious. The nurse was not coming to her bedside quickly and Janet was left without what she considered to be proper nursing care. So she was being frustrated at point A. At point B, her Belief System, Janet first had a quite rational Belief (rB): "What bad luck! Nine women on this floor had gynecological surgery yesterday. The nurses are obviously busy, but I'd like care when I want it and I'm not getting it. How annoying!"

If Janet had stayed with this rational set of Beliefs, she would have merely felt displeased, disappointed, and irritated with her nurse's behavior. And as a result of having these negative feelings, she might have taken some appropriate action such as, speaking to the nurse firmly but nicely about her "goofing"; or getting herself transferred to another floor where the nurses might be able to respond quickly to most of her calls; or arrange to hire a private duty nurse. But she would not feel very upset.

At point iB (irrational Belief), however, Janet had another set of ideas: "They *must* not arrange things so that I am on a gynecology floor with this many other postoperative patients! It's totally unfair that the nurses don't come immediately when called, as they *should* come when I'm in so much pain! How *terrible* that this neglect should have happened to me! How can they treat me this way? What an unbearable situation!"

Janet kept upsetting herself about the unpleasant Activating Experiences (A) with her irrational Beliefs (iB's). It was her own Beliefs, *not* the experiences themselves, that made her feel upset and angry. Although she tended to see these Beliefs as quite logical and warranted, they really had little to do with reality. They stemmed from her exaggerated *views* or *evaluations* of the facts of her life, and not from these facts themselves.

If you were one of Janet's health care professionals, how would you help her to give up her irrational Beliefs (iB's)? Mainly by talking with her along these lines:

THERAPIST   Why *must* they not arrange things so that you are on a gynecology floor with this many other postoperative patients?

PATIENT   I guess—well, really I suppose there's no reason why they must not. Maybe they're stupid about arranging things this way. Maybe it would be far better if they arranged it otherwise. But I can see that they don't *have to* arrange things the way that I would preferably want them.

THERAPIST   Right! They never *have to* act properly or well, even though it would be lovely if they did! And is it really unfair that the nurses don't come immediately when you call them?

PATIENT   No, I guess it really isn't. They do have the responsibility for the other patients on this floor, too. So if they mainly answered my calls, it might well be that they were acting unfair to the others.

THERAPIST   Yes, I'm glad that you see that. They probably aren't being unfair. But let's suppose, for a moment, that they were unfair and were neglecting you for some of the other patients whom they favored. Where is the evidence that they *should* not act unfairly, just because you're in pain?

PATIENT   Well, shouldn't they? Isn't it their job, their duty to relieve pain?

THERAPIST   Let's suppose it is. Is there any law of the universe that says that they *should*, that they *have to* carry out their job or their duty correctly? Was that law ever passed?

PATIENT   No, I can see what you mean. Obviously, there's no such law. I'm merely inventing it.

THERAPIST   And where will it get you, if you keep inventing nonexistent laws of the universe, like this one?

PATIENT   Uh—. Anger and a pain in the gut.

THERAPIST   Yes. You have your original pain, from the operation itself; and now you'll only have an additional, gratuitous, self-created pain, which we call rage. Not so good, is it?

PATIENT   No.

THERAPIST   And supposing, again, that the nurses on your floor are neglecting you. Where is the *terribleness* of this kind of neglect?

PATIENT   Well, isn't it pretty *terrible* to get neglected, in one's hour
             of need?

THERAPIST   It's pretty painful, yes. It's really obnoxious, yes. But to
             see it as *terrible,* aren't you really seeing it as *totally* ob-
             noxious and as *more than* obnoxious?

PATIENT   Yes, I guess I am.

THERAPIST   And is it really *totally* obnoxious, considering that the
             nurses do have other things to do; and that they do even-
             tually come to your bedside? And can it be *more than*
             obnoxious—say, one hundred and ten percent obnox-
             ious, if they neglect you, as we're supposing that they are
             doing?

PATIENT   Well, no. I can see that it's not exactly totally obnoxious or
             unfair. And of course it can't be one hundred and ten
             percent obnoxious.

THERAPIST   But don't you really think, when you're feeling enraged
             that is, that it *is* more than one hundred percent obnox-
             ious?

PATIENT   I never thought of it that way. But you're probably right. I
             do think that way.

THERAPIST   You said, "How can they treat me that way?" Well, what's
             the answer to that question?

PATIENT   I guess it is: "They can!"

THERAPIST   Yes, people can *easily* treat you unfairly, unjustly, and
             rottenly. That is their nature. They have no trouble, in
             fact, being that way; and they would have considerable
             trouble in always treating you fairly and well. Do you see
             that?

PATIENT   I see it, now that you're showing it to me. But I can see
             that I usually look away from seeing that reality.

THERAPIST   Yes, and thereby, by looking away, make yourself en-
             raged! You finally said, "What an unbearable situation!"
             In what way is this situation with the nurses unbearable
             or unstandable?

PATIENT   Well, it isn't in one sense. I probably won't die of it.
             Though, of course, if they really neglect me, I may!

THERAPIST   No, you probably won't die of it. But even over and
             above that: Couldn't you be happy *at all* if this situation
             persists? For when you say that something is unbearable
             or unstandable, you strongly imply that you could not get
             any happiness whatever in life if this situation persisted.
             Is that really true?

PATIENT   No, I can see it isn't. As a matter of fact, on several occa-
             sions when the nurses did not come to my bedside for
             fifteen minutes or more, I became so absorbed in some-

thing else, such as watching television, that I forgot about them and my ailments completely for the moment, and was almost surprised to see them finally show up. So I guess I can stand it.

THERAPIST Right! You can just about always *stand* what you don't like—as long as you think you can.

PATIENT I see what you mean. I think I'd better work on getting that idea more solidly into my head!

Similarly, as this woman's RET-oriented therapist, you can help her see that any given nurse, or the nurses as a whole, who neglect her are not rotten people. Her nurses may indeed, at times, act badly or neglectfully to her, but that merely makes them people who *act* badly and not *bad people*. And they are not damnable or condemnable for their poor behavior, but are again just people who act in a fashion that can be criticized.

You can, in other words, help this woman, and any of your other patients who upset themselves greatly about some unpleasant thing that occurs in a medical (or other) situation or about someone's unfortunate behavior to them, see that they have basically only three choices about this situation or about this person's behavior: (1) to discover some way to change it or make it more desirable; (2) to get out of the situation, and still get good results; (3) to stay in the situation, with its advantages and disadvantages, and to gracefully accept it.

In the event of your patients taking any of these three sensible choices, there is no good reason for their making themselves hostile. Even when others treat them indubitably badly or unjustly, their anger follows from their over*reactions* to this unfortunate behavior, from their puerile demands that someone whom they definitely do not control be absolutely controllable.

As usual, several interrelated actions and reactions are involved here. First your patients demand that others treat them well, and make themselves upset when these others do not. Then they dictate that people listen to their angry tirades, and they make themselves still angrier when this does not occur. Then they may anger themselves at their own ineptness in getting others to treat them fairly or to listen to their tirades. They also often upset themselves *about* their angry feelings. They feel that they *should* not be making themselves angry and feel guilty about this, or feel that this kind of discomfort that we call anger *must* not exist, and have low frustration tolerance or discomfort anxiety about these unpleasant feelings.

As shown in *How to Live With—and Without—Anger*, there are several "solutions" to the problem of anger that are commonly given by different schools of psychotherapy. Thus, it is often recommended that they pound a pillow or a punching bag to let off steam; that they go to an anger-encouraging encounter group and scream and whine about how awful things are; that they take out their anger indirectly by attending blood-and-thunder movies, prize fights, or other combative entertainments. The theory of "creative aggression" states that by "releasing" their anger in these ways, your patients will feel great and not actually be angry at real-life people who annoy them.

A fine theory! But it rarely works in practice. For if you help people use catharsis or abreaction to reduce their anger, they momentarily may feel better, but they still retain the underlying childish philosophies by which they keep angering themselves again. Often, moreover, they *reinforce* these views by their pillow punching or telling people off in encounter groups. You can prove this for yourself, if you wish. For if you feel very angry at someone, and you lambaste a pillow or a punching bag to "get rid of" your rage, what will you keep telling yourself as you do this kind of lambasting? Probably: "Take that, you worm! You *are* no good! I hate you! You really deserve to die for the cruel way you keep treating me!"

As Albert Bandura, Seymour Feshbach, and other psychologists who have done much research with anger have pointed out, you and your patients will tend to socially reinforce or augment your angry feelings as you "let out" your anger, symbolically or actually, against other people. And, while abreacting, you will tell yourself quite false things about these people: for they *are not* worthless, though some of their acts may be reprehensible. They do not *deserve* to suffer, even though they have treated you unfairly. They are merely screwed-up, highly fallible humans who are behaving badly, and who, if you do *not* make yourself enraged at them, may well behave better in the future.

So the usual, and often therapeutically recommended, cathartic and abreactive ways of "releasing" anger often work only temporarily. They make people *feel* better but *get* worse, and rarely achieve anything but short-term gain and long-term harm. This does not mean, of course, that you had better encourage your patients to avoid acknowledging their anger or to squelch all its manifestations. They had better fully and freely admit that they *do* harbor grudges and resentments against others; but also acknowledge that they create these resentments by foolishly and unrealistically demanding that these others *must* treat them fairly and *have to* give them what they want.

Expect your patients, then, to be exceptionally displeased and annoyed about the kind of health care they often get when they are ailing. For some of the physicians, nurses, and specialists who treat them will act stupidly, incompetently, and unjustly. Your psychotherapeutic job, therefore, is to help these patients gracefully lump or *accept* this occasional kind of poor treatment and often to be assertive about trying to get better treatment for themselves. The more rage they incite themselves to feel, the more they will probably interfere with good health care processes, and the more they may damage their thinking and their bodies. It will almost certainly be hard for them to train themselves to feel sorry, disappointed, and annoyed but not irate and upset about poor health services. But they can accomplish this kind of self-control with your RET-oriented help.

8
Overcoming Anxiety About Dying

One of the main anxieties of sick (or potentially sick) patients is their enormous fear of dying. In fact, a great deal of your patients' hypochondriasis, fear of diagnostic or therapeutic procedures, and other forms of "nervousness" really relate to their ultimate fear of death, particularly in the case of relatively young individuals who are often exceptionally fearful of dying "before their time." This chapter will therefore be devoted to several rational-emotive procedures that you can use to help people overcome their fear of dying, and all the other kinds of anxiety that frequently accompany this fear.

Since the vast majority of humans, including those who are not living very happily, strongly desire to remain alive, isn't it only natural for them to be exceptionally fearful about dying? That still does not mean that they *have to* indulge themselves in this fear. They can arrange, if they want to work at it, to be appropriately concerned about serious illness and death, and yet not inappropriately overconcerned or panicked.

Concern, if you think about it, is quite different from overconcern. If your patients had no concern or rational fear about dying, they might seriously interfere with their life processes.

They might, for example, court death in fairly short order by refusing a life-sustaining operation, by exercising vigorously after having a serious heart attack, or by smoking three packs of cigarettes a day with an asthmatic condition. Their being concerned about living, therefore, merely means that they *want* to do so and regularly watch out for and change those conditions that might interfere with their remaining alive. It means that they will tend to eat properly, to dress warmly when it is cold, to call in a doctor when they have sharp, continued pain, to look to the right and left when crossing a busy street, and otherwise to take reasonably good care of themselves.

So concern helps people stay alive and achieve some degree of happiness or pleasure while they are alive. Overconcern or anxiety, however, is something quite different! It means that people are overly cautious about the things they do, that they *dwell* on the possibility of dying, and that they are moved not merely to take proper precautions for their own safety but to take *too many* precautions, or, paradoxically enough, to become so obsessed with the "horror" of dying and to dwell so much on this "horror" that they often take too few precautions, and hasten rather than retard their own demise.

In my book, *How to Master Your Fear of Flying*, I [A.E.] give several reasons why anxiety or undue concern about dying is foolish and self-defeating. Let me restate and revise these reasons here, so that you can use them with your overly fearful patients (and also, perhaps, with yourself!).

1. *Anxiety about dying rarely does any good.* Your patients can die in too many possible ways for them to make certain that none of them will occur. They can leave this earthly vale by cancer, stroke, heart attack, or accident. Accidents can happen on the street, at the office, in school, at movies, in church, and especially (as statistics show) at home. They can be killed by a spouse, lover, child, parent, friend, clergyman, or by a perfect stranger. They can die of perforated duodenal ulcer, wounds, or tuberculosis.

Considering the multitudinous ways in which death can overcome your patients, they obviously cannot ward off all possibilites. Their incessant worrying and taking every "possible" precaution against dying will avail them little. It may moderately decrease their chances of dying in the near future, but it certainly will not eliminate them.

2. *Anxiety about dying may facilitate a quick demise.* The more overconcerned your patients become about dying, the more they

may bring about this eventuality. Thus, if they are very anxious about getting in a car accident, they will tend to make themselves more tense while driving and increase their chances of slamming into another car or pole. Safety requires vigilance, not overvigilance which distracts people from doing well at pursuits that involve real danger. When people focus on "Wouldn't it be awful to die!" rather than on driving conditions, they hardly help themselves stay alive!

3. *The more people worry about dying, the less pleasure they have while living.* Sensible individuals mainly try to live and enjoy. For if they live miserably for 93 years, who needs it? Your patients have little chance of living happily if they keep plaguing themselves about dying. They probably have no better way to assure that their remaining days will be miserable than to make themselves exceptionally anxious about how, when, and where they may die.

4. *Worrying does not magically ward off dreaded events.* Many people wrongly think that anxiety will prevent trouble, but it will not. For most of the dire things that might happen strike them from without—a pilot makes a mistake and their plane falls or a rat gets bubonic plague and transmits it to them. Worry, however, is in people's heads and hardly affects these external accidents and diseases that occur to them. Your patients' incessant and intense anxiety about how their physician will treat them will hardly make this physician a better diagnostician or specialist.

Anxiety cannot cure diseases! If they have something wrong with their bodily defenses or their blood volume, these things will not improve because they worry. Some of your patients may actually think that if they give themselves a pain in the neck by worrying, this kind of self-penalizing ritual will ward off some fatal disease or accident. Well, it won't! And if one of your patient's liver is badly scarred from cirrhosis, it is not going to repair itself because he or she worries about this. If anything, again, severe anxiety will hasten rather than interrupt disease processes.

5. *Worry over death does not lead to a fuller existence.* Many people worry about dying because they feel that they have not really *lived* yet. They have spent most of their lives anxiously inhibiting themselves, refusing to do enjoyable things, avoiding adventure, and sticking to dull routes. They consequently may think, "Wouldn't it be *awful* to die when I have not really lived yet!" But this idea, that it is horrible to die when one has not yet lived, will hardly make one's life more full or enjoyable! On the contrary, it will tend to make it more constricted, more depressing, and less alive.

6. *Worry about dying does not bring about help from God or from fate.* Many people think that by worrying about death and praying to God or fate to prevent it, they will insure themselves against dying young. Highly dubious! For there seems to be no evidence that God or fate specially favors worriers, and will arrange that they be free from illness or not die from their serious ailments. If your patients worry, therefore, *because* that will presumably induce God or fate to help them, the chances are that they will do themselves more harm than good since the worry itself will almost always interfere with health-preserving processes.

7. *Worry is sidetracking.* Your patients will find that simple caution or concern will often help ward off some accidents and diseases. Thus, if they eat well, get sufficient rest, exercise regularly, and follow other sensible health regimens, they will tend to be somewhat less prone to falling asleep at the wheel of their cars or catching pneumonia from overexposure.

On the other hand, if they make themselves unduly anxious they will tend to impair their health and make themselves more accident- and disease-prone. And they will tend to keep thinking so desperately about the possibility of their dying that they will (1) not have the time and energy to follow healthy routines, (2) not be duly cautious when driving, and (3) not have the good sense to keep away from overexposure. Caution and concern involve thinking about measures that may prevent fatalities. Panic about dying involves people's being so preoccupied with how awful it would be if they did get into health-related trouble that they sidetrack themselves from taking the measures that might well prevent such trouble.

8. *Worry, anxiety, and panic stem from an unrealistic demand for certainty.* When people are very anxious, they demand absolute certainty that no harm will come to them and that they will not die before their time. But this, of course, is quite unrealistic because there *is* no absolute certainty, as far as we can discover, in the universe. Only a high degree of certainty, at times. Thus, because your patients are now alive, they will probably live for a number of years. But there can be no guarantee of this! Some will die young and some will live until they are 105. Your patients, therefore, had better accept the fact that they have no guarantees of life or freedom from pain. Once they accept this, they can then unanxiously relax and *live.*

9. *Worry about death leads to avoidance of risk taking and to a less adventurous and duller life.* If your patients take risks, they

clearly may fail and come to some harm. But full living involves a good deal of risk taking; of trying for uncertain goals; of looking for some adventure; of experimentally discovering what is and is not enjoyable. The more they worry over serious illness and death, the more they demand certainty in this respect, the less risk taking, adventurous, and potentially enjoying they will probably be.

10. *No matter how much (or how little) one worries about dying, death will come.* Ultimately, perhaps, humans may find the secret of eternal life and prolong their existence indefinitely. But they haven't yet! No matter how much, therefore, your patients worry, they will still die. The chances are, these days, that they will live until their sixties or later. But when the end comes, it does! If you can help your patients to accept death as an unfortunate end to the goodness of living but not a "terror" or a "horror," then they will hardly give it a waking thought. They will meet it calmly when it comes.

Helping Patients Overcome Their Fears of Dying and of Death

As shown in the preceding section, worry or anxiety about dying and about being dead almost always do much more harm than good, and by pointing this out to your patients, you can often help them overcome their panic and their obsessive dwelling on death. As a health care practitioner, you will have to tend many patients who are overtly or covertly fearful in this regard. For the great majority of anxieties about medical problems are related, in one way or another, to people's fear of dying. Almost any illness, if it becomes serious enough, could lead to death; and the great majority of people are still enormously afraid of their existence prematurely coming to an end. They define the process of dying and the state of being dead as *horrible*; and behind their horror of it is the belief that they *must* not die, or at least *must* not die before their "natural" time.

You can often effectively help your patients to stop feeling terrified of death by using the following empirical and logical kinds of reasoning with them:

1. There is no reason, of course, why you *should* or *must* live a long and happy life. It may well be unfair if you die young and someone else lives until the age of 95. But who said that things *must* be fair?

2. The state of dying, as studies have shown, is usually a rather peaceful and not too painful state. People tend to sink rather than to fall into death, and they only rarely suffer greatly in the process.

3. If you are so unfortunate as to die painfully, there is probably nothing that you can do to avoid this. You can, of course, take good care of your health while living. If you do not smoke, for example, you may well avoid dying of lung cancer. But if you do happen to die painfully, then you do! At worst, such a death is only enormously unfortunate.

4. Worrying about dying at a young age will certainly not help you live, nor live happily! Worry itself will help bring on various physical conditions, such as ulcers or high blood pressure, that might lead to your dying sooner. And you will hardly enjoy whatever life you do have if you keep worrying about when it is going to come to an end.

5. It seems almost certain (although not absolutely so) that death is a totally insensate state. It is almost exactly the same kind of state you were in before you were conceived or born: a state of nothingness, of no feeling whatever. It is not a state as foolishly shown in films and plays like *Our Town* where you are alive and dead at the same time, that is, presumably dead, but actually knowing about and worrying about what is going on in "our town." When you're dead, you are *really* dead, and it is most unlikely that you will ever feel *anything* again. Since you are hardly fearful of the state you were in before you were born, you are quite silly if you worry about a similar state, that is, the one you will be in after you are gone.

6. Most dreadful fears or panic states that we have are not merely about some object or event, such as a fear of dogs or of riding in elevators, but about the feelings we know pretty well that we will have in case our fears are realized. Thus, if you are afraid of riding in elevators, you *know* that you will feel very uncomfortable if you do take such a ride. So you become afraid of your own feelings of fear, of your own *reactions* to riding in the elevator. You thus wind up with a fear of the elevator itself and of your fear of it. But after you are dead, of course, you will not have *any* reactions, including fear or panic itself. If you will just accept this fact, you will lose just about all fears of being dead and of having uncomfortable "feelings" after your demise.

7. A fear of dying "before your time" is really a demand for certainty. So is a fear of various medical procedures. If your patients, for example, tell themselves, "Wouldn't it be terrible if I

were hurt during a barium enema!" or "Wouldn't it be awful if I died during a gall bladder operation!" they are really demanding absolute certainty that they *know* what will happen during these procedures. Actually, however, there does not seem to be any certainty in the universe, except the fact that they will *eventually* die. There is no way of knowing exactly what will happen during any health-related procedure, including an operation.

You can therefore show your patients that all we have are the laws of probability, but that they often work on a high probability basis. Thus, there is a high probability that nothing untoward will happen during a barium enema; there is also a high degree of probability that no unusual complications, including death, will occur during routine gall bladder surgery. Since none of us can possibly get the certainty that we would like, your patients had better *accept* probabilistic living and take the small chance that something will go wrong during the barium enema or that they might die during routine operations. If they do not accept the laws of probability, but instead keep demanding absolute certainty, then they have a near-certain chance of experiencing continual feelings of anxiety. Every time, therefore, they tell themselves, and really believe, "Wouldn't it be *awful* if—" or "Wouldn't it be *terrible* if—" they are going back to a demand for certainty, and to the creation of their own anxiety.

8. The state of dying may well be quite painful, as against the state of being dead, which is not. But it is silly to worry about the worst possible process you may experience while dying, when you actually do not know what it will be, and when it may turn out to be (as it usually does) painless. Worrying about the assumed pain of dying will hardly make that pain, if it does come, any more comfortable. And, as usual, it will only make the pain of living much greater than it need be!

9. People naturally assume that it would be great if they (and others) lived forever. But this would not be true especially if the aging process continued while we live. They forget that if humans did live forever, they would have to put a stop to childbirth, for the earth, the solar system, and eventually the universe would become so overpopulated that there would be no standing room. Because we die, we allow room for those who are born after us. And for us, in the present, to be accorded the boon of life, we had better acknowledge that we can only get this boon by also receiving the release of death.

Even, moreover, if "eternal life" could be arranged for some of us, it would still not be truly eternal. According to the second law of thermodynamics, all matter in the universe will eventually "run down," and be evenly distributed throughout space. This means that every thousand (or perhaps million) miles of space would contain a droplet of inanimate matter. Nothing else! Eternal life for anyone does not seem to be a good possibility, not even in the distant future.

Too bad; but not *horrible, awful,* or *terrible.* This is often what you can get your patients to see. If they *think* it horrible to die, they will tend to *make it* horrible. If they will accept the likelihood that they will die, and will make the most of the indefinite number of years that are still available to them, they will live more happily. You can teach them, to paraphrase the writings of Marcus Aurelius, St. Francis, Reinhold Niebuhr, and Alcoholics Anonymous, to change the unfortunate things that they can change in this world, to accept gracefully those things that they cannot change, and to wisely recognize and accept the difference between the two. Death is simply one of those things they cannot change. But they can choose the wisdom that enables them to accept that reality!

9
Quick Assaults on Disturbances Related to Illness

No form of psychotherapy, including RET, is a miracle cure. Rational-emotive therapy does not get rid of all human disturbance, and, in a sense, it does not really cure a person of any emotional problem. For "cure," as often used in medicine, means that a person has a ruptured appendix or an ovarian cyst, and after some form of operation or other procedure this is removed or repaired, so that it does not bother the person again. Emotional disturbances, since they are largely *tendencies* to think, emote, and behave in dysfunctional ways, are rarely removed or repaired. Instead, they are ameliorated.

So RET, like other effective forms of psychological treatment, usually results in significant improvement—but rarely in complete cure. It has an increasing number of experimental and clinical studies behind it that show that people who are taught the use of RET methods, and who actually work at using them, not only tend to lose their symptoms but also to reduce (not eliminate but reduce) their basic tendencies to upset themselves needlessly.

RET works, we think, because it bases itself on an understanding of what so-called human nature is, how it often encourages people to think foolishly and emote inappropriately, and what can be

75

done to change their thinking and minimize their self-sabotaging emotion. If you, as a health care professional, use RET procedures, you will probably find that they constitute an easily understandable, direct method of uprooting disturbance that quickly gets at the main philosophic core of upsetness and gives troubled people a quick handle on helping themselves.

RET, as noted in the first chapter of this book, can be done on a long-term basis, and often it had better be. For many patients have long-standing, deeply held disordered ways of thinking and behaving, and require a reasonable period of time to understand what these are and to concertedly attack and change them. All individuals, in fact, who use RET successfully require a considerable amount of time to change. Even when they begin to use it effectively from the first session onward (or immediately after reading one of the RET texts), they will almost always be forced to *keep* using it, for week after week, and even year after year, before some of its procedures become second nature, and automatically take over their lives.

Effective therapy, therefore, is in some ways an essentially long-term, and even lifetime, process; somewhat like dieting. People can often learn how to diet in a short period of time, and can go on a successful diet in a period of a few weeks or a few months. But to *maintain* proper dieting takes forever, and to maintain proper self-control also takes virtually forever. After awhile, the new cognitions or philosophies one acquires in therapy jell and become spontaneous or permanent. But there never comes a time when no effort at all is required to maintain them.

Nonetheless, RET is often a highly effective short-term treatment, in that patients can be briefly and quickly shown what they are doing to disturb themselves, and, in some cases, can be helped almost immediately to change their long-standing dysfunctional ways, and can be encouraged to maintain their gains for a long time. For one of the beauties of RET is that it reduces people's problems to their main essentials rapidly, often in an amazingly brief period of time. Thus, both of the authors of this book find that they can see new patients and actually get to the philosophic roots of their problems, using the A-B-C-D-E's of RET, in literally a few minutes; and both of us often give public workshops where we demonstrate the principles of RET by speaking with people of whom we have no prior knowledge, and in literally a few minutes, we are able to reach their fundamental disordered emotions and the philosophic underpinnings of these emotions, and show them how the two are intricately related.

This does not mean that when you, as an RET-oriented therapist, are able quickly to understand your patients' basic disturbances and then to help them understand, too, that they can actually change their personality structure in a short period of time.
Few of them, if any, can! For once they truly comprehend their
own irrational Beliefs (iB's) and how these lead to their emotional
and behavioral disorders, they usually have to spend a decent
period of time—anywhere from a few months to a year or more—
in repeatedly Disputing (at D) these Beliefs, and repeatedly giving
them up. Only after this kind of repetition and by actively forcing
themselves to act differently from their previous ways are they
likely to make fundamental and lasting changes in their personality structure.

All effective therapy, including RET, takes time to work
through to near completion. But one of the great advantages of RET
is that, in some cases, it can very quickly prepare patients to get
started on this working-through process, and eventually they will
be able to continue it largely on their own. With the various kinds
of cognitive, emotive, and behavioral procedures outlined in this
book, you can frequently help some of the most difficult customers
(D.C.'s, as we call them in RET) at least make a good *start* along the
road to therapeutic self-help.

Are there any especially rapid methods that you can use to help
your patients understand and undermine their emotional difficulties and thereby interrupt their upsetting themselves about their
health problems? Yes, there are several such methods, which we
shall now proceed to outline. Almost all of these seem to be especially helpful when you take a few minutes to educate your patients
about their illnesses and disorders—and to explain any diagnostic
or therapeutic procedures to them.

Antiwhining.   Although we normally, especially if we are psychiatrists or psychologists, give complex, high-sounding names to
emotional disturbance such as neurosis, psychosis, borderline psychosis, psychopathy, and habit dysfunction, the truth is that the
essence of all these forms of disturbance is almost always some form
of whining—yes, *whining*. If you observe your patients clearly you
will see that when they are acting "neurotically," they are invariably whining that (1) "I *must* do well and win others' approval, and
isn't it *awful* when I don't—whine, whine!" (2) You *must* treat me
beautifully and love me when I want you to, and isn't it *terrible*
when you don't—whine, whine!" (3) "The conditions of my life
and the world around me *must* give me what I want immediately,

without too much effort on my part, and isn't it *horrible* when they don't—whine, whine, whine!"

Some of the more severe states of mental illness, such as schizophrenia and manic-depressive illness, consist of more than mere whining since they have a strong biological element in them, and can occur to nonwhiners. But, almost invariably, when people are afflicted with severe degrees of mental illness, they tend to whine and whine *about* their afflictions and the disadvantages to which they lead, so that these psychotics, too, have in their makeup and their relations with themselves and others an enormous amount of whining. It seems almost impossible to get at the root of the truly "emotional" component of mental disorder without revealing its whining aspects.

Consequently, one of the quickest and most effective methods of RET is to show your patients, albeit in an objective, nondamning manner, that they are whining, and that much of the pain and discomfort they get from their emotional disturbances directly stems from this whining. If you can convince them that they often whine, that they virtually never need whine about anything, you will help them considerably to overcome a large amount of their disturbance—and often to do so in a remarkably short period.

As an antiwhining measure, you can help your patients take their usual terms, "I can't stand it!" and "It's awful" and substitute two other words that will just about obliterate these whiney terms and the crooked thinking that underlies them.

"Do you mean," you may incredulously ask, "that there are two words in the English language that almost all my patients can easily understand and can instantly and effectively apply to practically any disturbance they may feel about their health or about anything else? Just two words that, if my patients use them properly and steadily, will just about wipe out their emotional problems?"

Well, no; not exactly. Your patients are sometimes bound to feel anxious, depressed, enraged, or worthless at least occasionally or intermittently, and to feel that way mainly because they are human. We would not ask you to be unrealistic and expect them to change completely in their emotional makeup just by saying two "magical" words to themselves.

"But you strongly imply that most of the time, or in nearly all instances, if I help my patients get into their heads and really believe two common words they can minimize or eliminate the greater part of their hangups, particularly their neurotic hangups. Is that right?" Quite right! We contend, as RET has shown for a good many years now, that people continually employ two words that cause almost all their psychological problems. And we likewise contend that they can substitute for these two words two others that they could use to surrender their devout irrational Beliefs (iB's) in these first two words, and that if they bothered to do so often, they would have minimal disturbance.

"Are you serious about this? Do you really mean that practically all the findings about personality maladjustment that have been discovered by Freud, Adler, Jung, Wolpe, and their followers during the past decade, not to mention all the discoveries of RET and cognitive-behavior therapy, can be accurately summarized in just two words? And do you mean that my neurotic patients can resolve their disorders mainly by determinedly believing two interruptive words?"

Yes, oddly enough, we mean exactly that. As you may expect, the two words that mainly cause "emotional" disturbance have many variations, but they largely have the same basic meaning. And the same is true for the few words or phrases that, if properly employed, can do wonders for psychologically distressed people.

"What you say just sounds too simple and miraculous to be true. What *are* the two words that people keep telling themselves that supposedly cause virtually all emotional upsets?"

They simply are: "It's *awful!*" Or, in some of the other main variations: "How *horrible!*" "It's *terrible!*" "How *catastrophic!*"

For example, whenever your patients feel, at what we call point C in RET, the disturbed Consequences or disordered feelings of anxiety, depression, worthlessness, or hostility, they believe and vigorously convince themselves that "It's *awful* that I'm not in perfect health!" "How *terrible* that hospital costs are so high!" and/or "It's *horrible* that I have to take insulin every day for the rest of my life!"

As we consistently note in this book, just about every emotional disorder that people have at present or that we can imagine them having in the future stems from an absolutistic *should* or *must.* This categorical imperative is almost automatically followed by "It's *awful* that this thing does exist, when it *should* not!" Or "It's *horrible* that that thing does not exist, when it *must!*"

Following directly from this kind of *must*urbation come the three main headings under which we can place health-related and other disturbances. Feelings of anxiety, depression, and worthlessness follow from "I *must* naturally have good health and do everything in my power to preserve it; *it's awful* if I don't; and what a *weakling* am I if I fail in this respect!" Feelings of hostility, anger, resentment, and rage follow from "You *must* absolutely help me with my health and other problems; *it's terrible* if you don't; and what a *louse* you are if you fail me in this respect!" Feelings of low frustration tolerance or discomfort anxiety follow from "Conditions *must* be easy and immediately gratifying, so that I stay in perfect health without too much effort; it's horrible if they aren't; and what a crummy place the world is if it fails me in this respect!"

"What you say seems almost incredible. You really seem to mean that when our patients feel, at what you call point C, the emotional and behavioral Consequences of self-downing, inability to get moving, procrastination, hatred, and other neurotic manifestations, they are awfulizing enormously, and condemning themselves, others, and the universe. And you think that they can quickly and easily undo their awfulizing if they really get after it?"

Quickly, but not easily. And quickly means that they can immediately give up their awfulizing, but that they usually have to give it up a thousand times before they *really* stop believing in it. Also they had better change the words and phrases with which they awfulize, but, more importantly, change their deeper philosophic Beliefs that underlie their terribilizing and horribilizing.

"And what is that deeper philosophic Belief that, according to your RET theories, leads to their awfulizing conclusions?"

The philosophy of *must*urbation. As I [A.E.] show in *How to Live With—and Without—Anger,* the three main forms of whining that humans employ when, say, they make themselves anxious and depressed over a physical (or other) condition that they dislike are (1) awfulizing, (2) I-can't-stand-it-itis, and (3) self-downing. Thus, when they have a tumor that might possibly be cancerous, they tend to whine: (1) "It's *awful* that I have such a horrible ailment, and it would be absolutely *terrible* if I suffered greatly or died of it!" (2) "I *can't stand* this utterly abominable condition and the uncertainty that I have about it!" (3) "Since I could have watched myself more carefully and gone for regular medical examinations, and I did not do this well enough, that is rotten behavior and I am an exceptionally stupid, *rotten person* for behaving in this manner!"

All these three forms of whining seem, from a philosophic standpoint, to be *derivatives* of *must*urbation. For if people never thought in terms of any absolutistic *musts* but only in terms of *preferences* and *desires,* they would probably tell themselves, when they had a possibly cancerous tumor, something like: "I heartily wish that this growth is benign, since I distinctly wouldn't want it to be cancerous. But if, at the very worst, it is malignant, taking care of it will only be highly unfortunate. I definitely *can* stand dealing with it, and even if I were partly responsible for not taking care of it earlier and contributing to its growth, that was merely a stupid, rotten act on my part and never in any way makes me a worthless *person."*

As soon, however, as humans escalate their desires into *musts* and demand that they absolutely *have to do* the right thing by themselves or others, they almost automatically conclude: (1) Since I didn't do what I *absolutely should* have done to ward off getting cancer, and since I now may have this baneful disease that I *must* not have, it's *awful* that I have it!" (2) "Because I of course *should have* prevented myself from getting cancer, and conditions *must* never be arranged so that I do get it, I *can't stand* getting it, and *can't possibly* have any joy whatever in life while I think about having it!" (3) "Since it is really my own fault that I may have or actually have cancer, and since I *must* not have *this* kind of a serious fault, I am a thoroughly *rotten person* who doesn't deserve any goodness in life!"

In other words, awfulizing, I-can't-stand-it-itis, and self-downing almost invariably "logically" follow from the irrational premises of *must*urbation. If you think with consistent flexibility, open-mindedness, and relativity, you will virtually never *must*urbate and thereby bring on the forms of awfulizing that we are discussing in this book. But if you distinctly *must*urbate about your, others', and the world's behaviors and conditions, awfulizing will clearly be your lot!

"It hardly seems possible that *all* my patients' emotional upsets result from their Beliefs that something is truly *awful."*

It may not seem possible. But in some 35 years of psychotherapeutic practice, I [A.E.] have yet to find anyone who appears to have what we normally call an "emotional" problem who is not actively awfulizing. Don't forget, in this connection, that many so-called psychological problems really are not "emotional," in any true sense of the word, though they may *lead to* "emotional" disturbances. Thus, dyslexia, epilepsy, and Huntington's chorea are basically physical or neurological difficulties rather than "neurotic" or "psychotic" disturbances. And even schizophrenia and manic-depressive psychosis largely seem to be disorders with a strong biological basis. All these deficiencies or "ailments" may easily give rise to, or serve as the Activating Experiences for, "emotional" difficulties. Thus, if John Jones has epilepsy, he may easily conclude that he *must* not have it and may seriously upset himself *about* having it. And if Mary Smith has dyslexia, she may insist that she *should* not be thus handicapped, that it is *awful* that she is, that she *cannot stand* suffering with such a handicap, and that she is a *crummy person* for being afflicted with it. But in these cases, again, what we call the "emotional" or "psychological" or "psychogenic" problem seems to clearly stem from John Jones' or Mary Smith's *musts* and not from their original physical disorders. So it may seem quite unlikely that virtually all "neurotic" difficulties stem largely from *must*urbation and *awfulizing*. But so far the empirical evidence shows that this seems to be true!

"Assuming that RET is right about this, how can I help my patients to stop *must*urbating and *awfulizing* by merely using two 'magical' words that you mentioned before?"

You cannot; there is no magic, as far as we know, in the universe. You can use, and help your patients vigorously and consistently believe in, two very potent words, if you wish to help them quickly undo a large part of their awfulizing. But there is no magic about these words.

"What are the words?"

The two words that we usually recommend are "tough luck!" or, for those who can call a spade a spade, the even stronger words, "tough shit!" If you can convince your patients to really believe these words, and the basic philosophy for which they stand, they will tend to start losing their disturbed feelings almost immediately.

"What do you mean by 'the basic philosophy' for which these words stand?"

We mean that these words represent a shorthand version of the longer philosophy: "Too damned bad: that's the way things are and may remain. Tough, but not *awful!*" Take your patients' feelings of anxiety, depression, and shame, for example. Suppose they keep smoking, when they have been warned not to do so, and they have these self-downing feelings. They note, using RET formulations, that they feel ashamed because they are telling themselves, "I *must* not keep smoking, as I do. It's *awful* that I continue this bad behavior. What a total schnook I am for acting so schnookily!"

Using, instead, the "Tough luck!" philosophy they could convince themselves: "Tough luck! That's the way I still behave: quite imperfectly. And I definitely could behave better and smoke much less or quit entirely. But if I never act better in this respect, and keep killing myself by continuing to smoke, that's still only tough luck! It is not *awful*, but only very stupid and inconvenient. And I can accept myself with my idiotic behavior and enjoy life to some extent, even when I continue acting stupidly."

"I see. Getting my patients to think, 'tough luck' about their own foolish behavior stops them from downing themselves for it and thereby encouraging themselves to continue it. How about the longhand philosophy that I can get them to use in regard to their feelings of anger and resentment?"

You can help them believe, if they are angry with their doctors, nurses, or medical technicians, something along these lines: "Tough luck! That's the way my technician is, neglectful. I'd better accept the fact that he is and see what I can do to encourage him to be more considerate and less neglectful. But if I can't succeed in this respect, I can't. It's still tough luck! He's not a bastard for acting neglectfully. He has the right to do wrong because he's a fallible, screwed-up human. Too damned bad!"

"I'm beginning to see what you mean. I wouldn't have believed that 'tough luck!' could be properly applied to almost anything that goes wrong in my patients' lives. But I see now that maybe it can be. How about their feelings of low frustration tolerance and what you call discomfort anxiety? How can it help them with those feelings?"

If one of your female patients undergoes a series of diagnostic examinations to check on her growing ovarian cyst, and finally her gynecologist strongly recommends pelvic surgery and she awfulizes about this and balks at going to the hospital because of the inconveniences involved, you can help her tell herself, and we mean *really* tell herself and believe, "Tough luck, it is truly unfortunate that I have this ovarian problem, while many other women never have a cyst and never require surgery. But that's the way it is, tough! It would be still tougher, of course, if I don't have the operation, develop complications, and suffer prolonged pain and perhaps death. But it's only highly inconvenient, this way; and I damned well *can* stand the inconvenience, though I'll never like it. It's really rough being a woman and having ovarian problems. So it's rough!" In this way, this woman could get herself to accept the gynecological adversities of her life, to stop awfulizing and whining about them, and to go through surgical and hospitalization procedures with a minimum of discomfort.

"So in practically every case of emotional disturbance, I can quickly locate the underlying whineyness and awfulizing, and can try to help my patients use the 'tough luck' philosophy to counterattack and surrender it?"

Yes, and if the words "tough luck" or "tough shit" seem offensive to you or to your patients, you can employ other variations, such as "that's tough" or "too bad!" You can even use and help them use the single word, "Tough!" or some similar variation. The main thing is to let them see that life often *is* tough, but only by their foolish, overgeneralized definition is it *awful* or *unbearable*.

"Aren't there any dangers in teaching my patients that they can use a 'tough luck' instead of an 'It's *awful!*' philosophy?"

Yes, there definitely are. For humans tend to go from one extreme to another, as noted in *Reason and Emotion in Psychotherapy*, one of the first major books on RET. When you are trying to help them say to themselves, at point B, "Too bad!" or "Tough!" when some serious medical or other problem afflicts them at point A, they easily jump over to "So what?" For example, if one of your male patients is very disturbed about the possibility of having a heart attack, he may then switch to, "It doesn't really matter if I have a coronary. So what?" The hell it doesn't matter! If he were wiser, he would convince himself that it definitely does, that it would be most unfortunate if he had a heart attack, and that he had better do everything he can do to ward one off.

That is partly why we advocate the "tough luck" or "tough" way of helping your patients interrupt their awfulizing and catastrophizing. For it *would be* tough (meaning, highly unpleasant) if they had heart attacks, developed hyperthyroidism, or were afflicted with glaucoma. They had better fully admit, and forcefully tell themselves, that it would be. But that still does not mean that it would be *awful* and *unbearable*, nor that the world would come to an end if these serious health problems arose.

Even if you help your patients say to themselves, "too bad" when some unfortunate health condition occurs, that may be a little too pollyanna-ish, since they can then follow this with: "Well, I guess I'll just have to accept my heart condition for what it is, and not do too much about it." "Tough" or "tough shit" however has several more practical connotations:

1. It shows that the Activating Experience (at point A) that interferes with your patients' functioning or happiness really is uncomfortable and obnoxious, and that they had better do something to try to change it.

2. It implies that the degree of unpleasantness occurring at point A preferably requires some concerted action by your patients to change it.

3. It means that if people can't change the undesirable situation they are in right now, at point A, they had better look around for some ways of changing it later. Thus, your patients may feel

upset about not having enough health insurance coverage, and may be in no position to increase it right now, but they may be able to do better in this connection later.

4. "Tough" strongly implies that no matter how rough things are, there is no reason that they *should not* or *must not* be that rough. It is really rough if one of your young patients has developed asthma and the parents are upset about this. But it will not kill her or them, and she *must* have asthma if she actually has it. No one promised her or them a rose garden; that is the way the world is. Tough!

5. If your patients really tell themselves "that's tough" when they are ill, and they cannot change the unfortunate situation that has occurred (e.g., developing diabetes at a relatively young age), they can convince themselves that it still is only tough but not *awful, horrible,* or *terrible*. They *can* continue to put up with this bad situation. They *do* have the possibility, or high probability, of leading a happy life even if their ailment never changes. What is continuing to happen to them, at point A, does lead to *some* degree of pain and discomfort, at point C. But this Activating Experience practically never makes them experience *all* pain and *no* pleasure. Only their utter refusal to accept it for what it is would lead them to experience almost complete discomfort.

You can often use, and encourage your patients to use with themselves, fairly strong expletives, such as "tough shit" and "screw it" in their attempts to cope with highly inconvenient health problems. For this kind of self-talk is quite vigorous and forceful, and often helps combat some of the vehement awfulizing that they tend to do. However expletives can be overused or abused. Thus, if one of your male patients were to tell himself, after his internist has diagnosed a recurrence of his active gastrointestinal disorder, "damn it" this might mean that he is cursing reality. Or if he were to say, about his internist, "damn him" this might mean, "Damn him! He has made a wrong diagnosis." Or, "That worm! He has not treated me well and is to blame for my intestinal disorder."

Colorful words, then, for all their usefulness, are better employed appropriately and accurately, not sloppily. Whether your patients say them to themselves or others, they had best use them discriminatingly. Using shorthand statements also has its real limitations, since they may help your patients gloss over some important aspects of their intra- or intercommunications. A woman who has emphysema and is literally smoking herself to death may say to herself, "Tough! That's the way it is!" She is right in one way, since

she will not do herself much good by damning herself for her continued smoking. But she is wrong in another way, because she probably means something to the effect of, "I tried to give up smoking
but I just couldn't do so. Tough! That's the way it is. I guess I'll just
have to accept the fact that I can't give it up."

This kind of shorthand, masking as it does the irrational Belief
that this woman *cannot* give up smoking and that she *has to* accept
that fact, will hinder her from trying to stop. For the chances are
that she can stop smoking and that she need not accept the "fact"
that she cannot. So your patients can use the "right" expletives, but
can still use them quite wrongly.

The main point is that we can still say that almost all emotional
disturbance about health or other problems that your patients have
can be traced largely to their employing, in one respect or another,
the foolish belief that "it's awful." Their anxiety and depression can
be quickly interrupted if you help them use, and truly subscribe to,
Disputing and challenging Beliefs like, "tough," "too bad," and
"tough shit."

We may properly note, in this respect, that awfulizing creates
more havoc in the health field than in almost any other area. For, as
has been noted for a half century now, many physical ailments have
a psychogenic origin. And, as Liam Hudson has pointed out, the
contribution of psychology to medicine is of prime importance, for
to understand diagnosis and treatment today we had better "understand those aspects of illness that have a psychological component;
not just psychosomatics but the fear, anxiety, helplessness and
panic that can become translated into physical terms or simply
make physical illness worse or more difficult to cope with."

This extremely important interrelationship between physical
illness and emotional disturbance makes it all the more important
that you, as a health practitioner, understand the enormous power
of *must*urbation and awfulizing and also recognize and use the fast-
est acting and most forceful approaches that you can find to help
people change their self-sabotaging thinking. Why not, therefore,
suggest to your patients that they try some of the verbal approaches
outlined in this chapter?

10
Emotive Techniques for Helping Individuals with Health Problems

The great advantage of the "that's tough" or "tough shit" technique of helping your patients or clients tackle any of their emotional upsets is that it actively combines cognitive and emotive methods of therapy, and that has some overtones of behavioral technique as well. For the words, "that's tough" or "tough shit" first of all have distinct philosophic meaning. In their longhand version, they really mean something like, "I definitely recognize that getting rejected or being dealt with unfairly is tough, and is something that I'll rarely if ever like. But I also clearly acknowledge that this kind of refusal or unfairness constantly occurs in my universe, that I cannot always avoid it, that it won't mean the end of my life, and that I can still live happily in spite of it."

Emotive words, such as "too bad" carry a very *strong* philosophy; and that is why they are often so immediately and dramatically effective to change thinking, emoting, and behaving. But they at the same time have a direct "emotional" effect, what Eugene Gendlin calls a *felt* meaning. If, when you experience refusal or injustice, you may merely say to yourself, "Oh, well; that's the way the world sometimes is," and "I suppose I can stand it and somehow get along in life," these words have an emotive quality, too, but a quite different quality than "too bad" or than "tough shit." That is why, in RET, we often use very "strong," highly expressive, emotion-toned words and phrases with our patients and clients, including the famous four-letter words, such as "shit" and "crap." These words have a much stronger and more *felt* meaning than their less emotional synonyms.

Consequently, if you can get your patients to use the correct emotional words and phrases to themselves, this frequently helps them enormously to overcome or cope with their "psychological" problems. If they can powerfully and often tell themselves sentences like "I *can* and *will* live happily in spite of So-and-So's rejecting me!" or "So the world *is* often tough and unfair! Too damned bad!" they will frequently feel differently about rejection and injustice much more quickly, thoroughly, and lastingly than if they believed the same philosophies mildly or namby-pambily. RET employs a good many other highly emotive, dramatic, confrontative methods.

Rational-Emotive Imagery

Imaging methods, particularly those that include positive imagery or positive thinking, hark back to Hippolyte Bernheim, a famous French psychiatrist and hypnotist, who in the 1870s realized that what we usually call hypnosis largely consists of suggestion, and that an individual's self-suggestion or autosuggestion makes him or her listen to the hypnotist and follow that person's suggestions. Emile Coué, another Frenchman who studied hypnotism and emphasized its autosuggestive aspects during the first part of the twentieth century, pioneered in the technique of "Day by day in every way I'm getting better and better," and helped produce some almost miraculous cures of physical and emotional ailments.

Following Coué—and sometimes giving little credit to him—a number of Americans, including Norman Vincent Peale, Dorothea Brande, and Maxwell Maltz, extended the technique of positive thinking and included in it a good deal of imaging. They mainly advised people with fear of failure to picture themselves very strongly as being *able* to write, read, play tennis, or do other things well, and showed that with such positive images they usually got much better results than with their habitual negative images of themselves failing (and ending up as utter turds for failing!).

Positive thinking and imagery often brings excellent results, partly because (as most of its practitioners fail to see) it also includes philosophic elements. Thus, if your patients picture themselves as continually failing at, say, social relations and feeling ashamed of such failure, and then they start deliberately picturing themselves as succeeding admirably at such relations, they change their basic philosophy from "I *can't* succeed and am therefore a crummy person!" to something like "I *can* succeed and am therefore a pretty good individual!" Quite a different outlook!

In spite of its frequent efficacy, positive thinking or positive imagery has several distinct limitations:

1. It tends to cover up, rather than really replace, patients' self-concepts as failures. It is quite possible, in fact easy, for them to imagine themselves succeeding at social relations and yet to still think that they have not succeeded *well enough* or *perfectly*, and to still rate themselves as fairly worthless individuals.

2. It falsely emphasizes success as a measure of human worth. It essentially reinforces the view, in most instances, that "I *can* do well and *therefore* I am a good person." But if one later fails—as, inevitably, one often will—one returns to the basic philosophy of self-downing: "Now that I haven't done well, what a *schmuck* I am!"

3. It is not, from a philosophical standpoint, a very depth-centered or cognitive restructuring technique. It fails to show your patient that he or she really *cannot* be, except by arbitrary definition, either a "worthwhile" or a "worthless" individual, that people never *have* to prove themselves in any way, and that *all* self-rating in a total or global manner is really illegitimate and ultimately self-defeating.

4. It is palliative rather than curative, because, when using positive thinking or imaging, one still retains the fundamental philosophy that one would be worthless if one failed. Your patient has to keep imagining him- or herself as succeeding and being approved by others. Rarely would he or she get to the point where *automatic* self-acceptance as a fallible human comes *whether or not* one succeeds or gains others' approval.

Partly because of these intrinsic limitations, the usual superficial and palliative forms of positive thinking and positive imaging have been replaced, in recent years, by the techniques of a number of outstanding psychotherapists, including Drs. Joseph Cautella, Arnold Lazarus, Maxie C. Maultsby, Jr., and Albert Ellis. In doing RET, Drs. Maultsby and Ellis have particularly emphasized the use of rational emotive imagery, which goes far beyond positive thinking and which can be quickly taught to almost any troubled individual.

You may employ rational-emotive imagery (REI) in two different ways, one especially emphasized by Dr. Maultsby and one usually emphasized by me [A.E.]. These are outlined in a pamphlet, *Techniques for Using Rational-Emotive Imagery (REI)*, published by the Institute for Rational Living in New York and reprinted at the end of this chapter.

Rational-emotive imagery (REI) can be used to help overcome many of your patients' potential or actual disturbances about their health problems. You can teach them to use it in regard to failing to take their medication, refusing to do their prescribed exercises, worrying over the consequences of a diagnostic procedure, and many other anxieties, worries, and health avoidances.

They can, for example, intensely imagine themselves failing to take their medication, let themselves feel quite self-castigating and depressed about this, change their feeling to one of regret and determination to take the medication in the future, and practice the new appropriate feelings instead of the old ones of self-damnation and depression. They can also, if you think it advisable, use positive imagery to imagine themselves habitually taking their medication, doing their prescribed exercises without due hardship, and going through other procedures that would be highly desirable for their health care.

As indicated in *Executive Leadership: A Rational Approach*, there are few potentially disturbing Activating Events to which REI cannot be successfully applied. People can vividly envision themselves making difficult decisions, taking real risks, going to boring social affairs, dealing with their mate's and children's inanities, experiencing sex failure; by using REI they can philosophically and emotionally acclimate themselves to virtually any kind of difficulty that is likely to arise. By all means, then, encourage your patients to convince themselves, by the steady use of rational-emotive imagery, that they *can* do many things that they think they cannot and have appropriate feelings that they think are beyond them. You will often find it good to push them along these lines; but, simultaneously, to show them that, even when they fail, they are never rotten people, but only people who have so far not succeeded. Once they work at viewing themselves with equanimity even when they indubitably fail, they will be much more able to practice failing tasks again, and increase their future probability of success. But success, again, is never *all*-important; it is only *important!*

Unconditional Acceptance

Carl Rogers, an outstanding clinical psychologist, has pioneered in the advocacy of "unconditional positive regard." In using this therapeutic method, you show your patients, by your words, tone, and actions, that you fully accept *them*, even though you often may deplore some of their self-defeating *behavior*. In RET, we do not like the term "unconditional positive regard," because "regard" still implies some kind of a rating of the individual. We would rather, as I [A.E.] have shown in a good many articles and books, encourage people not to rate themselves at all, but only rate their traits, deeds, acts, and performances—for the purpose of greater enjoyment rather than for "ego" raising or self-esteem.

In RET, moreover, we not only do our best to fully accept our patients, but to actively and directly teach them to accept themselves. By following RET procedures, you can do the same. Specifically, first convince yourself—and we would advise you to do so many times, and strongly—that humans really cannot legitimately be rated as a whole, no matter how well or badly they behave. Practice accepting your friends, relatives, mates, fellow workers, and others *with* their stupid or unfair acts. The more you are able to do this, in general, the more you will probably be able to do it with even some of your most difficult patients!

With your patients you would (1) Show them that some (or many!) of their performances are poor (e.g., when they refuse to give up smoking when they have emphysema or cardiovascular problems) and that you would greatly prefer their following medical advice; but that they do not *have* to do so and are not *contemptible people* if they don't. (2) Discuss their failings merely as problems to be solved, for their own good rather than for the good of the medical profession. (3) Patiently repeat instructions to them, and with the confident tone that they *are* able to carry out these instructions properly and promptly. (4) Refrain from bawling them out when they fail in some significant ways. (Be firm rather than stern!) (5) Show them how to focus on their good, as well as on their bad, points, and that *it* is good (that is, advantageous or self-helping) that they have the good traits, but that this does not make them good *people*. (6) Indicate that you like them in the sense that you would distinctly prefer them to succeed, especially in feeling healthier and enjoying themselves more, but that this is not a demand on your part, and that you will only feel disappointed and not damning if they do not. (7) Demonstrate that you are reasonably sure that they have more ability than they think they do. Even if they are lacking in specific ways, they almost certainly have the ability to accept themselves with their deficiencies and to enjoy themselves in spite of such deficiencies. (8) Teach them some of the general principles of RET and its views on self-acceptance and show them how to accept all people, including themselves, with their failings and their goofings.

Shame-attacking Exercises

RET specializes in shame-attacking exercises, which constitute both an emotive and a behavioral method. I [A.E.] created these a number of years ago when I realized that one of the main essences of all emotional disturbance is shame: the feeling that people bring on themselves when they believe that they have done something foolish, ridiculous, or stupid, and that others may look down on them for doing this kind of thing. In RET, we particularly get them to do their A-B-C-D-E's when they feel ashamed of something, and get them actively to dispute their humiliation-creating thoughts.

Thus, they can ask themselves: "Granted that others think me foolish for doing some stupid or unpopular act, what is really *shameful* about it? Why do I have to down *myself* for doing it and for getting their disapproval? How does this foolish *behavior* make *me* a no-goodnik?"

To which they can answer: "Nothing is truly shameful in the universe; although many acts, such as this one I have just done, have their distinct disadvantages and had therefore better be avoided. I never have to down *myself*, even when I behave very foolishly and know that others disapprove of me for behaving in this fashion. My silly *behavior* only makes me a *person who has acted* stupidly. It never makes me a truly *stupid individual*."

To insure that your patients really go through this kind of Disputing process, it is often good to give them active shame-attacking exercises: so that they at first truly experience the intense feeling of shame, and then are able to live with it and to rid themselves of it. Preferably, in this respect, they can do almost anything that they personally would feel humiliated about doing, such as wearing a garish outfit that they have purchased but have not dared to wear yet, or refusing to tip a waiter or a taxi driver when they have been given poor service. But they can also do prepared "outlandish" acts, which you can suggest to them if they cannot think of anything better, e.g., yelling out the time of day in public, or telling strangers that they have just been released from a mental institution, or shopping for a dildo in a sex shop.

In doing such "shameful" acts as homework assignments, your patients will tend to discover—and you can point out to them— that others are not as interested in their acts as they think these others are; that many simply ignore them, and that some do not even think of them as "shameful," but only as "amusing" or "interesting." You can also help them see that even when others do frown on their behavior and view them as "crazy," they do not have to accept such verdicts, but can keep their own counsel, realize that they have done their shame-attacking exercises for very sane and self-helping reasons, and that what others think of them for the most part does not really count that much.

Shame-attacking exercises, of course, are not to be recommended where your patients may suffer a real penalty for performing them. Don't have them walk naked in public and risk arrest or act foolishly at work and possibly get fired. Let them perform these exercises in front of friends or strangers, who may think them pretty "nutty," but who are not likely to penalize them in any severe fashion. And the more often they can get themselves to perform them and to work at getting themselves *not* to feel ashamed, the more they will automatically tend to feel sorry about the foolish and sometimes self-defeating things they have done—but not feel self-downing, not feel like worms.

Self-disclosure

Shame-attacking and risk-taking exercises have, as just noted, great value in helping your patients give up their feelings of worthlessness and inadequacy. You can help them to do a special form of these exercises: self-disclosure. For most people really *want* to talk about themselves and express their feelings, especially to a few others with whom they would like to have close relationships. But they are often afraid to do so for fear, again, of what these others will think of them—(1) for the disclosure of some "foolish" behavior and (2) for the hesitant, uncomfortable, or inadequate *manner* in which they make this disclosure. So they constantly monitor themselves and only reveal "safe" things. In doing so, however, they reinforce their underlying philosophy: "If I *did* let myself go and tell others how I feel and what I have done (or would like to do), and if they *did* disapprove of me for my disclosure, that *would be* terrible, I *couldn't* stand their disapproval, and it *would* make me a pretty rotten person!"

Psychotherapy often works best, therefore, if you can get your patients to reveal intimate, and especially, "shameful" things about themselves, and thereby help train them to be able to do so with others as well as with yourself. For self-disclosure is a skill that may well improve by *practice*. The first time a bottled-up individual reveals some "humiliating" material, he or she usually has great difficulty in doing so. But as this material is repeated to others, it becomes less "shameful" and "frightening." The fourth or fifth disclosure may not seem anxiety-provoking at all, and may actually prove to be enjoyable.

So often encourage your patients to reveal sex acts, stupid mistakes on the job, social ineptitude, and other failings that they would hesitate to admit to others. Just let them make sure that they do not get into serious practical difficulties, but only that they get into "trouble" in the sense that others think them "foolish" or "silly" but do not actually penalize them severely.

Role Playing

Another emotive-dramatic technique that is often used in RET— and one that is behavioral as well—is that of role playing. This technique has largely been originated by the famous psychotherapist, J. L. Moreno, and has been popularized by Fritz Perls and the Gestalt therapists. Following Moreno's and Perls' lead, role playing is usually done in an abreactive manner in order to promote the reliving of early emotional experiences and for cathartic release regarding those experiences. In RET, we have often found that this technique has its advantages for helping to open up people but that it also has its great limitations in that it concentrates on overdramatic methods of helping them to get immediate release and to *feel* better rather than to *get* better. Therefore we use it to bring things out in people but then to get them to use these feelings to understand themselves and to work through their irrational ideas, and to change these ideas.

We also use role playing as a dramatic form of behavior rehearsal. If, for example, any of your patients are blocked in their ability to talk to others, and especially to do so in a job interview, you can get them to role play the interview with you (or with a therapy group). In so doing, you may help blocked individuals to open up verbally, to feel the same kind of shame or embarrassment that they would normally feel, and to work through this feeling in the relatively safe but still somewhat "dangerous" atmosphere that is created in their dramatic enactment. Moreover, you can critique the role-played performance, show your patients where they have gone wrong, rerehearse the scene one or more times, and help them get to the point where they fairly easily, unhesitatingly, and smoothly enact the part that they want to act in real-life situations.

In RET role playing, moreover, whatever blocks come out in the behavioral rehearsal can be tracked down to the irrational Beliefs and sentences that your patients tell themselves to create these blockings; these can be disputed and surrendered in the usual RET cognitive-philosophic procedures. RET role playing, therefore, goes beyond psychodrama, Gestalt therapy, and other types of role playing in that it adds a greater understanding of what is going on in your patients' minds during the rehearsed sessions, and shows them how they can deal with their underlying self-defeating premises that cause them to be blocked, overexcited, anxious, or otherwise beset with disruptive feelings.

RET role playing, as is shown in *How to Live With—and Without—Anger*, can also be done when the patients are by themselves, in the form of homework assignments that they give themselves or that you work out with them. Thus, when they are alone they can role play in their heads, in front of a mirror, or with a tape recorder; they can do it with the help of a friend or a group of friends. Thus, one of my [E.A.] patients was afraid to go for a medical examination because he thought that his physician would tell him that he had to have a serious heart operation. By role playing with me, with his wife, and with his tape recorder, he was able to prepare for a relatively unanxious appointment with this physician, to ask all the questions that he wanted to ask about his condition, and to make the arrangements for a full diagnostic workup. Without this kind of role-played preparation, he might have delayed talking with his physician, or perhaps never made the appointment at all. The ironic end to this story is that the diagnostic workup showed that he had no serious heart condition but that his symptoms of physical discomfort were almost entirely the result of his anxiety about the possibility of his getting a heart attack! As we tackled this problem of anxiety, during the next several weeks, his heart "palpitations" and angina completely disappeared.

Other Emotive Procedures

RET makes use of a great many other emotive methods of therapy
from time to time. In my [A.E.] therapy groups, we use encounter
exercises fairly regularly, to bring out emotional material that group
members would normally not bring up themselves, or not even
know about, and then we deal with this material on an RET problem-solving basis. At the Institute for Rational-Emotive Therapy in
New York City, and in various other parts of the country, RET
therapists give rational marathon encounters, for periods of 14
hours or more. Many emotive exercises are used in these marathons, including some of those conventionally used in other types
of marathons and some that we have devised ourselves.

RET therapists also employ emotionally charged language on
some occasions to get ideas forcefully across to patients. They go
over with their patients—as you can go over with yours—emotionally toned words, phrases, and sentences that the patients can then
use with themselves as they go about their own lives in between
the therapy sessions. Thus, patients who have difficulty giving up
smoking can forcefully repeat to themselves, several times a day, "I
can get lung cancer from smoking. There is no special exemption
that I have in this respect!" People who are afraid of illnesses can
keep repeating to themselves, "Diabetes is only inconvenient, not
awful! It won't kill me—if I take care of it properly." They can also
carry around cards on which these forceful messages are written or
typed, or play to themselves taped cassettes on which they have
been recorded.

Almost any emotive therapeutic procedure can be used with
RET, as long as it is not the kind of a procedure that encourages
your patients to be overly dependent upon others, to forbear thinking for themselves, and to look for magical formulas instead of
trying to get at the core of their own self-created disturbances and
continuing to work at uprooting them. Some emotive procedures,
like the use of forceful self-dialogue outlined in the preceding paragraph, are in themselves rational. Other procedures, such as psychodrama or encounter techniques, may mainly be evocative or
confrontational, but they can be tied up with the A-B-C-D-E's of
RET and turned into highly effective rational-emotive techniques.
The more you develop a sensible outlook yourself and know how to
apply the basic cognitive principles and methods of RET, the more
versatile and effective you can be in using emotive-oriented procedures with your patients.

A final word on emotive methodology: rational, as used in RET, does not merely mean calm, passive, indifferent, serene, or unemotional. Emotions are a very valuable part of human behavior. They can show people how disturbed they are, help get at the ideas behind these disturbances, motivate them to work against their needless upsets and self-defeating behavior, and bring them immense pleasure. RET tries to help people become *appropriately* emotional rather than under- or overemotional. It helps your patients strongly desire without their direly needing. But it virtually never encourages them to give up wishing, wanting, and feeling. For then they would hardly be human!

Techniques for Using Rational Emotive Imagery (REI)

Rational Emotive Imagery was originated by Dr. Maxie C. Maultsby, Jr., when he was chief of the Outpatient Psychiatry Department of the University of Kentucky Medical Center and has been modified and developed by Dr. Albert Ellis, Executive Director of the Institute for Rational-Emotive Therapy in New York City. Specific techniques for using REI with negative imagery (usually favored by Dr. Ellis) and with positive imagery (usually favored by Dr. Maultsby) are presented in a pamphlet published by the Institute for Rational Living and reprinted on pages 98–101. Further details on REI are included in *Help Yourself to Happiness* by Dr. Maultsby, also published by the Institute for Rational Living.

Techniques for Using Rational-Emotive Imagery (REI)

MAXIE C. MAULTSBY, JR., M.D.
Dept. of Psychiatry, University of Kentucky Medical Center

ALBERT ELLIS, PH.D.
*Institute for Advanced Study in Rational Psychotherapy
New York City*

Would you like to think more rationally and make yourself less emotionally upset? Try these techniques of rational-emotive imagery (REI).

Negative Imagery

Picture to yourself or fantasize, as vividly and intensely as you can, the details of some unpleasant Activating experience (A) that has happened to you or will likely occur in the future. As you strongly imagine this event, let yourself feel distinctly uncomfortable–for example, anxious, depressed, ashamed, or hostile–at C (your emotional Consequence). Get in touch with this disturbed feeling and let yourself fully experience it for a brief period of time. Don't avoid it: on the contrary, face it and feel it!

When you have actually felt this disturbed emotion for awhile, push yourself–yes, **push** yourself!–to change this feeling in your gut, so that instead you ONLY feel keenly disappointed, regretful, annoyed, or irritated and NOT anxious, depressed, guilty or hostile. Don't think that you can't do this–for you can! You can, at almost any time you work at doing so, get in touch with your gut-level feelings and push yourself to change them so that you experience different feelings. You definitely have the ability to do this. So try, concentrate–and do it!

When you have let yourself, pushed yourself ONLY to feel disappointed or irritated, look at what you have done in your head to MAKE YOURSELF have these new, appropriate feelings. You will note, if you observe yourself clearly, that you have in some manner changed your Belief system (or Bull-shit!), at B, and have thereby changed your emotional Consequence, at C, so that you now feel regretful or annoyed rather than anxious, depressed, guilty, or hostile. Let yourself clearly see what you have done, what important changes in your Belief system you have made. Become fully aware of the new Beliefs (B) that create your new emotional Consequences (C) about the unpleasant Activating experiences (A) that you keep imagining or fantasizing.

If your upsetting feelings do not change as you attempt to feel more appropriately, keep fantasizing the same unpleasant experiences or events and keep working at your gut until you do change these feelings. Don't give up! You create and control your feelings. You **can** change them.

Once you succeed in feeling concerned rather than anxious, disappointed with your behavior rather than ashamed of yourself, or displeased about others' traits rather than hostile to them for having such traits, and once you see exactly what Beliefs you have changed in your head to make yourself feel badly but not emotionally upset, keep repeating this process. Make yourself feel disturbed; then make yourself feel displeased but not disturbed; then see exactly what you did in your head to change your feelings; then practice doing this, over and over again. Keep practicing, until you can easily, after you fantasize highly unfortunate experiences at A, feel upset at C, change your feeling at C to one of disappointment but not upsetness, and see what you keep doing at B to change your Belief system that creates and maintains your feelings. If you keep practicing this kind of rational-emotive imagery (REI) for at least ten minutes every day for the next few weeks, you will get to the point where whenever you think of this kind of unpleasant event, or it actually occurs in practice, you will tend to easily and automatically feel displeased rather than emotionally upset.

ILLUSTRATIVE EXAMPLE: At A, the Activating experience of Activating event, let us suppose that you have failed to do a job well and your supervisor or boss has severely criticized you for this failure. You feel depressed or self-downing about this (at C, your emotional Consequence) and you want to get over this disturbed feeling.

Let yourself strongly, vividly fantasize the details of your failing and getting criticized (of its actually occurring in the past or your imagining its occurring in the future). Let yourself feel, as you intensely picture this failure and criticism, depressed or self-downing. Feel this! Get keenly in touch with your emotions of depression and worthlessness! Keep in touch with them for a short period of time.

Now push yourself—yes, push yourself—while keeping this same unfortunate set of conditions vividly in your mind to make yourself feel ONLY disappointed and concerned. If you have trouble doing this, keep persisting until you succeed. You can fantasize failure and make yourself feel ONLY concerned and disappointed RATHER THAN depressed and worthless. Do this!

When you have begun to feel ONLY concerned and disappointed (and NOT depressed and worthless) look for what you have started telling yourself, in your head, to MAKE YOURSELF have these new, appropriate feelings. You will find that you probably have started telling yourself something like: "I guess it doesn't prove awful for me to fail and get criticized, even though I do find it unfortunate and highly inconvenient. The world will hardly come to an end if my supervisor or boss keeps criticizing me, even though I don't like this and wish I could make him or her stop. I can stand failing, although I'll never want to fail. While my acts seem bad and deplorable, they hardly make me a rotten person."

While you still vividly imagine your failing and getting severely criticized, keep practicing telling yourself these kinds of rational beliefs. And keep feeling the appropriate emotions of disappointment, regret, concern, and displeasure—and NOT depression or worthlessness.

Positive Imagery

If you would employ positive imagery and thinking, picture to yourself or fantasize, as vividly and intensely as you can, the details of some unpleasant Activating experience (A) that has happened to you or will likely occur in the future. If you want to do so, you can picture the situation at A at its very worst—the worst that you ever experienced it or will probably ever experience it in the future. Let yourself feel distinctly uncomfortable—for example, anxious, depressed, ashamed, or hostile—at C (your emotional Consequence). Get in touch with this disturbed feeling and let yourself fully experience it for a brief period of time.

As you feel upset at C, notice what you keep telling yourself at B (your Belief system or Bull-shit) to MAKE YOURSELF feel disturbed. When you clearly see these Beliefs, Dispute them (at D), as you would in the usual kind of Disputing that rational-emotive therapy (RET) or rational behavior training (RBT) teaches you to do.

Now, as you see these irrational Beliefs and vigorously Dispute them, strongly fantasize how you would feel and behave AFTER you started giving them up and AFTER you started believing, instead, rational Beliefs about what keeps happening to you at A. Intensely picture yourself (1) disbelieving your irrational Beliefs and believing your rational ideas about obnoxious events that may occur at A; (2) feeling appropriately displeased or disappointed rather than inappropriately depressed or hostile at C; and (3) acting in a concerned instead of an upset manner at E.

Keep practicing this procedure, so that you first imagine something unfortunate or disadvantageous; then make yourself feel depressed, hostile, or otherwise disturbed about your image; then see what irrational Beliefs you hold to create your disturbance; then work on changing these Beliefs; then strongly picture yourself disbelieving these ideas and feeling and acting in accordance with your new rational philosophies; and wind up by actually feeling only concerned and displeased rather than depressed or hostile.

ILLUSTRATIVE EXAMPLE: At A, the Activating experience or Activating event, let us suppose (once again) that you have failed to do a job well and your supervisor or boss has severely criticized you for this failure. You feel depressed or self-downing about this (at C, your emotional Consequence) and you want to get over this disturbed feeling.

Let yourself strongly, vividly fantasize the details of your failing and getting criticized (of its actually occurring in the past or your imagining its occurring in the future). Let yourself feel, as you intensely picture this failure and criticism, depressed or self-downing. Feel this! Get keenly in touch with your emotions of depression and worthlessness! Keep in touch with them for a short period of time.

Now actively look for the irrational Beliefs (at B) with which you keep creating your disturbed feelings, and make sure that you find them. Don't give up easily! Assume that your feelings get created by your own Beliefs and persist until you discover these Beliefs—especially the **shoulds, oughts,** and **musts** they almost invariably include.

You will probably find that your irrational Beliefs follow these lines: "I find it awful to fail and get criticized! If my supervisor or boss keeps criticizing me, my job will end, the whole world will practically end for me, and I'll never get a good job again or find happiness at work. I can't **stand** failing and getting criticized! If I keep failing like this, that proves me a thoroughly rotten person who remains incapable of succeeding at practically anything!"

Get yourself to see your own irrational Beliefs very clearly. Then vigorously, persistently Dispute them (at point D), until you see that you don't **have** to believe them and that you **can** give them up and feel much better about the obnoxious things, the failing and getting criticized, happening to you at A. Picture yourself, as vividly as possible, actually believing a radically different philosophy about yourself failing. Such as: "I don't have to find it awful, but merely inconvenient and disadvantageous, to fail and get criticized.

If my supervisor or boss keeps criticizing me, I probably won't lose my job but will merely keep getting criticized for not doing it well enough. If I somehow do lose my job, I'll probably get another good one again, and may even learn considerably from this bad experience. Although I'll never like failing and getting severely criticized, I certainly can stand it! Even though I keep failing, that only proves me a person with flaws, who cannot do as well as I'd prefer to do but who never turns into a rotten person, utterly incapable of succeeding at anything."

As you picture yourself believing this, also see yourself, as vividly as you can, responding appropriately to a critical supervisor or boss; looking around for better solutions to your problem of failing; seeing the possible loss of a job as a problem to get solved rather than as a catastrophe; and accepting yourself fully, no matter how poorly you do in job situations. Keep practicing these positive thoughts and images, until you easily and automatically begin to feel disappointed, concerned, and displeased rather than to feel depressed and self-flagellating.

Self-reinforcement

As noted above, if you use either negative or positive rational-emotive imagery, you will probably find it useful to spend at least ten minutes a day practicing one or both of these forms of REI for a period of two or three weeks. You may find them particularly useful if you expect an unpleasant or risky situation to occur—such as taking a stiff examination of some kind—and you fear you will get anxious or depressed when it does occur. If for several days or weeks before its transpiring, you vigorously employ these REI methods, you may find that you easily meet the situation, when it does occur, without the feelings of anxiety or depression you would usually experience.

If you frequently avoid homework assignments, such as REI, and you want to encourage yourself to carry them out, you may use operant conditioning or self-management methods (originated by B. F. Skinner, David Premack, Marvin Goldfried, and other psychologists). Select some activity that you highly enjoy and that you tend to do every day—such as reading, eating, television view-

100

ing, masturbation, or social contact with your friends. Use this activity as a reinforcer or reward by ONLY allowing yourself to engage in it AFTER you have practiced REI for at least ten minutes that day. Otherwise, no reward!

In addition, you may penalize yourself every single day you do NOT use REI for at least ten minutes. How? By making yourself perform some activity you find distinctly un-pleasant—such as eating something obnoxious, contributing to a cause you hate, getting up a half-hour earlier in the morning, or spending an hour conversing with someone you find boring. You can also arrange with some person or group to monitor you and help you actually carry out the penalties that you set yourself. You may of course steadily use REI without self-reinforcement. But you will often find it more effective if you use it along with rewards and penalties that you execute right after you practice or avoid practicing this rational-emotive method.

11
Behavioral Methods of RET and Cognitive-Behavior Therapy

RET is a truly comprehensive method of therapy because it includes a good many cognitive, emotive, and behavioral techniques—as we have been emphasizing throughout this book. In its general or less elegant form, it is synonymous with what is usually called cognitive-behavior therapy (CBT); but it also has a distinct emotive component, as outlined in the last chapter, and is therefore somewhat more comprehensive than many forms of CBT. In this chapter, we shall outline some of the main behavioral techniques that are consistently employed in RET. We cannot discuss all of them, of course, for that would take a book in itself. But the most common behavioral methods that rational-emotive therapists tend to employ include the following ones.

Operant Conditioning and Self-Management Procedures

The outstanding psychologist, B. F. Skinner, did a great deal of experimental work, using reinforcement schedules with animals and humans; in this experimentation he tended to show that if individuals (or pigeons!) are reinforced every time they do a certain act and are penalized (or deprived) every time they do not perform this act, their behavior may change enormously, so that they continue "naturally," easily, or "spontaneously" to perform the reinforced or rewarded act. Innumerable other experimenters who have been interested in helping people change their dysfunctional emotions and behavior (who are often called behavior therapists) have utilized Skinnerian techniques and have used them with good, and at times remarkable, effect.

One form of operant conditioning consists of what is called contingency management where people make one of their difficult behaviors, such as self-discipline, contingent upon one of their easy behaviors, such as eating or television viewing. David Premack found that effective reinforcers for contingency management need not be what are called primary reinforcers, such as food, water, or sex, but can also be secondary reinforcers, i.e., virtually any behavior that the individual considers to be easy and satisfying. Following Premack's lead, Lloyd Homme discovered that secondary reinforcers can be used even in the case of young children.

Thus, children find certain activities, such as talking to others, yelling, and walking around the room, much more satisfying than sitting in class or paying attention to their teacher for a prolonged period of time. But if the teacher tells them that if they pay attention for, say, ten minutes, they will then be allowed to walk around the room, to yell, or to talk to others, they are able to control themselves for this period of time in order to earn this reward or reinforcement.

You can teach many of your patients how to set up self-reinforcement schedules so that they can induce themselves to perform almost any kind of difficult or disciplined activity that they normally tend to avoid. Thus, if they are having trouble exercising regularly or keeping to some other medical regimen, they can talk to themselves in this manner: "Enough of this avoidance! Let me review the activities that I find truly enjoying to see which I can use to help discipline myself. What do I like? Well, having a good meal, for one thing. All right. I will permit myself to have a good dinner only after I have already devoted myself for at least a half hour to exercising. And no exceptions! At least a half hour a day playing tennis, jumping rope, or jogging—or only a crummy dinner!"

Similarly, your patients can use self-management schedules to diet, to give up smoking, to speak to their boss about getting a raise, to pay their monthly bills, and to help themselves do various

other kinds of tasks that they consider onerous and that they usually avoid. Take, for example, the office manager of a moderately
large buying office who came to one of the procrastination workshops that are regularly given at the Institute for Rational Living in
New York. His problem was to get himself to go for regular appointments with his family physician, since he usually gave himself
some specious excuse and kept avoiding either making these appointments or keeping them once they were made.

"Look," he told the workshop group. "I keep getting notices
from my family doctor, my dentist, and my eye doctor that I'd
better call to make an appointment, and I ignore practically all of
them. I must have several of them piled up in my drawer right
now—some of which I've had for months. You know how it is. I
just feel that I can't be bothered with going through the inconvenience of making and keeping the appointment. What can I do?"

In his workshop group, we showed him first of all how not to
down himself and make himself terribly guilty about not making or
keeping these medical appointments. He was certainly doing himself in by neglecting them, but this was only poor *behavior* on his
part and did not make him a rotten *person*. He thought that by
condemning himself roundly for avoiding the appointments he
would drive himself to make them. But he learned during the workshop that self-flagellation gets people to concentrate on themselves
and their rottenness, rather than on changing their *acts,* and that it
consequently interferes with instead of aiding their doing this kind
of changing.

While we were helping him work on the self-downing, we also
considered his low frustration tolerance (LFT). After, at point A
(Activating Experience), he considered making a medical appointment, he would at point C (behavioral and emotional Consequence)
procrastinate and avoid making it because at point B (Belief System)
he would at first rationally tell himself, "What a hassle to make and
come in for a doctor's appointment! I wish I didn't have to do this.
How annoying!" This was a set of rational Beliefs (rB's) because he
did not like these appointments and it would have been nice had he
been able to avoid them and not suffer the consequences.

But then he kept adding an irrational set of Beliefs (iB's): "How
horrible to go through this kind of a hassle! I *should not* have to go to
this bother! I probably don't have to go anyway, since I can wait till
I get sick and then call my doctor. Even if it's in the middle of the
night, he'll have to come and see me."

We got him to Dispute (at D) these irrational Beliefs: "Why is it *horrible* to go through this kind of a hassle?" Answer: "It isn't, of course. It's only annoying and inconvenient, but it will be even more annoying and much more inconvenient if I have an illness that easily could have been avoided had I gone for the examination." "Why *should* I not have to go to this bother?" Answer: "There is no reason why I *shouldn't* have to go through it. And there are several good reasons why I'd better have the examination, even though it takes time and trouble. If I want to remain in good health, I *had better* get examined regularly—for that will increase my chances of avoiding sickness." "Can I really wait until I get sick and then call my doctor?" Answer: "I certainly can, for there's no law against doing so. But how unwise that will be! Quite possibly, he won't be available in the middle of the night, and even if he is, who knows what will happen to me, especially if I have something serious like a heart attack? If I see him regularly, however, I will probably be able to ward off some ailments that would greatly inconvenience me if they did occur. So I'd better not rationalize and falsely believe that it is good to wait until I'm really sick before I call!"

In the workshop group we helped him Dispute his irrational Beliefs until he started giving them up. He still correctly thought that it was hard and inconvenient for him to make medical appointments, but not that it was *too* hard and that it *should not* be that hard. The workshop group also suggested a simple self-reinforcing schedule for him. He was to avoid having any kind of sex, including masturbation, until he first made and then kept an appointment with his family physician.

Since this man had an active sex life and did not want to give up one of his greatest pleasures, he immediately made an appointment for a medical checkup. This kind of reinforcement schedule worked so well that he kept using it for dental and other health care appointments, and always made them very quickly whenever he received a reminder to call for one. He wrote a follow-up letter several months later to the workshop leader:

> I'm certainly glad that I attended your procrastination workshop; and more than glad that I decided to take it seriously and work hard on changing my own behavior. I feel much better for several reasons: the visits to my doctors are no longer hanging over my head; I accurately know the state of my health; and, above all, I know now that I can manage my own life and think and act in a manner that is truly nondefeating. All this really helps me a great deal, and I am consequently doing better in several other ways that I never thought I could handle before. Thank you again for conducting such a fine workshop!

You can teach your patients self-reinforcement schedules and apply them to a variety of situations. At the Institute for Rational-Emotive Therapy in New York we continually use them to help our psychotherapy patients lose weight, cut down on excessive drinking, attend social gatherings, act better with their family members, give up smoking, and do many other things that they consider *too hard* or *impossible* to do. As soon as they really deprive themselves of some strong satisfaction and make their engaging in this activity contingent on their disciplining themselves, their self-discipline often greatly increases and frequently they get surprisingly good results.

Not that all of the people we see or those you will see are this easy to work with and to teach the methods of self-management! Many are D.C.'s (difficult customers). For these individuals, who will not really monitor themselves or who continue smoking or overeating and still indulge in the gratifying activities that they supposedly are going to give up if they smoke or overeat, we sometimes find that penalization is more effective than reward. For many of them will honestly say, "You know, there is nothing that I can think of that I could not easily forego in order to continue to smoke or to overeat. Reinforcing myself in this manner just won't work." And it won't—or, at least, they won't let it work.

Stiff penalties, however, sometimes will. As in the case of the woman with cardiovascular problems whose physician told her very strongly that if she did not stop smoking her usual two or more packs of cigarettes every day, she could very easily kill herself. She said that she wanted to stop and to stay alive; but she felt that she just *could not* give up smoking. I [A.E.] suggested several reinforcement schedules, but none of them worked. So I firmly said: "Look, smoking is so clearly gratifying to you, and stopping smoking so onerous, that you will continue to smoke even if it means missing good meals, giving up television, or refraining from socializing. You could, of course, not allow yourself to eat at all for the rest of the day whenever you have a single puff of a cigarette. That would probably work. But it doesn't look like you will stick to that regimen and let it work."

"You're right. I don't seem to have the ability to stick to the reinforcement schedules that we've used so far."

"You have the ability, but, again, you won't use it! But I can tell you something you can do, if you really want to give up smoking."

"What?"

"Severely penalize yourself immediately—and I mean *immediately*—after you have a single cigarette."

"Penalize myself? How?"

"Well, that depends on what you consider penalizing. I have one penalty that I am almost certain would work: but I unfortunately haven't been able to get anyone to use it yet."

"Which one is that?"

"Oh, a simple one: every time you take a puff of the cigarette, merely reverse it and put the *lit* end in your mouth for at least fifteen seconds."

"I couldn't do *that!*"

"Oh, yes you could. But you probably won't. So let's think of something a little more practical—and less dangerous to your mouth! What would you consider really penalizing, something you could do immediately after puffing on a cigarette?"

"I really can't think of anything."

"I'm sure you can if you really try!"

"Uh. Well. I guess I can think of something."

"What?"

"Well. Sending away a contribution to a cause I hate, like the Ku Klux Klan."

"Fine! How much will you send for every cigarette you smoke?"

"Well, uh. How about ten dollars?"

"Okay. But let's be clear. Not merely when you smoke, you send ten dollars to the Ku Klux Klan. But *every single time* you smoke. That means that if you smoke five cigarettes a day, or even start to smoke five cigarettes, that's a total of fifty dollars you have to send to the Klan that very day."

"Every single time I even start to smoke a cigarette? That seems rough!"

"Yes, but it's rougher if you smoke. You really could *kill* yourself that way!"

"You're right. Okay, ten dollars for every time I even start to smoke."

"Good. And if we find that that isn't a severe enough penalty, we can always raise it to twenty-five or fifty dollars."

"Oh, ten dollars will be quite enough, I'm sure!"

"We'll see!"

As this woman predicted, ten dollars was enough. She kept away from smoking pretty well, but in the first few weeks did send 60 dollars to the Ku Klux Klan. She felt so badly that she completely refrained from smoking.

Similarly, you can often induce your difficult customers not only to fail to reinforce themselves when they avoid important health disciplines, but to penalize themselves fairly severely. With less difficult individuals, you can show them how to use simple reinforcement techniques. And, as usual in RET, when either the reinforcements or the penalties do not work, you can go back to getting them to see what they are telling themselves to create and maintain their low frustration tolerance, and how to dispute these irrational self-statements.

Homework Assignments

Since I [A.E.] first started to use RET, it has always emphasized activity homework assignments, usually on an in vivo or alive (rather than an imaginative) basis. Rational-emotive imagery, as we have shown in the previous chapter, uses imagery techniques, and so do various other RET procedures. But we have found over the years, as a good many behavior therapists (such as Isaac Marks) have also discovered, that desensitizing in vivo homework assignments work best for many individuals who find it difficult to change their dysfunctional behavior.

Take the case of Joan F., who was exceptionally resistant to getting regular allergy desensitization injections because of her strong fears of having anything injected into her body with a needle. She had had this fear since childhood, and traced it down mainly to her several weeks stay in a hospital when she was seven years old and to the pain she experienced when they kept taking blood samples out of her arm for a series of tests. She said that she realized, today, that the pain of a needle was really not that bad, but she still felt terrified every time she even thought about getting an injection.

I [E.A.] went through the A-B-C's of RET with Joan, and induced her to Dispute the "horror" and the "can't-stand-it-itis" that she felt in regard to injections. This kind of anti-awfulizing only enabled her to take her antiallergy injections regularly, but not to give up her tremendous fears about them. In discussing homework with her, she herself suggested, though with great hesitation and with the obvious wish that I would veto the suggestion, that she could get a syringe and inject herself several times a day, until she became desensitized to this kind of procedure. I thought that was a great idea, and encouraged her to try it. I also showed her that, if she failed to go through with her homework, she could penalize herself by not allowing herself to talk to her close friends over the phone or in person until she had injected herself at least five times a day.

The suggestion seemed to work so well that she immediately got a number of plastic needles and started injecting herself with water at least five times, and sometimes ten or more times, every day. For the first few days, she was able to do so, but still with her usual fears. But when, a week later, she determined that she would routinely go ahead with the injections, no matter how anxious she felt about them, she suddenly realized that her anxiety had dropped, and that she was able to view them as mildly painful but not as *awful* or *terrible*. Apparently, as happens with a great many people, she had been using her feelings of anxiety to give herself an excuse *not* to go through with injections. Once she determined that *no* excuse would do, and that she definitely, come hell or high water, would go through with them, much of her anxiety left.

After a few more weeks of giving herself several injections a day, Joan completely lost her fear, even though she never enjoyed the injections. She was thereafter able to drop her homework assignment and to go regularly for her antiallergy shots without virtually any trouble. Her in vivo desensitizing procedure had helped her give up her deliberate, though unconscious, exacerbation of her anxiety, and it also helped her to get so habituated to taking several shots a day that going to her allergist twice a week for her medical shots seemed quite unimportant and mild.

Keeping cases like this in mind, you can often help your patients figure out some in vivo activities that they can keep doing regularly, in the form of homework assignments. Usually, these will be antianxiety assignments: doing something that they are afraid to do, such as going for a medical examination or even calling up to find out about the results of the exam. But they can also be related to their low frustration tolerance. For in RET we often get people to give themselves the tasks of staying in an obnoxious situation for the present, instead of copping out of it, and showing themselves that it *is not* terrible, that they *can* stand it, and that the world is *not* an impossible place in which to live while this obnoxious situation exists.

Thus, you can show a man who will not go to a clinic regularly, because he sees it as *too* hard and *terrible* to go through its frustrating procedures and to wait until the clinic doctor or nurse will see him, that he is not imagining the hardness but the *too*-hardness of clinic attendance. And you can get him to deliberately keep attending the clinic for awhile, instead of paying money that he cannot afford for private medical visits, until he overcomes a good deal of his low frustration tolerance. Once he sees that he can fulfill this assignment and not inwardly rage and scream about it, he *then* may be encouraged to look for easier ways of getting medical treatment. But it is often better for him, at least for the present, to stay in a bad situation and stop defining it as *awful* rather than arranging a better situation. Later, he can always arrange to get rid of some of the medical hassles in his life—*after* he has managed to increase his frustration tolerance!

Frequently, you will find it best to give your patients home-work assignments, particularly those that help desensitize them to anxieties, on a gradual basis. Thus, someone who is fearful of needles could inject herself, first, once a week, then twice a week, then once a day, and finally several times a day. But if you can get your patients to do their activity homework implosively and quickly, you will find that they frequently desensitize themselves to "fearful" stimuli much faster and more permanently.

This particularly goes for situations involving social anxiety. I [A.E.] once had a patient who was pregnant and was attending a course in childbirth and childcare but was too afraid to ask questions in class, for fear that she would ask them badly or that she would show her stupidity in not being able to understand the answers. Since the class was only going to last for a few weeks and I thought that it was a good opportunity to get her to desensitize herself to these types of social situations and to stop worrying too much about what others might think of her, I induced her to speak up in her class several times every day she attended. She had to either ask a question or make a comment when she spoke up. She was very reluctant to do this, but I pointed out what a fine opportunity it was for her to tackle her anxiety and to overcome it quickly.

When she forced herself to keep speaking up in class, in spite of her great fears of doing so, she was able to zero in much more specifically on her irrational Beliefs and to tackle them. She also, in just a few weeks, became quite unafraid to speak up in the class-room situation and then, without even at first talking to me about it, to give herself similar flooding exercises about speaking up in social groups, of which she was also quite fearful. In this short period, she made amazing gains in regard to her social anxiety, and she is typical of a good many other people whom I have seen over-come anxieties or phobias quickly and almost completely and do so with in vivo flooding methods.

Relaxation Methods

Joseph Wolpe pioneered, a good many years ago, in using Edmund Jacobsen's progressive relaxation technique as a reciprocal inhibition method. Thus, he would let people imagine things or events of which they were afraid, for example, riding in trains or speaking in public, and then, when they felt anxious about these imagined events, interrupting their anxiety with relaxing. After awhile, as many experiments have shown, they trained themselves to be less anxious when imagining these "dangerous" scenes and were ultimately able to face their fears in practice. A good deal of experimentation has subsequently shown that Wolpe's form of desensitization can be done with different kinds of interruptive methods, and without any kind of relaxing whatever.

However, relaxation is still a good method for helping people, at least palliatively and temporarily, to overcome their anxiety. You may often be able to use it successfully with your patients, as they face "dangerous" or "fearful" health situations, such as entering the hospital, going through certain diagnostic procedures, or even having a regular examination in a physician's office. To employ this technique, you learn one of several relaxation methods yourself, such as the Jacobsen or the Luthe and Schultz technique. You can then show your patients how to perform this technique, especially at times when they are quite upset. Or you can give them printed instructions or a tape recording that will teach them such a method.

Similarly, you can encourage some of your patients to use various meditative, Yoga, and other techniques which tend to help them relax their bodies and to turn away from obsessive-compulsive thoughts with which they may be bothering themselves. All these techniques, RET hypothesizes, involve a great deal of thought distraction. When, for example, you use Jacobsen's method of progressive relaxation, and keep focusing on relaxing one of your muscles after another, you are forced to think very concertedly about what you are doing to relax yourself, and while you are focusing your mind on this kind of problem, you will find it almost impossible to worry about anything else. Similarly, meditation, Yoga, breathing, television viewing, window shopping, and many other kinds of physical or mental relaxing methods are really forms of thought distraction or diversion, and they work cognitively as well as "physically."

You can therefore use these methods with your patients, and put them in an RET framework. You can realize yourself that they work largely because they consist of mental distraction; you can inform your more sophisticated and better educated patients about this. You can also let them know that such methods are usually palliative because they can easily return to the same anxieties a little later. For they have not discovered, through relaxing, the philosophic core of their anxiety-creation, and they have not Disputed this core, at what we call point D in RET.

Nonetheless, just as aspirin is palliative but often useful, so are various kinds of relaxing and distracting methods. This is particularly true when your patients are confronted by temporary situations such as a relatively short stay in the hospital. If you can show them how to relax physically or otherwise to distract themselves during this stay, they will often be in a much better frame of mind, and able to recuperate better from surgery or any other procedures. If they have overweening basic anxiety, relaxing methods will only work temporarily and had better also be accompanied by some of the other important RET methods outlined in this book. But if they are anxious only under certain limited conditions, relaxation procedures can be quite helpful.

Health problems often lead to lack of sufficient sleep, and by the same token, lack of sleep often leads to health problems. Relaxing and distracting methods can prove valuable to overcome such sleep problems. Thus, if your patients know how to perform progressive relaxation, or to focus regularly on their breathing, or to auto-suggestively tell themselves as they lie in bed, "Relax, relax, relax!" they may be able to get to sleep much more easily. At the same time, they can be shown that insomnia is not *awful* and *horrible* but only *highly inconvenient*. By using RET to help them give up their anxieties *about* sleeping, they will often sleep much better.

Skill Training

RET primarily emphasizes that people will help themselves and grow to a maximum degree when they change their basic thinking and take a risk-taking, adventurous outlook on life; it consequently prepares them philosophically to do so. But, as pointed out in the article "Rational-Emotive Therapy: Research Data That Supports the Clinical and Personality Hypotheses of RET and Other Modes of Cognitive-Behavior Therapy," when men and women receive training in certain skills, for example, in assertion, in socializing, in sex technique, or in values clarification, they frequently change their thinking, emoting, and other behavior and sometimes make themselves considerably less emotionally disturbed.

For example, suppose you have a patient who does not know how to communicate well with others, who is anxious about her social ineptitude, and who feels very depressed whenever she fails to get along well with a new person or group. Using RET, you show her that her anxiety and depression stem largely from her own irrational Beliefs (iB's) and not from the fact that at point A (Activating Experiences) she is having difficulty in communicating with others and is often failing at this kind of communication. She is probably telling herself, "I *must* communicate well and win the approval of others! Isn't it *awful* when I don't! I *can't stand* my social ineptness. I am a complete *schnook*, a pretty *worthless individual* for having such difficulty!"

Using some of the main principles of RET, you get her to Dispute (at D) her irrational Beliefs, and to work toward a saner philosophy or new cognitive Effect (at point E): "Well, it would be distinctly preferable if I communicated well and kept winning the approval of others. But I am a highly fallible human, and will always do some things poorly and fail to win many people's acceptance. How annoying and frustrating! But it *isn't* awful and I definitely *can* stand it. My worth as a human, moreover, has nothing to do with my various traits and skills, and even if I always am fairly poor at communicating, that is merely *a* failing and it doesn't make me a *failure*. I can still lead a reasonably happy, though less happy, existence with this deficiency. Now let me see what I can do to make up some of my deficits in communication."

Doing her A-B-C's in this manner, and winding up with a new cognitive Effect (E), this patient will feel much better and be ready for skill training in communication. Without this kind of RET Disputing (at D), she might take the skill training, focus on what a worm she is for having to do it less than perfectly and interfere with her learning how to talk better to others. So in using skill training, you would usually place it in this kind of an RET framework.

Forget RET for the moment and let us suppose that you merely help this woman to improve her communication skills. In private talks with her, or as a member of one of your therapy or workshop groups, you teach her, as Robert Liberman would do, how to look people in the eye, speak up more firmly, listen more carefully to what they say, smile at them encouragingly, etc. So, even though you have done little as yet to help her change her disturbance-creating philosophy, she follows your teaching and develops better social communicative skills.

If so, you have usually helped her to change at least *some* of her self-defeating ideas. For among other things, she tends to believe, "I *can't* communicate adequately," and as a result of skill training she now changes this idea to: "Perhaps I can communicate better," or even, "You know, I'm getting pretty good at communicating." But this woman, before you teach her communication skills, probably also tends to hold such irrational Beliefs as, (1) "Social communication is the most important thing in life and the be-all and end-all of existence." 2) "If I communicate imperfectly, *no one* will like me or have anything to do with me." (3) "If I can't communicate well, I can't do *anything* properly." (4) "If I learn to socialize better with others *all* my emotional problems will be solved," etc.

By teaching this person good communication skills and getting her to practice these in her actual life situations, many or all these ideas will tend to be almost automatically disputed and surrendered. For her new skills and the activities she goes through as a result of acquiring them consist of *behavior* that is incompatible with some of her crazy thinking. By changing herself *behaviorally* she will also tend to change herself, at least to some degree, *philosophically*. She will therefore not only do better in communicating with others, but may make a significant philosophic and emotional change in herself that will then enable her to gain confidence, not in everything she does but at least in her ability to communicate, and therefore to improve even more in this area.

Skill training in itself, consequently, often (though not always!) leads to profound ideational or philosophic changes, and that is one reason why it has become so popular in recent years. However, the change that your patient makes in this case through your helping her communicate better may be only rather superficial and somewhat misleading. She may wind up, for example, with the philosophy, "I now know that I can communicate much better than I did before. But suppose I don't do *as* well in this area as I want to do. Or suppose I lose some of this skill later. Or suppose I communicate well and *still* don't get the kind of social or love relationships I want. Wouldn't *that* be terrible! I then *couldn't stand* my relative ineptness, and I would go back to being a *rotten person*." In other words, she would have made a highly inelegant, partial philosophic change and would still be, at the very least, underlyingly anxious, and easily disturbable.

Anyway, there are often valid aspects of skill training that you can teach your patients or can have them learn elsewhere. These, like problem solving, are a regular part of RET. Even though we mainly focus on people's Belief System and get them to change their iB's (irrational Beliefs), in order to help them change their C's (behavioral and emotional Consequences), we often also help them to change some aspects of their A's (such as their failing behavior) which trigger their irrationalities. If they can behave better at A, and most of them can, they will have little need to tell themselves these irrational sentences. As noted above, they can also tell themselves good philosophies about the desirability, though not the necessity, of succeeding.

In the field of sex, for example, you can easily learn, and then teach your patients, some of the skills that people can use to help themselves function more effectively. Following the lead of Masters and Johnson, Hartman and Fithian, and Helen Kaplan, as well as using the sex techniques that I [A.E.] have been teaching and writing about since the early 1950s, you can help your patients use pleasuring methods, avoid intercourse until they have learned to bring each other to orgasm noncoitally, and use their imaging and fantasizing ability to heighten their sex drives. You can also encourage them to practice various coital positions that are often more satisfactory than conventional ones, rehearse themselves in the course of their masturbatory experiences so that they later can enjoy sex more with a partner, and learn various other sex skills. Naturally, as a physician, nurse, or other health professional, you cannot expect to be a skilled teacher of every important human skill. Nor can professional psychotherapists expect this kind of competence either. But you can learn how to teach a few basic skills such as sex, marital communication, and interpersonal relations that you can use with a good many of your patients. And, as ever, you can teach these skills within a general RET context, rather than merely in their own right.

Stimulus Control

RET distinctly emphasizes helping people to change their B's (Belief Systems) rather than merely changing their A's (Activating Experiences or environmental events of their lives). But in the course of its behavioral methods, it sometimes also shows patients how to control certain kinds of stimuli, so that they are less likely to resort to dysfunctional, addictive behavior.

Take, especially, the problem of helping your patients control their overeating tendencies and to lose and maintain the loss of superfluous weight. Since such large numbers of people in Western civilization are overweight and since obesity contributes significantly to many of their health problems, this is an important area for you to know about and with which you can try to help your patients. As usual, you can largely and elegantly do this by showing them that their addiction to overeating significantly stems from their low frustration tolerance (LFT), that is, their *must*urbatory irrational Beliefs: "I *must* not suffer immediate deprivation, and it is *awful* if I do! I *can't bear* continual frustrations, like dieting; and my life is horrible if I am forced to diet for the rest of my life in order to maintain good health and get other satisfactions that I want."

This kind of short-range hedonism basically causes many—perhaps most—people in our culture to fail to discipline themselves in many important ways, including sticking with a proper diet regimen. And, using RET, you can show your patients that they have a self-defeating philosophy, can teach them how to actively Dispute it, and can help them acquire much higher frustration tolerance, and thereby set the stage for better dieting procedures.

But this is often not enough. You still had better see that your patients acquire sufficient dieting skills, and consequently do some skill training with them. You might, for example, see that they learn something about calorie counting, about nutrition, and about various other aspects of dieting. In addition, you might well teach them some of the basic aspects of stimulus control. For, obviously, most people diet poorly and less rigorously when they are around people who overeat, when they have improper foods easily available to them, and when the conditions of their lives are conducive to easy overeating.

You might therefore teach them how to control some of the food-related stimuli in their lives by having them follow specified rules: (1) Restructure the environment to reduce temptations to eat. For example, if pastry is served during the office coffee breaks, you could immediately get only the coffee and take it to your desk to drink, and leave the coffee break itself until it is over. (2) Avoid the purchase of problematic foods. Take a list of suitable foods to the grocery or supermarket and bring only enough money to cover the cost of these foods. (3) Do not serve certain foods to children or mates, but train these individuals to take their own desserts or other fattening foods themselves at mealtimes. (4) Clear all plates at mealtimes directly and swiftly into the garbage pail, and refuse to leave any tempting food on the plates, where you may later eat it yourself. (5) Leave the table soon after finishing a meal. (6) Eat slowly and do not gulp down food. The faster one eats, the more one tends to eat. (7) Eat at least three meals and preferably four or more meals a day, so that your calories are divided and you do not feel tempted to eat too much at any one meal. (8) Only eat at a meal; do not watch TV while eating or give in to other distractions that may keep you from only eating the right amount of food at each meal. (9) Stock the eating environment in your favor. For example, do not keep candy or unusually tempting food in the house or apartment. (10) Use relaxation exercises or other diversions that will keep you from feeling anxious and eating because of anxiety. (11) Use a small plate rather than a large dinner plate; this will help give the illusion of eating more. (12) Do not use condiments at meals that have a high caloric content. (13) Engage in regular exercise, such as moderate walking, that helps burn calories. (14) Eliminate from the diet various high calorie foods, such as alcohol, cake, bread, and butter. (15) Encourage family members to be supportive of your patients' dieting efforts.

   While using these techniques of stimulus control, you can also help your patients to use specific cognitive techniques of dieting, such as counterattacking their all-or-nothing attitudes: "Now that I've gone off my diet and eaten one doughnut, I have ruined things completely. So I might as well eat six doughnuts." Or attacking perfectionist attitudes: "Because I've only lost a few pounds, it will take me forever to lose the amount of weight that it would be desirable for me to lose." If you can help your patients keep working at their cognitions while they also use behavioral methods of weight control, they can stay on their diets much more easily and can also maintain such diets for a long period of time.

Practicing and Reinforcing Rational Cognitions

   You can use RET to help your patients Dispute their self-defeating cognitions and to substitute, in their stead, new philosophies or better coping statements. Thus, in regard to weight reduction, they can Dispute the irrational Beliefs that that they cannot lose weight, that it is too hard for them to continue to diet, and that they should be able to eat whatever they want and still not get fat. They can substitute new Beliefs and coping statements for their dysfunctional ones, such as, "No matter how hard it is for me to continue to diet, it is much harder for me to continue to overeat!" "I definitely *can* lose weight and keep my weight down," and "I am not a worm for letting myself be as fat as I now am, but this is very wormy behavior because of the harm that I keep doing to myself by retaining this weight."

   Such sensible philosophies, however, get stabilized mainly by steady practice and not by repetition. People, therefore, had better keep doing this practice—or work activity. RET, as is pointed out in several of its basic texts, particularly *Reason and Emotion in Psycho-therapy, Humanistic Psychotherapy: the Rational-Emotive Approach,* and *Handbook of Rational-Emotive Therapy,* fosters three kinds of insight. The first insight consists of the view that A (Activating Experiences) do not directly cause C (emotional Consequences); rather, B (our Belief System) does. Therefore, people are largely responsible for their own emotions and behaviors, including their emotional disturbances. The second insight is the view that no matter how disturbances originally arise, during early childhood or partially as a result of what is often called conditioning or learning, people now, in the present, carry on the irrational Beliefs (iB's) by which they upset themselves. So, at the very least, they *continue* believing what they once believed, and it is this continuation of their disturbance-creating philosophy that "causes" them to be self-defeating today. The third insight is the knowledge that there normally is no other way than *work and practice* to give up one's original and continuing irrational Beliefs and to thereby make profound changes in one's emotions and behaviors.

In using RET, therefore, you can keep emphasizing to your patients that they had better work and practice to change their ideas, emotions, and acts, when these are self-sabotaging. This work and practice is the main behavioral component of RET and stems directly from its theories. It includes, moreover, cognitive as well as emotive and behavioral practice. I [A.E.] introduced cognitive homework at the very beginning of my using RET in 1955, and some of my associates, such as H. Jon Geis and Maxie Maultsby, Jr. also have emphasized it for a good many years now and pushed their patients to perform it. Dr. Maultsby has created a rational self-analysis form that helps people to do their cognitive homework and to Dispute their irrational Beliefs.

At the Institute for Rational-Emotive Therapy in New York City we have developed our own Self-Help Report Form that incorporates the basic A-B-C-D-E theory of RET and that encourages people to practice Disputing day after day, week after week, until it becomes a semiautomatic aspect of their lives (the Self-Help Form and two samples of filled-out forms are reproduced here). We use this form with practically all of our regular clients or patients at the Institute, and find that if they keep employing it, they not only can rid themselves of almost any feelings of emotional disturbance rather quickly but also can imbibe the essence of a rational philosophy of life and after awhile cease to create many new symptoms.

Sometimes the form is used in connection with self-manage-

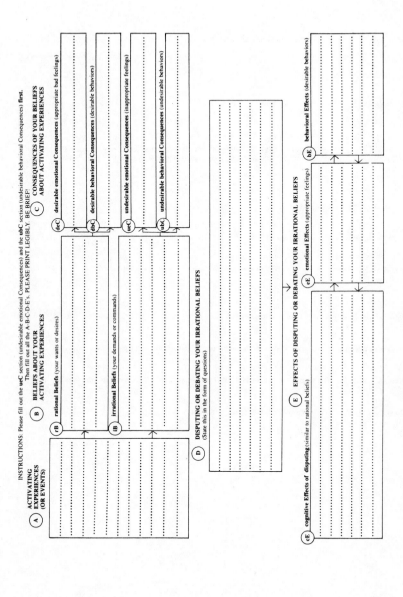

INSTRUCTIONS. Please fill out the **ueC** section (undesirable emotional Consequences) and the **ubC** section (undesirable behavioral Consequences) **first.**
Then fill out all the A-B-C-D-E's. PLEASE PRINT LEGIBLY. BE BRIEF!

(A) ACTIVATING EXPERIENCES (OR EVENTS)

(B) BELIEFS ABOUT YOUR ACTIVATING EXPERIENCES

(rB) **rational Beliefs** (your wants or desires)

(iB) **irrational Beliefs** (your demands or commands)

(C) CONSEQUENCES OF YOUR BELIEFS ABOUT ACTIVATING EXPERIENCES

(deC) **desirable emotional Consequences** (appropriate bad feelings)

(dbC) **desirable behavioral Consequences** (desirable behaviors)

(ueC) **undesirable emotional Consequences** (inappropriate feelings)

(ubC) **undesirable behavioral Consequences** (undesirable behaviors)

(D) DISPUTING OR DEBATING YOUR IRRATIONAL BELIEFS
(State this in the form of questions)

(E) EFFECTS OF DISPUTING OR DEBATING YOUR IRRATIONAL BELIEFS

(cE) **cognitive Effects of disputing** (similar to rational beliefs)

(eE) **emotional Effects** (appropriate feelings)

(bE) **behavioral Effects** (desirable behaviors)

Rational Self-Help Form. © 1976 by the Institute for Rational Living, Inc., 45 East 65th Street, New York, N.Y. 10021.

1. FOLLOW-UP. What new GOALS would I now like to work on? ....

....

....

....

What specific ACTIONS would I now like to take? ....

....

....

2. How soon after feeling or noting your undesirable emotional CONSEQUENCES (ueC's) or your undesirable behavioral CONSEQUENCES (ubC's) of your irrational BELIEFS (iB's) did you look for these iB's and DISPUTE them? ....

....

....

How vigorously did you dispute them? ....

....

If you didn't dispute them, why did you not do so? ....

....

3. Specific HOMEWORK ASSIGNMENT(S) given you by your therapist, your group or yourself: ....

....

....

4. What did you actually do to carry out the assignment(s)? ....

....

5. How many times have you actually worked at your homework assignments during the past week? ....

....

6. How many times have you actually worked at DISPUTING your irrational BELIEFS during the past week? ....

....

7. Things you would now like to discuss with your therapist or group ....

....

....

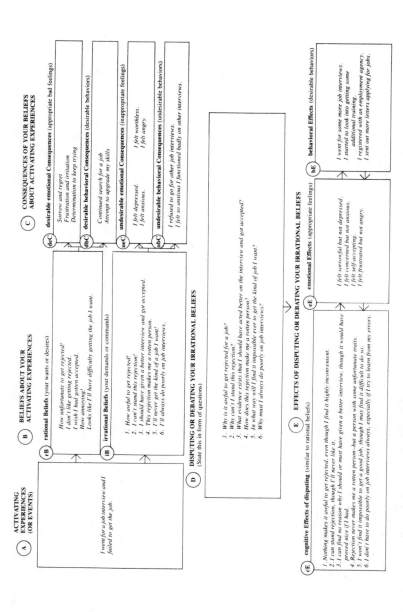

Sample Rational Self-Help Form. © 1976 by the Institute for Rational Living, Inc., 45 East 65th Street, New York, N.Y. 10021.

(A) **ACTIVATING EXPERIENCES (OR EVENTS)**

My mother and father promised to lend me money and for no good reason refused to go through with their promise.

(B) **BELIEFS ABOUT YOUR ACTIVATING EXPERIENCES**

(rB) rational Beliefs (your wants or desires)

How unfortunate that they backed out!
I don't like their behavior.
I wish they had kept their promise.
How annoying and irritating!
I'll try to get the money elsewhere, but will find that quite a hassle.

(iB) irrational Beliefs

1. How awful for them to act that way!
2. I can't stand their unfairness!
3. They should have lent me the money!
4. Because they didn't do what they should, that makes them rotten people!
5. People will always treat me unfairly like this! How horrible!

(C) **CONSEQUENCES OF YOUR BELIEFS ABOUT ACTIVATING EXPERIENCES**

(deC) desirable emotional Consequences (appropriate bad feelings)

Frustration and annoyance. Sorrow and regret.
Determination to help change parents' attitudes

(dbC) desirable behavioral Consequences (desirable behavior)

Continued attempts to persuade parents to change
Attempts to get the money in other ways

(ueC) undesirable emotional Consequences (inappropriate feelings)

I felt angry. I hated my parents. I felt depressed.

(ubC) undesirable behavioral Consequences (undesirable behaviors)

I screamed at my parents.
I refused to consider other ways of getting the money.
I pouted and sulked.

(D) **DISPUTING OR DEBATING YOUR IRRATIONAL BELIEFS** (state this in the form of questions)

1. What makes it awful for them to act that way?
2. Why can't I stand their unfairness?
3. What evidence exists that they should have lent me the money?
4. How does their unfair treatment of me make them rotten people?
5. How do I know people will always treat me unfairly? And must I view it as horrible if they do?

(E) **EFFECTS OF DISPUTING OR DEBATING YOUR IRRATIONAL BELIEFS**

(cE) cognitive Effects of disputing (similar to rational beliefs)

1. Nothing makes it awful, but only inconvenient for them to act that way.
2. I can stand their unfairness, though I'll never like it.
3. I can find no evidence that they should have kept their promise to me though I would have found it very nice if they did.
4. Their unfairness doesn't make them rotten people, but merely people who have acted rottenly to me in this respect.
5. People won't always treat me unfairly—though they may often do so. And if they do, tough! It won't kill me!

(eE) emotional Effects (appropriate feelings)

I felt irritated and annoyed but not angry.
I felt very disappointed and concerned but not depressed.
I still basically loved my parents but hated some of their traits.
I felt determined to find other ways of raising the money.

(bE) behavioral Effects (desirable behaviors)

I spoke to my parents about my feelings of disappointment and irritation.
I attempted to persuade them to change.
I investigated other means of raising money.

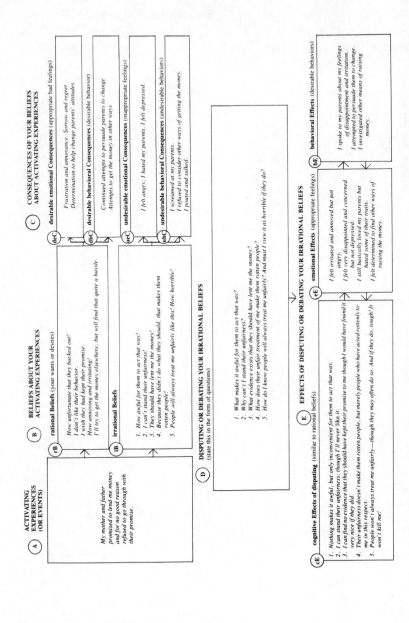

Sample Rational Self-Help Form. © 1976 by the Institute for Rational Living, Inc., 45 East 65th Street, New York, N.Y. 10021

ment or operant conditioning principles. Users agree with themselves (or with a therapist or a therapeutic group) that they will fill out a Self-help Report Form every day or at least once a week about some problem with which they are bothering themselves. If they carry out this agreement, they get a stipulated reward or reinforcement (such as reading, television viewing, taking a pleasurable vacation, or conversing with people they care for) while if they fail to carry it out they get a stipulated penalty (such as burning a 20 dollar bill, vacuuming their home for at least an hour, or conversing with someone with whom they would much rather avoid talking). Most people, we find and as you will probably find in your own practice, will do this written homework report without requiring reinforcements or penalties to help them do so. But some do their homework more easily or more regularly when they use reinforcement schedules.

Another common mode of practicing and reinforcing rational cognitions that you can use in RET is the steady assignment of bibliotherapy. As noted before in this book, RET practitioners use a great deal of bibliotherapy and get their patients or clients to read articles and books outlining the essentials of RET, to listen to tape recordings, to use slides and film presentations, and to use any other kind of bibliotherapeutic procedure that appears useful. But again, bibliotherapy requires work and practice. You can therefore regularly assign your patients to use, view, or hear RET materials. They can report back to you to discuss what they have gone over since their last appointment, and you can give them tests to see whether they truly understand the material. You can assign them to talk it over with their friends and relatives.

According to RET theory—and this again is why we use a good deal of behavioral material—humans tend to acquire new habits of thinking, emoting, and acting mainly from a great deal of repetition. They can fall back into their old habits because they fail to keep up this repetition. Therefore, almost anything you can do to help your patients keep repeating rational messages to themselves and continue to Dispute irrational messages will help them really get the RET philosophy in the first place and keep it in the second place. Some of them, of course, will not like this kind of repetition, especially in the form of homework assignments, and will try to avoid it. But even many of these difficult customers will tend to find, if you keep after them for awhile, that the rational philosophies of life become easier to learn, to retain, and to follow after some amount of practicing them has occurred. So do not fail to encourage them in any way you can to do sufficient practice!

12
Additional Cognitive Methods of RET

We have outlined in this book some of the main cognitive, emotive, and behavioral methods that are most commonly used in RET, but this does not mean that we have demonstrated all of them. Theoretically, any of the usual methods or, for that matter, the unusual methods of psychotherapy can be used by a rational-emotive therapist, as long as they are not irrational and self-defeating, and as long as they do not, preferably, *only* help people to feel better and not to get better.

Even that last caution has its limitations. Occasionally, you can see patients that you are fairly sure, for one reason or another, will not benefit from any elegant mode of RET, because of their inherent deficiencies or the restricted conditions of their lives. People, for example, who are senile, brain injured, seriously autistic, or in the lower grades of mental deficiency may not be capable of any of the regular forms of psychotherapy, including RET. With such individuals, therefore, you may at times attempt purely palliative methods, such as support, reassurance, environmental change, or directly telling them how to run their lives.

With the vast majority of individuals, including most diagnosed psychotics, you may well be able to use some of the more elegant aspects of RET, especially if they also can benefit from the major tranquilizers, antidepressants, or other antipsychotic drugs. Through a combination of such drugs and RET you may well be able to help seriously disturbed people quite appreciably—though not, usually, to the degree that you will be able to help run-of-the-mill "neurotics" and "normal" individuals with dysfunctional habits.

Theoretically, there are literally hundreds of forms of therapy that are distinctly or mainly cognitive, especially if we acknowledge the fact that virtually all the so-called emotive and behavioral therapies such as Reichian, Gestalt, and conditioning therapy have pronounced cognitive elements. I [A.E.] pointed this out in several papers a number of years ago and Victor Raimy, who once was a leading client-centered therapist but is now largely in the cognitive camp, has nicely expanded on this point in his book, *Misunderstandings of The Self*. For almost all of the psychotherapies (as well as, even, the drug therapies) are informative, instructive, persuasive, and suggestive, and most of them include large elements of focusing, imagining, interpretation, and covert or overt philosophizing, all of which are highly cognitive processes.

Humans, unless they are exceptionally deficient, cannot avoid thinking, so that, no matter what you get them to do therapeutically to help themselves, they will inevitably *think about* (1) what you are telling them, (2) what your attitudes and feelings toward them are, (3) to what extent they can trust what you are saying, (4) what ability they have to follow your directions, (5) what the chances are of your therapy actually working well with them, (6) what experiences they are having as they follow your directions or otherwise respond to you, (7) what kind of person they are if they respond to therapy well or poorly, etc. Consequently, as many experiments in psychology have shown, even if we strongly "condition" people externally, that is, control their environment and reinforce them for doing the "right" thing and/or penalize them for doing the "wrong" thing, they still *think about* what we are putting them through and they literally talk to themselves before, during, and after this "conditioning."

Try to be keenly aware, therefore, of the enormous element that cognition or philosophizing plays in human affairs and in helping your patients to become emotionally disturbed about anything and in aiding them in overcoming their disturbances. If you do this, you have potentially scores of cognitive methods that you can employ therapeutically—most have been already described in the literature, but some of which you can invent or recreate yourself. One very effective cognitive intervention is to explain tests and procedures to patients, as well as to educate them in general about their disabilities. In the rest of this chapter, we shall outline some additional cognitive methods that we have barely mentioned previously in this book.

Suggestion and Autosuggestion

Even Sigmund Freud, who was keenly interested in deeply exploring people's past lives and interpretively connecting them with their present disturbances, realized that the gold of psychoanalysis is almost invariably mixed with the dross of suggestion as he cleverly put it. He could just as well have said that all psychotherapy tends to include a great deal of suggestion. For humans largely believe what they want to believe, rather than the empirically-backed "truth." And they give enormous and often magical power to an impressive therapist, particularly one who has a great deal of "personality," charm, or charisma. Moreover, once they take a therapist's suggestions seriously, even though these may be quite misleading or harmful, they tend to autosuggestively carry them on themselves. In fact, as Hippolyte Bernheim partly realized many years ago, and as Emile Coué more specifically saw, almost all suggestion is effective largely because people turn it into autosuggestion, and actively carry on what some "authority" has told them is true.

Since your patients are highly negative thinkers who tell themselves continually that they cannot do something that they really can do, that others are rotten people for not doing what they want, and that the world is *too* hard a place in which to live happily, you can often dramatically get them to change this negative thinking by showing them how to replace it with "positive thinking." This therapeutic technique has been successfully applied and taught by many individuals, including Coué, Dorothea Brande, Norman Vincent Peale, and Maxwell Maltz. There is a vast amount of clinical and experimental evidence that shows that it often works "miracles." People who have been depressed, paralyzed, and almost pandemically anxious sometimes use positive thinking or beneficial autosuggestion to convince themselves that they can do well at various tasks and that they can enjoy themselves despite many adversities. There is little doubt that many such people feel and perform much better by its use.

You, therefore, can quite authoritatively, and sometimes almost dogmatically, use suggestion to convince your patients that they can overcome their physical complaints, that they will be able to lead more efficient and productive lives, that they do have the fortitude to go through diagnostic or surgical procedures, that they can bear pain and frustration, and that they have the ability to do many things that they negatively view as too difficult or impossible. You will find this kind of positive suggestion particularly valuable when employed with people who have limited ability to respond to more elegant forms of RET, such as young children and rigidly thinking older individuals.

As you employ positive thinking with your patients, recognize its distinct limitations. People who feel better as a result of suggestion, autosuggestion, positive thinking, religious conversion, or other forms of dogmatic change are "improved" to some significant degree. As Jerome Frank has shown, this kind of conversion process lies at the core of much of what we call psychotherapy. But, in RET terms, they usually do not make fundamental or elegant changes in their basic self-downing and self-pitying philosophies. They disturb themselves by the strong conviction, after perceiving their own flaws or the unniceties of the world (at point A, Activating Experiences), that things *must* not be this bad, that they cannot *stand it* when they are, and that they are *bad people* or that the world is *too hard* for them to live in happily. Then, as a result of some kind of suggestive or conversion process, they usually strongly convince themselves that what they perceive at point A is not really that true or that bad. Thus, they autosuggestively "see" that things are better than they thought they were, at A; or that they can succeed instead of failing; or that they have some kind of magical helper (a shaman or a god) on their side who will help them cast out evil and bring about good.

With these radically new autosuggestions, they feel much better, and sometimes finally realize that they can exist happily *whether or not* they fail or meet miserable conditions of living. But mostly they still fool themselves into believing that conditions are (or will be) fine, rather than that they can bear it fairly nicely even if conditions are somewhat uncomfortable or miserable. Knowing this, you had better use suggestion sparingly and carefully. Sometimes let your patients know that suggestion is palliative and that they can still try for a more elegant RET-orientated philosophy of accepting themselves, others, and the world in spite of their meeting up with less-than-ideal conditions.

The Norman Vincent Peale version of positive thinking relies too much on pure faith, rather than in faith founded in fact. As Kenneth Briggs points out, Peale offers three "formulas" for human happiness: (1) "to love one another," (2) to "have faith," and (3) to believe that the good life increases in proportion to the amount of faith one has. These formulas have distinct advantages, particularly for people who think negatively, and who have "faith" that they will fail and be contemptible. But, from a scientific standpoint, you cannot very well convince all your patients that they must love one another since they will often meet people with highly unlovable traits. To *accept* one another is fine; for that merely means that they accept the fact that the others exist and have a right to their own existence and happiness, and not that they must like others' behaviors.

Your patients are likely to ask you, moreover, *"Why* should I have faith that good things will happen to me and to others, when reality shows that this is often not true?" A good question! They can always, if they work at it, have faith that they can meet the bad things in life and not upset themselves about them. But how can they scientifically or validly have faith that good things will keep occurring? Obviously, they cannot.

Instructive in this connection is the case presented by David H. Barlow and his associates on "Gender Identity Change in a Transsexual: An Exorcism." These therapists saw a male who was about to have his genitals removed, after a lifelong history of cross-dressing and believing he was really a female, and who completely gave up his transsexualism and made a good heterosexual adjustment after a fundamentalist physician had a three-hour session with him in the course of which the physician told him that he was possessed by evil spirits, exhorted and prayed for him to give up his transsexualism, and put his hands on his head and shoulders. After this physician supposedly exorcized 22 evil spirits from his body, the patient immediately discarded his female clothes, announced he was a man, and went to the barber shop to have his long hair cut into his current short, masculine style. He later followed up this exorcism session with Bible reading and a visit to a well-known faith healer, and he remained quite heterosexual thereafter.

A case like this dramatically shows how cognitive suggestion, followed by strong autosuggestion, can result in pronounced change in an individual's symptoms and personality. True! But from Dr. Barlow's report, it seems obvious that this "cured" transsexual left conversion therapy with some continuing, and even some more pronounced, disturbances, and that in some ways his "cure" was hardly, in RET terms, elegant. Therefore realize the power of suggestion and autosuggestion and at times use these techniques with suitable patients, but cautiously and with full knowledge of their limitations. Elegant RET attempts to help people be less suggestible and more self-choosing and independently thinking. But this ideal result of RET is hardly going to occur with all of your patients all of the time!

Interpretation of Defenses

One fairly accurate observation of the Freudian and other psycho-analytically-oriented therapists, which Eric Berne also went along with in his transactional analysis, is the fact that instead of honestly admitting many of their failings and inadequacies, humans tend to become defensive and to resort to all kinds of escape mechanisms, such as rationalization, projection, avoidance, forgetfulness, and lying. Many of your own patients, in all probability, will make use of these defenses. What can you do to help them avoid this kind of defensive thinking and behaving, especially since it bars them from acknowledging some of their most important symptoms (especially hostility and anxiety) and therefore gives them little chance to rid themselves of such symptoms?

The psychoanalytic answer to this question consists of showing people, through a long-winded therapeutic process, how their defenses originated (presumably in their early childhood, especially in their relationships with their parents) and very gradually revealing the defensive pattern to them during this process. In RET, we usually take a much more direct view. We assume that defenses largely stem from self-condemnation, and that if patients damn themselves for having a symptom, especially a socially criticizable symptom like hostility, they will often resort to various kinds of defenses to keep this symptom out of their consciousness and even deny that it exists if someone brings it to light. We therefore start them, right at the beginning of therapy, on an antiawfulizing, antimusturbational process that shows them, often in a few sessions, that they certainly commit many errors and defeat themselves in various ways, but that they are never contemptible or damnable for these errors. We show them, as indicated in many parts of the present book, that they can always accept themselves *with* their behavior, and then do their best to eliminate the dysfunctional behavior.

Take Jordan Y., for example, who was in a therapy group that the authors of this book led together at the Institute for Rational-Emotive Therapy. This 23-year-old graduate student of philosophy was fanatically compulsive about keeping his apartment clean and in order, and ruined his relationship with several females because he was always late to appointments with them. Even if they visited his apartment and tried to leave for, say, a ballet that was to start at 8:30, which meant that they had to leave at 8:00 in order to arrive on time, he would not allow himself to leave the apartment before, say, 8:25 P.M., because he just *had* to wash some dishes, sweep the floor, make the bed, or otherwise put things in order before they left.

At first, we and his therapy group made no inroads whatever on his compulsive cleaning and tidying since we tended to laugh at its ridiculousness and merely to show him how it interfered with some of his basic goals. But he would not even admit that he was seriously compulsive, and kept asking, "What's wrong with being tidy and wanting to keep my apartment in order?"

To get at his compulsiveness, we first showed him how he could accept himself with it and with his other self-defeating symptoms, including sexual anxiety and impotence, procrastination on his term papers, and fear of public speaking. We spent several group sessions mainly showing him—largely on philosophic grounds since philosophy was his major interest in life—that no one is ever to be condemned as a human for any behavior, including self-defeating behavior. Once he started to see this, he began to undefensively admit the extent of his compulsiveness, and to tell us details about it that he had previously hidden from the group and from his closest friends and relatives. Then, not being absorbed in defending himself or in trying to keep his symptoms out of consciousness, he was able to see that he had a dire need for certainty, that the kind of safety and security that he demanded in life just did not exist and that he could base his existence on the laws of probability and chance. At this point, he began to do his anticompulsion homework, which he had resisted doing before, and forced himself to leave the house promptly at least a half hour before his appointments with anyone; in a few months he had made notable inroads against his compulsiveness and also began to relate much better to the woman he was currently dating.

In treating defensive patients, you can often confront them very quickly with their defensiveness, and show them, with evidence, that they have symptoms that they are stoutly denying. But do so within a general RET framework, which is by concomitantly showing them that no matter what "stupid," "incompetent," or "shameful" behavior they perform, they are not bad humans for performing it poorly. Within this context of fully accepting them yourself and actively teaching them how to unconditionally accept themselves, you can usually get them to admit their "horrible" symptoms, and then to work at eliminating them.

Presentation of Alternative Choices and Actions

All psychotherapy largely rests on the assumptions that human behavior is not completely determined by hereditary or early conditioning influences and that people have a good measure of "free will" in recognizing and changing their dysfunctional symptoms. Even psychoanalysis, which is more deterministic than most therapies, finally acknowledges the ability of people to change themselves, although after many years of preparation with an archeologically-inclined analyst who obsessively-compulsively digs through their past and relates it to the present. RET is much less deterministic than psychoanalytically-oriented therapies and classical behaviorist therapies. Even though it firmly tends to uphold the idea that human disturbance has strong biological elements, that we bring our biological *selves* to our early and later experiences, and that we therefore have strong predispositions to disturb ourselves no matter in what good or bad conditions we are reared, it also states that we have a large degree of choice or will and can, though with considerable amounts of work and practice, partly determine how we now feel and act. It believes, along with Abraham Maslow and the human potential movement, that humans are also born with strong tendencies to actualize themselves, to think about what they are doing "badly" or "poorly," and to strive for greater fulfillment. It believes that they can, with effective therapy, be shown how to do this much more readily and thoroughly.

The view that people have a good measure of free choice has been stressed by many well-known therapists and educators, including Alfred Adler, Robert Assagioli, John Dewey, Albert Ellis, Myles Friedman, Fritz Perls, and Carl Rogers. It has been especially stressed by Harold Greenwald, in his decision therapy, which significantly overlaps with RET. You can use this view and help convince your patients that they have many more alternatives than they think they have. For they easily tend to think that their choices are limited and that they *must* do this and must *not* do that; and that they *cannot* do what they would often like to do, particularly in regard to changing themselves.

Joanna F., for example, came to therapy sessions with me [A.E.] almost completely depressed, inert, and uninterested in life. She said that, up to the age of 30, she had tried all kinds of activities and relationships, thrown herself actively into them, and had proven to herself that none of them were any good. Now, at the age of 38, she was more convinced than ever that she couldn't possibly get an interesting job, maintain a good relationship with a man, or find anything exciting in life.

I quickly showed her what her main irrational Beliefs were, especially, "I MUST accomplish everything I want quickly and easily; it is *horrible* when I don't; and therefore life is completely shitty and worthless!" I tried to induce her to combat these beliefs, but at first with little success since her inertia was carried into her therapy. She mainly was coming to see me at the insistence of her mother, who herself had been helped considerably by reading *A New Guide to Rational Living*. So she only reluctantly paid attention to our sessions, and virtually never did any of the activity-oriented homework that I assigned.

I kept stubbornly pointing out to her alternative modes of thinking and behaving. When she said that she could not find any good places to go in New York to meet men or any other sources of meeting them, I showed her how she could choose from a dozen different places and how she could employ a number of meeting techniques that had never even occurred to her, including attending large conventions where high-level males would be present, and interviewing top-flight executives (who she said were most attractive to her) for an article that she might write about them. When she claimed that she never could find an interesting job, I sent her to the library to look up the *Dictionary of Occupational Titles*, which provided her with a number of possible occupations she hardly knew existed, some of which seemed interesting and for which she was educationally qualified. When she insisted that she could not find anything exciting in life, I had her make lists of things that she had really wanted to do in the past or that she thought that she might want to do now. Forced to do this assignment, she came up with several avocational pursuits, including the study of botany and horticulture that she had not thought about in years.

By insisting that this woman *did* have many alternatives to which she normally gave no thought and reviewing a good many of them with her, I found that she became much more animated and less depressed during the next several months, and that she started looking for a new job and getting into a solid relationship with a man for the first time in years. Whenever she said things like, "I don't know what to do," or "I don't know what I really want," I pointed out that she was not bothering to explore several possible alternatives, and I guided her into doing so. Invariably, she really *did* know what to do and what she wanted when she started to do some actual exploring of possibilities.

Similarly, you can assume that some of your patients have many more potentialities and abilities than they are using, but that they are sticking in the mud of depression or indecision because they only let themselves think of a few limited ways, or no ways at all, out of their dilemmas. Also, when they hit upon a given "solution," and it turns out to be less than ideal, as, for example, picking a certain course of study or a mate, don't let them assume for no good reason that they have to stay with this situation indefinitely, when of course they do not. Show them, in such cases, one or several alternatives. Get them to see that humans normally decide their own destiny, and that they have great abilities for redeciding and rechoosing. Help them out of their rigidities by providing several alternative paths they can take or, better yet, encouraging them to think out such alternatives themselves. Widened and flexible choice is one of the essences of emotional health. Help your patients to acquire such flexibility!

Semantic Precision

As indicated in the introductions to several books on RET, especially, *How to Live With a Neurotic, A New Guide to Rational Living,* and *How to Live With—and Without—Anger,* human thinking is distorted partly because of imprecise language and, conversely, the use of imprecise language follows from distorted thinking. Alfred Korzybski, the founder of general semantics, was one of the first to point this out in detail, and many of his students, such as S. I. Hayakawa, D. David Bourland, Jr., John G. Lynn, and Wendell Johnson, have added to his theories and have sometimes applied general semantics to the problems of emotional health.

In RET we make good use of many of the principles of general semantics. The books noted in the last paragraph are all written in E-prime, a form of English that does not use any form of the verb *to be,* and therefore avoids many kinds of overgeneralization, allness, and the *is* of identity and of predication. As a professional person who would help some of your patients psychotherapeutically, you would do well to acquire some knowledge of general semantics and to use some of its principles. In particular, you can help your patients acquire semantic precision and to radically change some of their irrational thinking by correcting their language in some of the following ways:

When your patients state, "I *must* not get cancer!" or "I know that I absolutely *should* not make myself depressed," you can interrupt them with, "It *would be preferable* if you did not get cancer; but if you do it won't be the end of the world, and you can usually do something effective about it." You might also say "It is *highly desirable* if you stop depressing yourself. But you don't *have to*, and you are not a worm if you don't!"

When your patients say, "I can't consistently diet" or "It's impossible for me to quit smoking," you can intervene and try to get them to change these sentences to: "I *can* consistently diet, even though I find it quite difficult to do so." "So far, I haven't stopped smoking; but that doesn't prove that it's *impossible*, merely *difficult*."

When your patients claim, "I *always* do badly *every* time I try to make regular dental appointments" you can point out that they can change this to "I *usually* (or *often*) do badly *most* of the time that I try to make regular dental appointments. But there is no reason why I cannot do better in this respect in the future."

When your patients insist, "It would be *awful* if I had to go for an operation!" or "How *terrible* if this operation doesn't completely cure my complaint!" you can try to get them to think, instead, that "It would be highly *inconvenient*, but that's *all* it would be, if I had to go for an operation" or "What a *hassle* if this operation doesn't completely cure my complaint! But I can live happily in spite of such hassles!"

When your patients state, "I am a *bad person* for drinking so steadily and ruining my health!" or "I am a *worthless individual* because I won't even do the exercises that my doctor gave me!" you can help them to say to themselves, instead, "It is highly unfortunate that I foolishly keep drinking so steadily and keep ruining my health. But that silly behavior doesn't make *me* a *bad person*." They can also say "I definitely am sabotaging my own health when I don't do the exercises that my doctor gave me, and that means I am acting very stupidly. But I cannot legitimately rate *myself*, my *totality* as either worthwhile or worthless because of my actions. So I'd better get back to working to change these foolish actions instead of downing *me!*"

When your patients contend, "I *need* my mate's help to get me over this illness!" you can try to get them to think, instead, "I greatly *desire* my mates' help to get me over this illness, but I certainly don't *need* it, and can come through even without it."

When your patients declare, "I'm *supposed* to think rationally, now that you have shown me how to do so, and I *have to* stop this irrational thinking!" you can help them change this to, "I *had better* use RET to help me think more rationally, but I don't *have to*. If I don't, I shall merely suffer needlessly; and I am determined to try to suffer less!"

In these and various other ways, you can closely attend to your patients' imprecise, exaggerated, overgeneralized ways of thinking, talking to themselves, and conversing with you and others. And if you undamningly, nicely keep correcting them, you may encourage them similarly to correct themselves and to learn to think more clearly and rationally.

Teaching Coping and Rational Philosophies

Some cognitive-behavior therapists, such as Donald Meichenbaum and Michael Mahoney, question the efficacy of the highly active RET techniques of Disputing irrational beliefs because they wonder if they are too disputational for certain clients. Quite possibly this is true, though little evidence as yet exists bearing directly on this point. In any event, an alternative technique, if you do not want to use cognitive restructuring of a disputational nature with your patients is to teach them coping statements or rational philosophies that they can use instead of the irrational Beliefs (iB's) that they frequently employ.

Thus, you can teach your clients to use and to practice such statements as, "Nothing is *awful* in the universe, though many things are highly inconvenient." "I never really *need* what I *want*." "I can distinctly *stand* obnoxious things that I don't *like*." "Rating *myself* and other *people* is illegitimate, though rating my *traits, deeds,* and performances may be quite helpful." "I'd better go for *longrange* instead of merely *shortrange* hedonism."

These statements are not exactly the kind of positive thinking that we mentioned previously in this chapter, since they include the notion that many things may be bad or inconvenient and that your patients may easily fail and act stupidly. This is still "all right," in the sense that they can still live happily, though not *as* happily as they might live under better conditions.

The trouble with teaching people coping statements and rational philosophies is that it may not show them *why* these ideas are rational and *how* they may be distinguished from irrational notions. Consequently, your patients, when they are entirely on their own, may not have a good ability to figure out for themselves, whenever they are depressed or anxious, what they are doing to create their inappropriate feelings; and they may not be able, even if they see their irrational ideas, to keep surrendering them. The form of logical and empirical Disputing taught in RET, therefore, tends to put people more on their own, and seems to be a somewhat more elegant solution to their problems than simply teaching them coping and rational philosophies. But this latter technique is still a good one, and you may use it effectively on many occasions.

Reattribution Therapy

It has been found, in studies by a great many social and experimental psychologists, that people often tend to attribute motives, reasons, and causes to others and to external events and internal physical states. By doing this kind of attribution, much of which is false and misleading, they significantly influence their own emotions and behavior and sometimes contribute to their own disturbances. Thus, paranoid individuals, in particular, observe that others treat them "badly" and attribute hostility to these others when it may be largely or entirely nonexistent.

I [A.E.] am diabetic, and I therefore eat regularly (eight times a day) to balance the one injection of N.P.H. U-100 insulin that I take before breakfast every morning. I usually explain this to my patients, and they are able to take this fact in stride. But a few of them attribute my regular eating of sandwiches, sometimes during therapy sessions, to various "intentions," such as the "fact" that I am not interested in them, that I am not hospitable enough to offer them some food, too, or that I eat white bread to show that I am opposed to their views on nutrition. All of these ideas, as I sometimes try to show them, are nonsense!

Look not so much at the facts your patients present. But investigate their attributions about these facts. Thus, their parents may have indeed treated them unfairly at times, but was this because these parents really *wanted* to, or because the parents had certain desires of their own that they put before those of their children? Again, their mates may have truly acted in an unloving or unkind manner. But was this because these mates felt quite unloving or hateful to them, or because they, again, had their own fish to fry, and had other motives than lack of love or hatred for their actions?

People, of course, sometimes do things in order to hurt others or to show these others that they have very little interest in them. But they frequently do not! Much more commonly, in fact, they do the "bad" or "harmful" things out of their own disturbances, that is, their own self-downing or low frustration tolerance. And you can show your patients how to look for this kind of disturbance in others, rather than to attribute their actions to "meanness" or "complete lack of interest."

One of my [A.E.] female clients, for example, insisted that her husband always deliberately left her hanging sexually, that he wanted to see her suffer, and that his refusal to give her orgasms the way she wanted to have them, by clitoral manipulation, proved that he had no interest whatever in her. I doubted whether this was so, and pointed out to her that, from the other information that she gave me about her husband, he seemed to have severe feelings of inadequacy and distinct low frustration tolerance. Therefore, I hypothesized, it was quite possible that he was refusing to satisfy her sexually because, first he felt that he *had* to satisfy her with his sacred penis, else he was not really a man, and, second, he found it too hard, after a difficult day at the office (where he had severe feelings of inadequacy) to take a full half hour of petting to bring her to the kind of orgasms she wanted.

She checked up on my hypotheses, had a nonhostile talk about sex with her husband, and found that I was exactly right. He loved her sincerely and would have been much more upset about any breakup of their marriage than she would have been. But he irrationally felt that he *had* to give her an orgasm during intercourse, and he also had a considerable amount of "laziness" or low frustration tolerance. Once they had this discussion, and she unangrily understood where he was at sexually, it was not difficult for her to get him to agree on regular noncoital methods of bringing her to orgasm, and they started to have a remarkably good sex life.

Whenever, then, your patients complain that someone is deliberately doing them in or that conditions are especially arranged so that they unduly suffer, check to see if they are not inventing all kinds of groundless attributions. If so, work with them to give up these attributions and to see if they cannot do something practical to solve their complaints. You will find that once they stop misattributing nasty intentions to others and once they cease thinking that the world's stupidities are specifically set up to hassle them, they will feel much better and have an easier time getting through life.

Distraction Methods

A great deal of psychotherapy actually consists of distraction, though some of the users of this form of treatment do not seem to be fully aware of how and why they are employing it. As Joseph Wolpe has pointed out, once people become anxious about anything, they can use different forms of distraction, or what he calls reciprocal inhibition, to divert themselves away from their anxieties and to make themselves feel better. What is more, if they do this a sufficient number of times, they begin to see that they have an effective technique of anxiety control, and they then may lose certain fears entirely.

Although many distraction methods, such as relaxation, Yoga, and sports, seem to be physical, they are really quite cognitive. For according to RET theory, we make ourselves anxious, depressed, or hostile by focusing or concentrating on some *awfulizing* thought, such as, "Wouldn't it be terrible if I failed at the talk I am going to give tomorrow! I *must* give a good one! I would be a pretty stupid and rotten person if I came across badly!"

As we keep showing in this book, an elegant and semipermanent solution to this kind of awfulizing consists of logically and empirically Disputing these thoughts and replacing them with a new philosophy (or cognitive Effect) that it definitely would be disadvantageous but hardly *awful* or *catastrophic* if we failed at this approaching talk. However, for one reason or another, we may not do this kind of anti-awfulizing and instead may distract ourselves in a number of different ways, such as engaging in conversation with others, reading, looking at television, doing strenuous exercise, meditating, or using Jacobsen's technique of progressive muscle relaxation.

All these and many other distractions often work because while we are doing them we are *concentrating* and *focusing* on what we are doing, and because of this kind of focusing and the limited way in which our minds normally work, we are unable simultaneously to focus on worrying or awfulizing. Of course, this kind of distracting ourselves with thoughts about *x* (a relatively pleasant preoccupation) and thereby diverting ourselves from thinking about *y* (a relatively unpleasant preoccupation) has its distinct limitations. For one thing, our unpleasant thoughts may not be entirely destructive since they often include appropriate concern as well as inappropriate anxiety or panic, and getting rid of them may rid us of constructive problem solving. Second, cognitive distractions may be a form of denial since if we frequently resort to them, we may drive our anxieties, hostilities, and other negative feelings out of consciousness and be out of touch with them. Third, distraction normally only lasts temporarily; after we return from focusing on physical activities, pleasant daydreams, meditation, or what not, we are still left, usually, with the same basic problems as before.

The writers of this book, for example, have frequently treated devotees and even teachers of meditation, Yoga, and relaxation methods, and have seen these individuals appreciably benefit from using this technique on themselves. They are able, for periods of twenty minutes to a few hours a day, to focus beautifully on non-worrisome or pleasurable states. During this time, they are truly nondisturbed, and sometimes almost ecstatic. They still, however, have considerable and sometimes overwhelming basic anxieties, rages, and depressions; not even the hundreds or thousands of times they have resorted to their distracting methods have made great inroads against their fundamental disturbances.

You can, however, recommend various kinds of cognitive distractions to your patients, especially for use as temporary respites from overweening anxiety. If they are confronted by medical or dental procedures that they view as "horrendous" or "debilitating," you can show them how to employ Jacobsen's or Luthe and Schultz's relaxation methods, can recommend Yoga and other exercises, can teach them how to meditate, can direct them into sports, or can advise them to get involved in various kinds of other distracting activities.

One of the best involvements in this respect is what we call, in RET, a vital absorbing interest. Humans, as shown in *A New Guide to Rational Living*, naturally seek enjoyable pursuits. But many such pursuits are of a short-lived nature and therefore lead to boredom and to the seeking of newer activities, which are sometimes not easy to find or to pursue. Consequently, if your patients can get involved in long-range, large-scale interests, they are often better off than if they only have ephemeral goals.

Some long-range, constructive pursuits might be marrying and building a family, for example; specializing in absorbing vocational interests, such as medicine, astronomy, or biochemistry; endeavoring to be an outstanding novelist, painter, or musician; becoming an authority on some sport, on the theater, or on politics; traveling to every important corner of the world.

If you can help your patients become absorbed or continue to maintain a high level of interest in one of these engrossing fields (or even two or three such areas) they will often tend to be almost permanently diverted from some of their worst worries and depressions, and will tend to lead much happier lives. Do not let them cavalierly convince you that they have not, nor could possibly ever have, such a large-scale absorption. Almost everyone can if he or she really tries to find one. Persist with them, in many instances, in looking for this kind of vital interest and see if you can help them discover one.

Imaging and Fantasy Methods

We have spoken, previously in this book, about the method of rational-emotive imagery, and shown how effective it can be. In addition, you can use various other imagery procedures as you employ RET with your patients, as has been pointed out by leading therapists and researchers, such as Barry Brown, Aaron T. Beck, Albert Bandura, Joseph Cautela, Arnold A. Lazarus, Jerome Singer, Thomas Stampfl and D. J. Lewis, and Joseph Wolpe.

Cautela, for example, has pioneered in covert sensitization and covert desensitization. Employing this technique, you can have your patients who are afraid of surgery imagine that they will have pleasant experiences and results from undergoing an operation. Or using the Stampfl and Lewis method of implosion or imaginative flooding, you can have your patients who are exceptionally afraid of medical procedures intensely fantasize, over and over again, that they are going through these procedures, until they desensitize themselves to these images. Again, using the Wolpe reciprocal inhibition methods, you can have them imagine undergoing medical procedures that they intensely fear, gradually let them get closer and closer in their minds to experiencing these procedures, and have them interrupt their anxious feelings by using relaxing techniques, such as Jacobsen's progressive relaxation.

All these methods induce your patients to keep facing (at least in their imagination) people and events that they feel terribly afraid of and get them to "see" that these Activating Experiences (at point A in the RET A-B-C system) are not really as "fearful" or "horrible" as they think they are. People, we might say, really *imagine* "awful" occurrences, then bring on "gruesome" symptoms, such as uncomfortable feelings of panic, then exaggerate the significance of these feelings, and then become afraid of their feelings even more than they are afraid of the original "awful" occurrences. They start with a fear of a thing or an event and they wind up with a fear of their own fear, or of the "horrible" feelings they get when they are fearful. Their secondary symptoms, or discomfort anxiety, often become worse than their primary symptoms, or anxiety about some object, person, or occurrence. They therefore keep withdrawing not only from the original event, but from any symbol, idea, or representation of it.

Typically, for example, a child has an unpleasant experience swallowing a large pill or being injected with a needle and therefore makes itself afraid of the pill or needle. But, learning that it will experience extreme anxiety when presented with swallowing a pill or being injected with a needle, the child then becomes exceptionally afraid of this uncomfortable feeling of anxiety. Thereafter, any mention of a pill or a needle, or any picture of it, or any image of it will be sufficient to "drive" the child into a fit of terror. This terror may remain for the rest of his or her life. Keep in mind that people are anxious about their anxiety so you can combine RET explanations and Disputing with any imaging techniques to get them to face, in their imaginations, the originally feared objects and thereby help them overcome their discomfort anxiety, or their fears about their fears. You can use rational-emotive imagery (REI) to get them to imagine that they are facing, say, a series of feared injections, and are very anxious about it. You can ask them, "How do you feel about your feelings of anxiety?" Usually, they will reply, "Terribly upset and nervous. Very uncomfortable!" Then you can instruct them, "Fine. Now, as you see yourself feeling very anxious about the prospect of getting a series of injections, make yourself feel *only* sorry and disappointed, and not anxious about your anxiety. *Only* let yourself feel sorrow and disappointment, and not anxiety."

They almost always will be able to do this. You then ask them *how* they made themselves feel sorry and disappointed instead of very anxious about their feelings of anxiety, and they will usually reply, "I told myself that it was only uncomfortable, and not awful, to be anxious," or "I saw that anxiety is only a bad feeling and that it certainly won't kill me." You then get them to practice this same

REI procedure every day for the following 30 days or so, until they can fairly easily imagine themselves feeling anxious and face this kind of feeling with some real degree of equanimity.

With a combintion, then, of imaging techniques and of explaining and combating severe feelings of anxiety with the A-B-C-D-E's of RET, you can help your patients face and overcome almost any overwhelming fear (or fear about being fearful) that they have created. The beauty of the Disputing or challenging aspect of RET is that it helps you, as a therapist, to understand more of what is going on in the patient's thoughts and feelings, and that it enables you to give him or her a much more thoroughgoing picture of what is occurring and how it can be understood and changed.

Overcoming Feelings of Worthlessness

As we have just noted, many emotional problems that you will encounter in your work as a health professional are concerned with low frustration tolerance or discomfort anxiety. In the field of medicine, perhaps more than in any other field, people have a rational fear of illness, disability, and medical procedures, and then they exaggerate these into a highly irrational set of fears. They naturally dislike discomfort and possible death, and they easily escalate the real inconveniences and disadvantages of these states into "holy horrors" or "terrible happenings." This kind of LFT then creates in them serious feelings of nervousness, anxiety, anger, or depression, and they make themselves so inordinately uncomfortable about such symptoms of disturbance that they become, very often, more disturbed about the symptoms than about the original medical problems. Where their primary symptoms break off and their secondary ones begin is sometimes almost impossible to ascertain. But you can safely go on to the assumption that much or most of the time they have both sets of disturbances.

If your patients had very high frustration tolerance, most of their emotional problems about illness and disability would probably disappear. But they still would be left with other serious disturbances; namely, those that involve ego anxiety. For discomfort anxiety (or LFT) is a very common form of emotional difficulty, but ego anxiety is also pandemic among humans.

Ego anxiety largely stems from the first of three major irrational premises that people bring to the events of their lives: "I *must* perform well and win the approval of significant others, and if I don't do what I *must* in these respects, it's *awful*, I *can't stand* it, and I am a *rotten person!*" It results, at point C (emotional Consequence) in deep-seated feelings of depression, anxiety, inadequacy, and worthlessness. Although you cannot be sure that your patients have these feelings or the thoughts that create them, you can be reasonably sure that the great majority possess them to at least some degree, either overtly or underlyingly. So keep looking to see if they do.

If you do find your patients displaying almost any form of ego anxiety, you can use the general A-B-C-D-E's of RET, and especially focus on D, or Disputing their irrational Beliefs (iB's) that directly seem to lie behind this kind of anxiety. More specifically, you can show them or teach them the following counterattacking philosophies:

1. You are definitely not, or do not equal, your traits. Your traits, deeds, acts, and performances are certainly important *aspects* of you. But if you have an exceptionally bad characteristic, such as that of consistent stupidity or immorality, this is only *one* of your major aspects. To say, therefore, that *you*, a total human, are bad or worthless because this characteristic (being self-defeating and conducive of lesser happiness) is bad or fairly worthless is a vast overgeneralization and cannot be logically or empirically validated.

2. *You*, or your totality as a human, are so complex that you cannot possibly be given, on any legitimate basis, a global rating. You have literally thousands (if not millions) of traits and performances. Sometimes these are good (self-helping and aiding others to live happily) and sometimes they are bad (self-defeating and needlessly sabotaging others' happiness). Most of these traits are quite different. They consist, in a sense, of apples and pears. They keep changing all the time. Therefore, how can you or anyone else add or multiply them, divide by the total number of characteristics involved, and come to any general rating of your you-ness? Not very accurately!

3. You are an ongoing, ever-changing *process*. You have a past and a present, and, until the day you die, will always have a future. It hardly seems legitimate to give any kind of a global rating to this kind of a process. How are you ever going to know about or very accurately predict how you will behave in the future?

4. When you rate yourself, your you-ness, or your totality, you may seem to be trying to help yourself live and enjoy, but you are really going, almost always, for other, magical goals. You are trying to prove that you are either "better than" or "worse than" other

humans, that you are truly "special." This means, in effect, that you are trying, on the one hand, to be noble, godlike, or superhuman in order to get into heaven; or that you are trying to prove that you are ignoble, devil-like, or subhuman in order to get into hell. This is a futile pursuit since it is very unlikely that you will ever be superhuman or subhuman or that you will reach heaven or hell.

5. When you feel inadequate, self-downing, or worthless, you are consciously or unconsciously assuming that there is some kind of special force or fate in the universe that spies on you (and other people) to see whether your traits and deeds are good enough and that distinctly damns and punishes you during your entire life on earth and perhaps into eternity. This kind of an all-seeing force that gives you, as a whole, "deservingness" or "undeservingness," definitely cannot be proven and has little likelihood of existing. If, moreover, you believe in it, you will tend to feel "undeserving," and will not try to improve your characteristics or performances. Anyway, such a sadistic force or fate has very little chance of existing, and you are foolish if you base your feelings upon belief in it.

6. The ostensible purpose of your rating yourself or your totality, as well as your various acts, is to help yourself live longer and more happily. For if you only rated your behaviors, and rated them in relation to your goals of surviving and enjoying, you would have an important corrective element and would tend to improve the ways you think, feel, and behave. But as soon as you start this rating, you usually wind up by doing yourself immense harm: (a) You deflect yourself from your goal of changing your traits and instead focus on your self, on what others think of you, on damnation, and on other irrelevancies that will absorb much of your time and energy and make you less effective in changing. (b) You create overwhelming feelings of anxiety, despair, depression, and worthlessness. When you are in the throes of these feelings, you are again unable to concentrate very well on changing your deeds and traits for the better. (c) Since you are human and fallible, if you aspire to any kind of total or universal goodness, you will inevitably fail, because you will keep making serious errors and behaving in dysfunctional ways. Consequently, you will tend to see yourself as mainly or totally "bad," and will think that a bad *person*, such as you, is hardly able to change his or her *traits*. You will also make self-fulfilling negative prophecies about your doing badly in the future, and you will thereby often bring about the poor behavior that you stoutly predict for yourself. (d) Even when your self-rating works and you view yourself as a "good" person, you have gained

only a temporary or pyrrhic victory. For you then have to *maintain* your "goodness," and consequently have to watch yourself and your behavior incessantly, to make certain that you do not appreciably fail in the future. At best, therefore, you remain underlyingly anxious, even when you are temporarily feeling "adequate."

With arguments such as these, you can show your patients how to give up their self-ratings and *only* stick to evaluating their acts, deeds, and performances. You can justifiably warn them that, because they are human and reared in human society, they have strong biological and sociological tendencies to slip from trait-rating to self-rating, and that they never are likely to be perfect nonraters. You can also show them that it is often quite desirable for them to rate their actions and traits, and for them to try to improve these. But you can keep before them the ideal of not rating their selves, their totalities, at all, and you can often help them greatly in this respect.

The Use of Humor and Paradoxical Intention

RET has always emphasized the use of humor and paradoxical intention in psychotherapy. As I [A.E.] emphasized in a somewhat (in)famous talk at the American Psychological Association meeting in Washington (when for the first time in the previously staid and respectable history of this Association I gave a presentation on "Fun as Psychotherapy" in the course of which I actually sang— yes, in my faded baritone sang—some rational humorous songs), emotional disturbance largely consists of taking life too seriously and exaggerating the significance of things; that is what I have called, with humor aforethought, catastrophizing, awfulizing, or horribilizing.

If people tend to be not merely serious but overly serious about their desires and frustrations, one method of helping them overcome this is to reduce their irrational Beliefs (iB's) to absurdity in a humorous manner. In RET, we often do this—and thereby overlap with several other outstanding modern therapists who have emphasized humor, paradoxical intention, evocative language, irony, and various other kinds of jocularity. Notable in this respect are the procedures outlined by Eric Berne, Allen Fay, Frank Farrelly, Viktor Frankl, Harold Greenwald, Jay Haley, Arnold Lazarus, Buzz O'Connell, and Carl Whitaker.

As shown in the paper "Fun as Psychotherapy" (which is reprinted in Albert Ellis and Russell Grieger, *Handbook of Rational-*

Emotive Therapy), you can use humor with your patients in several respects which are integral parts of RET. First, you can help them take responsibility for their own disturbances and not cop out by claiming that someone else hurts them emotionally or that their overwhelming impulse to eat or smoke *makes* them do so. When patients cop out in this respect, you can humorously say something like: "What do you keep telling yourself immediately before you cram that food down your gullet and into your craw? 'I hate food?' 'I just eat to keep up my strength?' 'I'll fix my dead mother by showing her that I can eat all I want without getting fat?' Or do you mean to tell me that the food automatically jumps out of the refrigerator, onto your plate, into your mouth, and forces you to swallow it?"

Second, you can help your patients unconditionally accept themselves by humorously and paradoxically pointing out to them what horrible people they really are for making mistakes or defeating their own ends. Thus, if a member of a therapeutic group confesses some stupid act and keeps condemning himself or herself for this act, you can say something like: "Of course, no one else in this group ever makes that kind of mistake! Maybe we all had better boycott you for life!"

Third, you can make fun of your patients' perfectionism. When they show inordinate fear of dancing, playing tennis, speaking, or doing something else imperfectly, you can make a comment like, "And of course, if you do dance poorly, everyone on the dance floor will stop and guffaw, do nothing else but think about you all night, and keep remembering your crummy dancing for the next forty years. Right?"

Fourth, you can employ humor to help your patients fully accept, or gracefully lump, many aspects of reality that they do not like. If, for example, they procrastinate and invariably do difficult things at the very last minute, you can say something like, "Yes, and by putting things off to the last minute, these things finally get easier or magically do themselves. Your term papers or business reports write themselves the day before they fall due. Is that correct?"

Fifth, you can humorously go after your patients' absolutizing and demanding utter certainty. Thus, when my [A.E.] group therapy members keep asking for a guarantee that they win someone's love or succeed at school, I may interrupt with, "Well, you really have luck today! We just happen to have printed a beautifully engraved certificate which guarantees that you will get exactly what you want. Just ask for it downstairs in the office and we'll gladly give it to you, absolutely free!"

One of the newer techniques of RET, which was introduced to the public in the paper, "Fun as Psychotherapy," is the use of rational humorous songs. These songs are cognitive, in that they each include a rational philosophy or a satirical excoriating of an irrational Belief. They are emotive, in that they are musical and often set to songs that already have an evocative and dramatic quality for the singer and his or her audience. They are behavioral, in that they are designed to repetitively go around and around in your patients' heads, like the advertising jingles that they hear over radio and TV stations, and thereby to have their messages sink in and influence the person who sings them aloud or internally "hears" them.

One of these rational humorous songs, for example, is this one, which I [A.E.] have written to the tune of the famous Yale "Whiffenpoof Song" (which was actually composed by a Harvard man in the 1890s!):

> *I cannot have all of my wishes filled—*
> *Whine, whine, whine!*
> *I cannot have every frustration stilled—*
> *Whine, whine, whine!*
> *Life really owes me the things I miss!*
> *Fate has to grant me eternal bliss!*
> *And if I must settle for less than this—*
> *Whine, whine, whine!*

(Lyrics copyrighted 1977 by the Institute for Rational Living, Inc.)

Another rational humorous song you can try with your patients is "Perfect Rationality," set to the tune of Luigi Denza's "Finiculi, Finicula":

> *Some think the world must have a right direction—*
> *And so do I, and so do I!*
> *Some think that with the slightest imperfection*
> *They can't get by—and so do I!*
> *For I, I have to prove I'm superhuman,*
> *And better far than people are!*
> *To show I have miraculous acumen—*
> *And always rate among the Great!*
> *Perfect, perfect rationality*
> *Is, of course, the only thing for me!*

How can I even think of being
If I must live fallibly?
Rationality must be a perfect thing for me!

(Lyrics Copyrighted 1977 by the Institute for Rational Living, Inc.)

Two more rational humorous songs that you can have your patients use (and that are included in the songbook, *A Garland of Rational Songs* and the recorded cassette with the same title published by the Institute for Rational Living, 45 East 65th Street, New York, N.Y. 10021) are:

I AM JUST A LOVE SLOB!
(To the tune of "Annie Laurie")

Oh, I am just a Love Slob,
Who needs to have you say
That you will sure adore me
Forever and a day!
If you won't guarantee
Forever mine to be,
I shall whine and scream and make life stormy,
And then lay me doon and dee!

(Lyrics copyrighted 1977 by the Institute for Rational Living, Inc.)

OH, HOW I HATE TO GET UP AND GET GOING!
(To the tune of Irving Berlin's "Oh, How I Hate to Get Up in the Morning")

Oh, how I hate to get up and get going!
Oh, how I love to procrastinate!
For the hardest thing I know
Is to hear the whistle blow,
"You gotta get on, you gotta get on,
You gotta get on and stop slowing!"
Someday, I promise that I will get going—
Someday, but never, of course, today!
I think I'll still procrastinate
And always get my ass in late,
And piss the rest of my life away!

(Lyrics copyrighted 1977 by the Institute for Rational Living, Inc.)

With these methods and various other forms of humor that you may devise and adapt, you can often help your patients laugh at themselves and thereby accept themselves with their vulnerabilities and fallibilities. With the use of humor, you can also clarify some of your patients' self-defeating behaviors in a nonthreatening manner; relieve the monotony and overseriousness of many repetitive points that often seem essential to effective therapy; help your patients to develop a kind of objective distancing by participating in your own humorous distancing; help them paradoxically think and act oppositely to some of their usual dysfunctional ways; and show them the absurdity, realism, hilarity, and enjoyability of life.

13
Treating Sexual Problems with RET

Doctors, nurses, and other health practitioners particularly are asked to deal with sexual problems. Males come to them because they are unable to achieve full erection and complete intercourse; they easily lose their erections once they begin to copulate; or they have no trouble achieving erection but then tend to come too quickly, or to have "premature ejaculation," after they start intercourse. Females come to health practitioners because they do not easily become aroused sexually or because they have little difficulty in getting aroused but find it next to impossible to come to orgasm, especially during intercourse. Both men and women patients may also talk to doctors and nurses about sex because they happen to consult them about other health problems and would be ashamed to go for specific sex treatment to a psychologist, psychiatrist, social worker, or sex therapist.

You may well expect, therefore, to do a good amount of sex therapy, whether or not this is your particular field of expertise. Fortunately, if you are well versed in RET, you may frequently do this kind of therapy, and may often help people with sex problems in a relatively brief period of time.

Details of the rational-emotive approach to sex and love problems are included in several of my [A.E.] publications, especially the books, *Sex and the Liberated Man* and *The Intelligent Woman's Guide to Dating and Mating* and the articles, "The Treatment of Sex and Love Problems in Women" (in Violet Franks and Vasanti Burtle, *Women in Therapy*) and "The Rational-Emotive Approach to Sex Therapy." We shall now present a summary of this approach in the present chapter. Following the example of the other material on RET that we have outlined in this book, you may take cognitive, emotive, and behavioral pathways to unraveling and improving the sexual inadequacies of your patients.

Cognitive Techniques of Sex Therapy

Sex counseling originated in the works of the late nineteenth-century and early twentieth-century sexologists, especially in the writings of Richard von Krafft-Ebing, Havelock Ellis, August Forel, and Magnus Hirschfeld. Their pioneering research and clinical activity was followed, in the 1920s, 1930s, and 1940s, by W. F. Robie, Th. Van de Velde, Robert Latou Dickinson, G. Lombard Kelly, and Alfred C. Kinsey and his associates. Finally, from 1950 onward, a group of other clinicians and researchers, including Albert Ellis, Alex Comfort, J. H. Semans, Joseph Wolpe, Arnold A. Lazarus, William Hartman and Marilyn Fithian, William H. Masters, and Virginia E. Johnson, pushed back the boundaries of sex information and dissemination, and since the 1970s Helen Singer Kaplan, Patricia Schiller, Jack Annon, and others have continued to publish significant findings in this field.

The one thing that almost all these authorities on sex have in common is that they believe in corrective information and education. The old style sex therapy—and that which I [A.E.] practiced for a dozen years before I created RET and with it rational-emotive sex therapy—was built on the proposition that sexual inadequacy is largely rooted in ignorance and misinformation. Men often do not know what to do to get and maintain their erections and women are ignorant of the proper techniques they could use to arouse themselves fully and bring themselves to orgasm. Tell them what to do, help them get rid of their ignorance, and most of their sex problems vanish—and sometimes very quickly.

There is considerable truth to this information-giving theory of sex therapy. For I have used it efficiently for some 40 years now, and it brings some excellent results. If you want to employ it with your patients, get a considerable amount of accurate sex information, and then see that you objectively and unprejudicially impart it to them. Teach them, for example, the following facts of life: (1) Sex does *not* equal intercourse, but can be enjoyed in a variety of non-coital as well as coital ways. Orgasm achieved noncoitally, especially in the case of many women, is frequently as good as, or even better than, that achieved through penile-vaginal copulation. (2) Though one of the greatest of natural or biologically-based pleasures, a good sex life between a given man and woman frequently had better be worked out and worked at, and does not arise merely because they are mated and care for each other. (3) Love and sex are often closely related—but not always! People can have great sex with those they do not care for and poor sex with those they deeply love. (4) Sex technique will not always work and has its distinct limitations, but knowledge of technique and experimentation with a variety of methods frequently helps the sex lives of certain partners. (5) Various special techniques, such as the sensate focus and the squeeze technique made famous by Masters and Johnson, serve as cognitive distractions that relax sex partners, at least temporarily allay their anxiety, and often enable them to function better with a desired partner.

In RET-oriented sex therapy, you can employ a good many information-giving methods and clearly explain to your patients what they are probably doing to interfere with their sexual arousal and satisfaction, and how to behave otherwise for greater compatibility. But if you use RET, you put these explanations within an antiawfulizing framework. For, like most sex therapists, RET practitioners assume that sex blocking is basically caused by unnecessary anxiety on the part of the blocked people, and that this anxiety has a fundamental philosophic cause, not, as the Freudians would suggest, rooted in early childhood experiences or parental teachings, but rooted largely in the basic *must*urbatory and absolutistic thinking of children and adults.

Take a typical male problem—inability to get or maintain an erection that will make intercourse possible and enjoyable. Such a problem may arise for many physiological and psychological reasons. Assuming that it is not of physical origin, however, the emotional reasons are usually pretty much the same: your impotent patient is worrying so powerfully about the possibility and the "horror" of his not getting and maintaining a stiff erection that he often fails himself in this respect. For sex, even more so than other "sports" like golf or tennis, does not work very well if the male

partner is focused on virtually anything except the sexual attractiveness of his partner and what great pleasure he is probably going to
have in copulating with her. That cognition—"Boy! how attractive
she seems and what a great time in bed we'll probably have!"—is
usually enough to get his penis into the most upstanding position
imaginable, while any other thought, such as, "I wonder what will
happen to my General Motors stock tomorrow," or "Will it stay up?
And won't it be awful if it doesn't!" is almost certain to interfere
with his erectile ability.

In RET sex therapy, then, as well as in RET-oriented general
therapy, you quickly look for your patients' *shoulds* and *musts* that
are interfering with their sex lives and rendering them "inadequate." Your male patients, almost always, think that they *must* get
erect immediately and fully and that they *have to* last a reasonably
long time in intercourse and give their partners a coitally induced
orgasm. Your female patients, for the most part, irrationally believe
that they *must* get aroused quickly, have *got to* enjoy sex thoroughly, and *ought to* have one or more orgasms within a few minutes after they go to bed with someone. All these patients need is
one or two *shoulds* and *musts* like these, and they don't *have to* fail
sexually, but they most probably *will*!

You can quickly find many of these *musts* by assuming that
they are probably there, and asking yourself which ones fit your
assumptions. Then you can check your hypotheses out with your
patients. Thus, if you see a male who is compulsively seeking sex
partners below the age of 12, you can assume that he is probably
telling himself, "I *must* have sex with young children rather than
adults." You can see if your guess is true, and if so, you can then go
on to Disputing: "Why *must* you? What are you afraid would happen if you tried older sex partners?" In answering questions like
these, he will usually turn up with other absolutes, such as, "I *must*
not fail with an adult, and children will not expect me to succeed or
will not notice my failing sexually in case I do fail." Or, "It's too
hard to get adults to have sex with me and like me; and it *shouldn't*
be that hard! With children, it will be easier."

In other words, with sexual problems, you look for the same
kinds of *shoulds* and *musts* that you look for with nonsexual problems; and you will almost certainly find them pretty quickly. For
such problems usually stem from (1) "I must not fail sexually; and
isn't it awful if I do!"—leading to anxiety, depression, and actual
sex failure; (2) "You *must* not treat me badly, and isn't it terrible if
you do!"—leading to hostility and the kind of sex problems linked

with hostility (e.g., deliberately not allowing oneself to get aroused by one's partner because of hatred for that partner); and (3) "Sexual conditions *must* be nice and easy; and isn't it horrible if they aren't!"—leading to low frustration tolerance (LFT), hostility, or depression, and consequent avoidance of sexual situations.

Once you find these *shoulds* and *musts* that make your patients anxious, hostile, and avoidant and that interfere with their sexual functioning, you do the usual RET thing: help these patients Dispute, challenge, and question their absolutistic thinking and give it up. In a typical case, for example, I [A.E.] saw a young woman who had lived with a man for two years, enjoyed sex with him in a two-sided manner, felt that she really loved him and had little hostility toward him, but never reached orgasm in any manner, coital or noncoital, and felt very ashamed of her "terrible problem." Our dialogue during the first session went as follows:

THERAPIST   What are you ashamed of?
PATIENT   George tells me that every other woman he's ever been with has fairly easily had orgasms, at least clitorally. And I can't ever get one in any manner!
THERAPIST   *Can't?*
PATIENT   Well, it certainly looks that way. I've tried everything— and I mean everything. You name it: George's hand, my own masturbation, a powerful vibrator—hell, even orgies. Nothing. Not one goddamned orgasm!
THERAPIST   All right. Let's suppose you really have tried everything, and that so far nothing works. That still doesn't prove that you *can't* get an orgasm, does it?
PATIENT   Well, no; not technically. Haven't yet; quite probably never will, from what I see. But I suppose I can't prove that I *can't*.
THERAPIST   Yes, haven't *yet* reached orgasm. That certainly seems proven in your case. And you've really tried, from what I've seen. But let's suppose the worst. Let's deliberately suppose—though it's almost certainly untrue—that you never, never in your whole life, achieve a single orgasm.
PATIENT   *Never?* You don't mean I'll nev—.
THERAPIST   No, I don't mean that you never will. But I'm deliberately trying to get you to suppose the worst. If you can imagine that and *still* not upset yourself unduly about it, then you've really got it made. You'll lose your shame. And, paradoxically enough, you'll most probably start getting orgasms.
PATIENT   You really think I will?

THERAPIST   Yes, most probably. But let's go back to supposing the worst. Suppose that you really, truly never get a single orgasm in your entire life. You stand on your goddamned head and you still don't reach orgasm. What then?

PATIENT   That would really be awful! Especially when all of George's previous women, according to him, have tended to have them so easily.

THERAPIST   Yes, let's suppose that, too. He may have actually been fooled by these women, or some of them. They may have pretended to have terrific orgasms, as many women do, and never had them at all. But, again: let's suppose the worst. All the other women George has ever known easily and greatly had orgasms. And you never have a single one. Now why would that be *awful*?

PATIENT   Well, I certainly wouldn't be getting what I wanted to get—orgasm.

THERAPIST   No, you wouldn't And why would *that* be awful?

PATIENT   To not ever get what I want?

THERAPIST   Yes, we're deliberately supposing you never got it. Never got an orgasm.

PATIENT   But I wouldn't—. Well, I wouldn't get one of the most important things in life. And, uh, others would. Other women would.

THERAPIST   So?

PATIENT   Well, wouldn't that be pretty awful?

THERAPIST   How? Why?

PATIENT   How can you really ask? Isn't it obvious?

THERAPIST   Not to *me*! I can see the inconvenience, the disadvantage, of course, of your being orgasmically deficient for the next 50 years or so. You'd lose pleasure. You'd feel frustrated. You might even—especially if you make a federal case about this, as you now seem to be making—lose your lover, lose George. But why would any of these things be *awful, horrible*?

PATIENT   Well, they'd surely be bad!

THERAPIST   Right! Bad. Not good. Bad. Obnoxious. Deplorable. Frustrating. But how—*awful*?

PATIENT   Aren't you merely playing on words? Isn't a thing that's that bad really *awful*?

THERAPIST   No, not quite! *Awful* means, of course, that something is bad, or even very bad. But it means *more* than that. What *more* does it mean?

PATIENT   More? Uh. Well, I guess I mean, by *awful*, that it is not only bad that I don't reach orgasm but that it will *continue* to be bad, probably forever. And that's pretty *awful*!

THERAPIST Yes, you mean it will continue to be bad. But that's still within the range of *very* bad. But don't you also mean, by *awful*, that it's *more than bad* that you're not having any orgasms; and that it *shouldn't be* as bad as it is? That it must not be *that* bad?

PATIENT Well, *should* it be?

THERAPIST Of course it should be—if it is! Anything that exists indubitably exists. And if your lack of orgasm does exist and it is bad, then it *should* be just as bad as it is!

PATIENT I—I never saw it that way. But I can see, now that you point it out, that it really should exist, if it does. No matter how much I don't like it to exist!

THERAPIST Right. And is it *more than* bad that it exists?

PATIENT *More* than bad? What do you mean by that?

THERAPIST Is it one-hundred and one percent bad? Or one-hundred and fifty percent bad?

PATIENT No, I guess not. How could it be?

THERAPIST Right! It couldn't be! It could only be, at most, ninety-nine percent bad. But not one-hundred and one percent or one-hundred and fifty percent bad. But isn't that what the term *awful* really means: more than one-hundred percent bad? And more than it *should be* bad?

PATIENT Maybe. I'm not sure.

THERAPIST Well, don't take my word for it. Think about it. See for yourself whether, when you call anything *awful*, you really don't mean that it is more than one-hundred percent bad and that it *must* not be as bad as it is. Think about it.

PATIENT Maybe you're right. I will think about it.

THERAPIST Another thing that is equally important. When you say, "It is awful if I fail to achieve an orgasm, and especially if I never achieve one," how do you feel about *yourself*?

PATIENT About myself?

THERAPIST Yes, you're rating *it*, your failure to get an orgasm, as a bad, and indeed an *awful*, thing. But are you also giving *you*, yourself some rating for engaging in this bad or *awful* performance?

PATIENT Oh, yes. I see what you mean. Yes, definitely. I am rating myself badly—seeing myself as a rather rotten person for being in this position, achieving this bad thing, that is, lack of orgasm.

THERAPIST And especially putting yourself down, rating yourself as a bad person, if you *never* achieve it?

PATIENT Definitely! For if I merely don't achieve it now, but do later, then I'm not so different from all the other women in the world who have difficulty coming to orgasm. But if I *never* in my whole life ever get an orgasm, then I really *am* different from them. And that makes me pretty deficient, pretty rotten, doesn't it?

THERAPIST   No, it doesn't. It makes you a person who's is doing a somewhat rotten, or at least defective, thing. But how does a person who has a deficiency, and even one who has it forever, amount to a deficient or rotten *person*? How does your bad act—or even series of them, over the years—make *you* bad?

PATIENT   Well, I can see that if I merely do a bad thing, like failing some of the time at sex, that doesn't label me as a totally bad person. But suppose I *keep* doing this defective thing, keep it up forever. Aren't I *then* somewhat bad?

THERAPIST   Yes, you are *somewhat* bad—meaning that you have some bad *aspect*. Your orgasm capacity would then prove to be bad or defective. But is your orgasm capacity *you*? Does it amount to, equal your entire person?

PATIENT   Mmm.

THERAPIST   Well?

PATIENT   Uh—no.

THERAPIST   I see you're quite hesitant about that answer. You really believe, as far as I can tell, that if you have a *big* deficiency, such as lack of orgasm, and that if you have it forever, then you, a total human, are defective or deficient. And that that defectiveness makes *you* bad.

PATIENT   Uh—. I guess I do think that.

THERAPIST   And where, if you have that kind of belief, is it going to get you?

PATIENT   Where will it get me?

THERAPIST   Yes, what results will such a belief bring? If you believe that you have a bad or poor trait, such as lack of getting an orgasm, then you tend to look at that trait as a disadvantage, and usually work as hard as you can to improve it, to correct it. But if you are a bad *person* for having that trait, how can a bad *you* correct anything about you? Wouldn't that bad *you* supposedly be doomed to be forever bad, and to be unable to correct its, *your*, poor traits?

PATIENT   I see. If *I'm* bad for having no orgasms, then how can bad *me* work at producing better orgasms? Quite a bind I've got myself in there!

THERAPIST   Yes, quite a bind! Now if we can get you to keep acknowledging that your trait, your lack of orgasm, is bad or disadvantageous, and get you to stop downing your-

self, your you-ness, for having that trait, then there's no
reason why you can't change it, the trait.

PATIENT   Can I really change it? Do you really think it's possible?

THERAPIST Oh, yes. In all probability, you can change it, the trait. *If*
you stop telling yourself that you *can't* get an orgasm, and
tell yourself instead that so far you *haven't* got one. And if
you stop seeing *yourself* as a bad *person* for having this
highly frustrating trait. If we can help you to work on
giving up those two nutty ideas—that you *can't* change
and that you're a no-goodnik because you can't—then the
probability is very high that you can change, and can get
orgasm either occasionally or even steadily.

In this dialogue, and in several subsequent ones that went
along similar lines, I showed my patient that she was awfulizing
about her sex problem and putting herself down for having it. I
then helped her Dispute (at point D) her irrational Beliefs (iB's) and
begin to surrender them. At the same time, I worked with her on
imaging methods, and got her to imagine several different kinds of
fantasies which she personally found exciting. In her particular
case, she found excitement in the fantasy of picturing herself as a
strip teaser, seeing herself on the runway of a burlesque theater
arousing the sex interest of hundreds of men in the audience, all of
whom immediately wanted to have her. As she kept this picture in
mind and simultaneously masturbated by massaging her clitoral
region, she was able, a few weeks after I first saw her, to have the
first orgasm she had ever experienced in her whole life. Then, as
she continued to experiment with this imagery and to try other
things, she was later able to have an orgasm while her lover mas-
saged her clitoral region. Finally, on occasion she was able to come
to orgasm in regular intercourse, though she never managed to do
this consistently.

Along with giving this woman some relevant sex information,
showing her how to Dispute her *mus*turbation and her awfulizing,
and use her head to imagine things that would fully arouse her and
help her come to orgasm, I also used the psychoeducational approach of RET. She read several of the regular self-help RET books,
especially *A New Guide to Rational Living* and *Humanistic Psychotherapy: the Rational-Emotive Approach*. She also read some relevant sex
books, including my own *Art and Science of Love* and *The Sensuous
Person* and Alex Comfort's *Joy of Sex* and *More Joy of Sex*. And she
listened to several RET tape recordings, on sexual and nonsexual
subjects, particularly "How to Stubbornly Refuse to Be Ashamed of

Anything." Although the imaging technique worked beautifully with this patient, and although the therapy she received might never have fully been effective without it, she acknowledged that the antiawfulizing that she learned from the therapy sessions and from the reading and tape-listening served to prepare her for doing the fantasizing, and that otherwise she would have felt guilty about it and perhaps never have persisted at it.

Emotive Techniques of Sex Therapy

Almost invariably, RET includes several emotive techniques that are used with patients who come for sex therapy. For one thing, you show them, by word as well as manner and deed, that you fully accept them with their deficiencies, and that in no way do you condemn them or put them down for having these defects. The female patient I referred to in the previous section of this chapter could see that I, a man, could easily accept her even if she never had an orgasm in her life, and if, into the bargain, she did various other wrong or stupid things, including putting herself down and making herself anxious and depressed (which is certainly a no-no in RET!). Similarly, you can show any of your patients who has a serious sex problem or deficiency that you may well deplore or feel very sorry about their behavior, but that you never condemn them for performing it.

Instructive in this respect is the example of Alfred C. Kinsey, the great sexologist. I [A.E.] knew Kinsey personally, and once spent literally an entire day with him, from 9:00 in the morning until past midnight—even to the extent of going to the public urinal with him twice during that day! The thing that impressed me most about Kinsey was not his vast knowledge of the field of sex, but his remarkably objective and accepting attitude toward any person he talked to, no matter how peculiar or even antisocial that individual's sex behavior. Wardell Pomeroy, one of Kinsey's early and closest associates, tells me that Kinsey at first really hated straight males who pretended to be homosexual, induced a homosexual male to admit his inclinations to them, and then savagely cursed him or even beat him up. But he trained himself, although always loathing their acts, to accept them undamningly as fallible humans. Consequently, he was able to get along well in his interviews with them (and almost everyone else he interviewed) and to get them to reveal information that they would have revealed to virtually no one else.

If you, then, will take an attitude of unconditional acceptance, and refuse to think badly of your patients no matter what sex peculiarities or inadequacies they have, they will tend to accept themselves as you accept them, to tell you virtually anything about which they are bothered, and to work more successfully on their problems. The more accepting you are, the more they will tend to acknowledge their sexual problems and disturbances but to refuse to down themselves for having these symptoms.

Another emotive technique of RET is rational-emotive imagery (REI), which we explain in detail in Chapter 10 of this book. In using REI for sex problems, you get your patients to imagine the worst possible thing that might happen to them, such as extreme sex failure. They then let themselves feel anxious, depressed, or self-hating about this kind of failure. After getting in touch with this inappropriate feeling for a short while, you ask them to change it to a more appropriate feeling, such as sorrow, regret, or annoyance at failing sexually. When they have succeeded in doing this, and virtually all of them can make themselves feel sorry or disappointed rather than depressed and self-hating about failing sexually, you ask them how they changed their feeling.

They will often answer that they changed some kind of irrational Belief (iB) to a rational Belief (rB). Thus, if one of your male patients feels terribly ashamed of his failing to get an erection when he is with a woman he cares for, and he makes himself feel, instead, only disappointed or sorrowful, rather than ashamed, he will do so by telling himself something like, "It certainly is very inconvenient and regretful when I don't get an erection with her. But it isn't the end of the world! And it doesn't mean that I'll never get one again. It's only unpleasurable and annoying. Too bad!"

You then get him to keep imagining, for five or ten minutes a day, that he fails sexually with this same woman; to let himself at first feel anxious or depressed about this, then to change his thinking, in the way he already did or in some other manner, until he feels regretful and annoyed but *not* depressed or self-downing. As he keeps practicing, he will tend to automatically feel that way in case he actually does fail sexually with this woman. Then, as he loses his feelings of shame, he will also be able to work more successfully on enjoying sex with her, and finally get to the point where he usually succeeds.

You can also help your patient do various kinds of shame-attacking exercises, which we also explain in detail in Chapter 10. He can start with nonsexual exercises, such as wearing "loud" clothing in public or asserting himself with rude waiters, and then add more sexually oriented shame-attacking exercises, such as acting assertively and forwardly with members of the other sex or asking a partner to do something that he particularly likes, such as oral sex, that he might consider "dirty" or "far-out." As he does these exercises and you discuss with him why it is *not* "shameful" or "awful" to do them, he will tend to become desensitized and lose his embarrassing or self-downing feelings about them.

You can help sexually blocked or inadequate patients to use highly emotive or powerful verbalizations (as we again note in Chapter 10) to overcome their problems. For when they feel horrified about certain sex acts or when they unduly inhibit themselves from engaging in activities that they would prefer to perform, they are not merely telling themselves negative things about these acts and about themselves but are *strongly, powerfully* verbalizing these things. Thus, they vigorously and forcefully tell themselves, "I *can't stand* failing my partner sexually!" or "It's *horrible* that I have to go through such a hassle to enjoy myself in bed!" or "If So-and-so doesn't make it easy for me sexually, he/she is an utter *louse!*"

To counteract this powerful kind of self-propagandization, you can help your patients forcefully and repetitively tell themselves: "I'll never like failing my partner sexually, but I damned well *can* stand it!" "It really is a pain in the neck to have to take so much trouble to enjoy myself in bed, but it's a much *worse* pain if I don't!" "If So-and-so doesn't make it easy for me sexually, I certainly will be frustrated; but he/she *has* a right to do anything he/she wants, no matter how much I get frustrated! People *should* do what they do—because that's the way they behave!"

Behavioral Sex Therapy

As emphasized throughout this book, RET-oriented therapists just about invariably employ a good many behavioral or activity-slanted methods of therapy, and you can use such methods in relation to sexual as well as to nonsexual problems. I [A.E.] outlined some of these activity homework assignments in my 1954 book, *The American Sexual Tragedy*; and they were later expanded upon and systematized by other sex therapists, such as Masters and Johnson, Hartman and Fithian, and Heiman, LoPiccolo, and LoPiccolo.

Following this RET behavioral methodology, you can use various activity homework assignments with your sexually blocked patients. If they are anxious about succeeding at intercourse, you can assign them to pleasure each other and do every conceivable noncoital act without actually copulating, that is, use the sensate focus of Masters and Johnson. If they are afraid to do certain harmless sex acts with their regular partners, you can encourage them to do these acts, to prove to themselves that there is nothing frightening about them. If they seem to be bored with their usual sex outlets, you can suggest that they experiment with unusual outlets or different kinds of partners. If they are hostile toward their regular mate, and therefore cannot have good sex with this mate, you can assign them to deliberately stay with such a partner while working to overcome their hostility, rather than to cavalierly leave this partner and thus "get over" their hatred. If they are inept at some sex positions or other activities, you can encourage them to practice these acts over and over again, until they acquire adeptness at them.

As usual, RET homework assignments in the sex area are often interspersed with A-B-C-D-E-ing. For if your patients agree to take an assignment—whether it consists of having more sex or less sex—and they fail to follow up on this agreement, you can always come back with: "What were you telling yourself just before you decided to go through with this assignment and then copped out on it?" And, examining their replies, you can find the *musts* and *shoulds* they internally employ to stop themselves. Thus, one of my [E.A] young female patients was given the assignment to ask her husband to have oral relations with her at times, instead of the conventional penile-vaginal copulation that they always had and to which she was somewhat indifferent, and when she failed to carry out this homework and I asked her what she kept telling herself to stop her from doing it, she said: "I guess I keep telling myself, 'I shouldn't *have to* tell him what I want sexually. If he really loved me, he should know!' " Once she began to surrender this absolutistic, super-romantic kind of thinking, she had no trouble in asking her husband for oral-genital relations, and, much to her surprise, he had no trouble in engaging in them with her.

When your patients are difficult customers and will not carry out their homework assignments even when they keep promising you and themselves to do so, the use of operant conditioning or self-management principles is often useful. One 30-year-old male I [A.E.] saw several years ago refused to have any relations with his sex starved wife, even though he said he loved her dearly and wanted to keep their marriage together. She thought her own desires were most reasonable, since she merely requested that he satisfy her in any way he desired, and by no means was demanding intercourse. Moreover, they agreed, he could fairly easily give her an orgasm in less than five minutes of clitoral manipulation. Nonetheless—nothing; no move on his part whatever to initiate sex or even respond adequately when she made the overtures.

"O.K.," I said. "Since you won't have sex with her without specific reinforcers, what could you use to reward yourself immediately after you do have it? Something you really like, that you prefer doing almost every day in the week?"

"Smoking," he replied. "I mainly smoke at home anyway, since the kind of work I do, playing around with chemicals all day, makes smoking very dangerous at the office."

"How about agreeing, then, that in order to allow yourself to smoke at home tomorrow, you have to try to satisfy your wife sexually tonight. And unless you regularly attempt to give her an orgasm every three days, as she says she really wants it, no smoking at home until, first, you try the sex again and, second, you make up for the number of tries you missed?"

"Let me get that straight," he said. "If I satisfy—or at least try to satisfy—her sexually tonight, I can smoke at home tomorrow. I can also smoke, if I try sex, for the next two days after that. But if I don't make a pass at her after that, no smoking for me at home until I do. Right?"

"Yes. And if you miss out on trying sex with her for, say, two weeks, then you owe her four tries. And until you make them up, no smoking! Okay?"

He agreed. Whereupon he stubbornly held out on her sexually that night and for the entire next week. But by that time he felt so deprived of smoking that he made sure that he had some kind of sex with her regularly, every two or three days, for the next several months that I kept track of this couple. And not only did their marriage improve considerably, but as I had predicted to him, his complete lack of interest in her body vanished, and he began to get aroused himself at least half the time. I still see this couple from time to time, as they keep coming to the Friday night Workshops in Problems of Everyday Living that I conduct almost every week at the Institute for Rational Living in New York City. And from what they both tell me, the homework assignment that I gave to the husband and that he finally carried out so well probably would not have worked at all had not a specific reinforcement, smoking *after* he had completed some form of sex with his wife, been made a regular part of it.

Some cases are even more difficult than this, since they require, in addition to reinforcement or reward, a stiff penalty. For although young children and many adults are fairly easily reinforceable by rewarding them after they do the right thing, many more troubled individuals with a long history of undisciplined behavior just do not move themselves at this kind of urging and require aversive penalties instead. In RET individual and group therapy, including sex therapy, we therefore often employ penalties that are to be immediately accepted if a patient does not carry out an agreed-upon homework assignment. Thus, a male who avoids encountering females socially or making any overtures to them when he does meet them may be given the assignment of talking to at least three women each week and trying to make dates with them. If he fails to carry out this assignment, he may agree to clean his bathroom for an hour, have a long conversation with someone he finds very boring, or burn a 20-dollar bill. Although such penalties may seem, at first blush, to be harsh and unsexy, we have found that they often work beautifully to encourage people to do their sex therapy homework and to overcome some of their worst forms of inertia.

RET has always included, in its therapy sessions and in the course of its homework assignments, a good deal of assertion training. One of the most popular RET-oriented self-help books, *The Intelligent Woman's Guide to Dating and Mating*, the first edition of which was published in the early 1960s, showed how women can be just as assertive as men if they work on their fear of rejection. It included a chapter, "How to Be Assertive without Being Aggressive," which clearly distinguished between these two forms of behavior and sparked many of the distinctions later made by Alberti and Emmons, Lange and Jakubowski, Wolfe and Fodor, and other leaders of the assertion training movement.

You can teach your patients, including your unassertive women patients, that they have a perfect right to assert themselves—to show others what they really want and do not want—without being aggressive, that is, trying to take away others' rights or deprive them of what they want. For self-acceptance means that people are willing, just because they fully accept their own aliveness and their own desires, to take the chance that others will refuse or reject them, and that they will still assert themselves sexually, affectionately, financially, attitudinally, and otherwise with those with whom they associate. And if you show your patients how to refuse to down themselves or hurt themselves when others do not like their particular assertions, you will undercut the main reason for their lack of going after what they want and refusing to do what they do not want.

More specifically, you can help your female patients, when they are too shy and retiring, to make friendly overtures to attractive males in public places, to phone their male friends instead of waiting passively for the men to call, to make sexual overtures when they wish to do so, to invite their partners to participate in sexual practices that they especially enjoy, and to engage in other behaviors that are sometimes considered "unfeminine" in our society but that are actually quite legitimate for any self-accepting female to follow. You can do this kind of assertion training through coaching, role-playing, and giving your patients activity homework assignments that will encourage them to get practice at honest, unhostile assertiveness.

Your male patients, too, will often be exceptionally afraid of assertive behavior. Falsely led by the belief that they have to do well in every encounter with a potential sex or love partner, and that they are crummy persons if they do not, they hold back from all kinds of sex-love assertiveness, and often fritter away the best years of their lives in grim inactivity. Where some forms of assertion training help these shy individuals to do better in their sex and love relationships by giving them training in communication techniques, RET-oriented assertion training does this and more. It helps them change their basic philosophy of awfulizing about rejection and of downing themselves if they fail in their assertions, and at the same time shows them, by role-playing, skill training, and other active-directive teaching methods, how to function better in the sex-love area. Some RET-oriented therapists, such as Arthur Lange, Patricia Jakubowski, Janet Loxley, Janet L. Wolfe, Iris Fodor, and the authors of this book, specialize in this kind of assertion training and give regular workshops along these lines.

In summary, people have sex-love problems largely because they are ignorant of some of the main things they can do to function better in this area and because they have anxieties and blockings that make them feel uncomfortable with the kinds of sexual experimentation that would normally get them over their inadequacies. Many practical and effective methods of sex education and therapy are available today to help these blocked people assert and express themselves and to encourage them to function better in the sex-love area. You can learn these methods by reading, by attending sex and communication workshops, and by getting more specific training and professional guidance. In so doing, you will find it exceptionally helpful to see your patients' sex problems within a general philosophic framework and to understand that they are usually tied up with the same kinds of awfulizing and *must*urbation that create and maintain nonsexual emotional disturbances.

If you understand this, and if you do sex therapy within an RET frame of reference, you will not only tend to achieve better and quicker results with many of your sexually troubled patients, but you will also help them with their social, vocational, academic, and other difficulties. We frequently find that people who come to us because they are exceptionally anxious about failing sexually, and who overcome this kind of anxiety and start to function adequately in their sex-love relations (sometimes after only a few RET sex therapy sessions), report: "You know, I'm not only pleased with my progress sexually. But, from what we've been going through in these sessions, I could see that I had exactly the same problems in my work (or school or social) life as I've had in the sexual area, and I've been applying the RET principles I've learned here to that part of my life as well. I'm really startled by some of the good results I've obtained in this other realm, and I am delighted that RET works so well in general as well as with my sex difficulties."

Not that RET is a panacea for all human ills. Not quite! But the fact that it tries to get at the deepest and most philosophic sources of any particular emotional blocking or malfunctioning, and that it often can do so in a remarkably short period of time, makes it a therapy of choice that you can use with a wide variety of disturbed individuals. When you employ it with people who have sex problems, you can indeed help them with the particular deficiency or symptom that they bring to you as a health practitioner. But, over and beyond that, you can help get them started on a general understanding of themselves (and their basic tendency to create all kinds of other symptoms) that may be of immense benefit to them for the rest of their lives.

14

The Use of Psychotropic Medication with RET

As a result of the widespread prescription of psychotropic drugs, and our belief that the appropriate use of these medications is sometimes indicated with RET, it is worthwhile for RET practitioners to have some knowledge of the most commonly prescribed drugs, whether or not they themselves prescribe medications. But first we think that it is important to point out that studies indicate that there are not any negative interactions between psychotherapy and appropriate drug therapy. One highly-regarded book devoted to this issue, *Pharmacotherapy and Psychotherapy: Paradoxes, Problems and Progress* by The Group for the Advancement of Psychiatry, concludes,

> *A careful review of the literature shows that there is no systematic evidence whatsoever that appropriate psychotropic agents, at appropriate dosages, interfere with the psychotherapy of schizophrenia, depression, or neuroses. Statements to the contrary are editorial and opinionated and clearly based upon ideological commitments. Evidence is never presented to support these views by those expressing them.*

But an impressive body of evidence does indicate that, as in most nonpsychiatric disorders, correct diagnosis is essential for ap-

167

propriate treatment and for assessing likely prognosis—at least in regard to major mental disorders, such as schizophrenia, syndrome depression, manic-depressive illness, the hyperactive child syndrome, and organic brain syndromes. As I [E.A.] pointed out at a National Conference on Rational-Emotive Therapy, there is now substantial evidence that we had better diagnose for these major mental disorders prior to giving RET.

We suggest that you as a health professional do just that in much the same way as you would diagnose organic illnesses—by taking the history of the signs and symptoms of a given entity, as well as a family history, then noting the pathological symptoms as they appear at the time of the interview. In other words, perform a mental status exam.

Keep in mind that no one symptom is diagnostic of an entire syndrome. For example, the symptom of depression can be present both in the syndrome of depressive neurosis and in schizophrenia.

Donald Klein and others have shown that correct diagnosis is essential for appropriate psychotropic drug treatment. Other studies have also shown that psychotropic medication is often extremely effective for certain diagnostic entities when compared to placebo.

Neuroleptics, or so-called major tranquilizers, have been shown to be effective for schizophrenia and other psychotic conditions. In the same way, Lithium is effective for manic-depressive illnesses, antidepressants for the depressive syndrome, as well as for phobias, and tranquilizers such as Valium or Librium for nonpsychotic anxiety.

Cadoret and King warn that if medication is used, it is only to be administered in adequate doses under proper control of a physician. They observed that a common problem in the treatment of outpatients is the tendency of the physician in charge to administer doses of medication that are too low. Drug failure is often the result of inadequate doses rather than inappropriate medications.

Drugs that have worked before for an individual, notes psychiatrist Allen Fay, are likely to work again. If the patients have not had the medication previously, it is useful to keep in mind that their first degree blood relatives may have similar response patterns.

In the matter of drug doses, many doctors tend to prescribe psychoactive medications two to four times a day. This schedule is often desirable early in the treatment program, especially in dealing with possible side effects. It has been shown, however, that for most patients the entire day's medication can be given at once. Often the best time to take these drugs is just before bedtime, because (1) the drugs' sedative properties can be utilized, (2) the once-a-day routine encourages compliance, and (3) larger doses usually cost much less than the same amount in divided doses.

Prescribed drug-free intervals, or drug holidays, are very effective, especially with antianxiety and antipsychotic agents. This can be achieved by skipping drugs on alternate days or on weekends. Many informed clinicians believe that the traditional prescription of antianxiety agents in equally divided, uninterrupted doses, can usually be abandoned.

Antianxiety medication is very popular these days. Diazepam (Valium) and chlordiazepoxide (Librium) rank first and third, respectively, in the class of all prescribed drugs. In fact, diazepam is the most commonly prescribed drug of any class.

As a health professional you may note many somatic equivalents of anxiety that affect essentially every organ system. Several that are seen most often are fatigue, bowel disturbances, insomnia, headaches, palpitations, and muscular aches, among others. You have undoubtedly seen many medical and surgical cases in which anxiety was a complicating factor, as such anxiety is often a secondary symptom of a physical disorder.

In regard to appropriate drug strategy remember that, as with antidepressants, equivalent doses of antianxiety agents lead to a wide variety of plasma concentrations. These drugs are also long-acting and can, therefore, maintain an effective plasma concentration with relatively infrequent administration.

Bearing these points in mind, Professor Leo E. Hollister of Stanford University believes that the minimally effective hypnotic dose of the drug should first be established. The optimum dosage can be found by instructing the patients to take the medication 2 to 3 hours before bedtime and to watch which dosage causes an enforced sleepiness and a minimal "hangover." The dosage can be gradually increased on successive nights to establish the required dose. Daytime doses, if needed, can be established at one-third to one-fourth of the nighttime dose.

Dr. Hollister also asserts that antianxiety drug treatment can often be limited to the course of the anxiety, which frequently is episodic. These treatment periods might last only a week. Unfortunately, many patients are chronically anxious. And data suggest that many anxious patients have relatively enduring symptoms for which a short-term drug regimen proves inadequate.

Regarding the drug treatment of chronically anxious patients, the University of Pennsylvania's Karl Rickels has said, "First, this investigator is convinced that many anxious patients do, in fact, require a more protracted course of pharmacologic treatment than is generally provided." He adds that some people may even need a form of maintenance treatment. This therapy would be similar to diabetics taking insulin. When treating patients such as these, doctors may stop the drug treatment from time to time. Then they can assess whether there is a recurrence of anxiety and more medication is needed. By reducing the drug in two or three steps, physicians can almost abolish withdrawal symptoms.

Of particular interest to the RET health practitioner, Dr. Rickels adds, "It is also true that some anxious patients who fail to respond to drug treatment within conventionally short periods of time may need such nondrug approaches, either alone or in combination with drug treatment, as family therapy, marriage counselling, or group or individual psychotherapy."

Evidence suggests that psychotherapy appears especially indicated for the following patient groups: 1) those only mildly anxious; 2) those high in obsessive-compulsive and performance difficulty complaints; 3) those who have marked problems in their interpersonal relations. Rickels notes that unrecognized depressed individuals are sometimes in the group not responding well to antianxiety medication. Such people may benefit from treatment with antidepressants.

Some of the "somatic equivalents" of depression are similar to those of anxiety: fatigue, gastrointestinal disturbances, headache, and insomnia. But before we outline the use of antidepressant medication, a statement by Dr. Frederick K. Goodwin of the National Institute of Mental Health seems relevant: "The more completely the clinical picture fits the description of the depressive syndrome the more certainly are drugs indicated." In assessing this "fit" the health professional evaluates the extent and duration of dysfunction and then notes the so-called endogenous cluster of symptoms. These include altered eating and sleeping patterns (especially middle and late insomnia), psychomotor changes, and general dysphoria.

Goodwin and M.H. Ebert suggest that, using imipramine (Tofranil) as a prototype, for most individuals treatment can begin with 50 to 75 mg on the first day. This is best taken in divided doses, largely because of side effects. Then the dose can be increased by 10 to 25 mg per day until limited by side effects. These limiting side effects are urinary retention, confusion, visual accomodation problems, and severe tremors. These authorities recommend waiting for five to seven days to assess patient response, after 150 mg per day is reached. If the patient has not responded at the end of this second week of treatment, the dose can be raised by 25 mg every two to three days. The upper limit is usually 300 mg, but severe individuals may require even more.

In considering antidepressant drug dosage, remember that the sedative tricyclic antidepressants, such as amitriptyline (Elavil) and doxepin (Sinequan) are exceedingly hazardous as suicidal agents. So limit your prescriptions of these medications to days rather than weeks, and with no refills.

Keep in mind the significant effects on the cardiovascular system from antidepressants. We suggest, therefore, that you refer patients with significant cardiovascular or cerebrovascular disease to an experienced psychopharmacologist.

We would like to make a few points about the use of psychiatric drugs with older and elderly patients. First keep in mind that organic diseases, such as cardiac failure or respiratory problems, often precipitate psychiatric symptoms in this age group. In this case, your diagnosis and treatment of the underlying organic disorder is more important than prescribing psychotropic medication.

But let us assume that organic factors have been ruled out, and you are faced with treating a paranoid, disorganized, agitated elderly patient. "What do the experts recommend?" you might ask.

According to psychopharmacologists Jonathan Cole and Bernard Stotsky, in these cases "One should begin with an almost homeopathic dose (e.g., 0.25 mg of haloperidol [Haldol] or 10 to 25 mg of thioridazine [Mellaril] and work upward." They suggest raising the dosage gradually until the patient is calm, if the individual is agitated after initial treatment. They add that decreasing the dosage of antipsychotic medication is preferable to continuing antiparkinsonian medication.

For insomnia in the elderly, many physicians have found modest amounts of alcohol helpful. But when you prescribe antianxiety agents for this age group, whether or not primarily at night, informed opinion advises beginning treatment with very low dosages.

In conclusion, we believe that proper dosages of appropriate psychotropic drugs are sometimes indicated along with rational-emotive therapy. Whether or not you yourself prescribe medication, you will undoubtedly see cases where you think that combined drug therapy and RET may be called for. "But," you might say, "What if I get cases that I need to refer?"

Of all doctors, usually psychiatrists are most familiar with psychotropic medications. Pharmacotherapy is becoming something of a speciality of its own, though, and the best referral of this kind is generally to a psychiatrist who is considered a psychopharmacologist. However, a good number of nonpsychiatric physicians are interested and competent in prescribing psychoactive drugs, and of course would be suitable for these referrals.

So help your patients with RET, by all means! But at times you may also feel that medication is indicated. And evidence suggests that combined RET and appropriate drug therapy make a powerful mix that can substantially help your disturbed patients!

15
Helping People Get Vitally Absorbed in Life

Rational-emotive therapy, although it attempts to be practical, down-to-earth, and unmystical, overlaps in at least one important respect with some of the more religious or spiritual ways of life, because of its heavy emphasis on self-discipline and daily homework exercises. While many of the groups that advocate Zen Buddhist, Christian born-again, Sufi, Hasidic, or other "transcendental" pathways seem to be full of crackpotism, they also urge their devotees to go through rigorous rituals and disciplines, and it is to be wondered whether it is not mainly these disciplines, rather than the mystical outlook of these groups, that actually help their followers to achieve the happiness and relative freedom from anxiety that they sometimes gain.

Be that as it may, RET distinctly espouses a highly disciplined, work-oriented point of view. For, peculiarly enough, most humans had better work to be happy. They *naturally* and *easily* give themselves a hard time and bring on themselves needless feelings of anxiety, depression, and hostility. They are helped in this respect by their parents, their teachers, and their culture. But, even during their days of childhood "innocence," they have a remarkable talent for thinking crookedly and emoting miserably. And they require an appreciable amount of self-discipline and steady hard work to over-come their innate self-defeating tendencies.

When, using RET or other effective methods of undoing their self-destructive thoughts and behaviors, people acquire a "good" (meaning, efficient and self-helping) philosophy, they still do not become automatically productive or happy. The mere fact that they no longer interfere with their own satisfactions does not insure their achieving their full potential and does not necessarily propel them into finding maximum happiness. Some of them, fortunately, do beautifully in this respect. They come for psychotherapy because they are emotionally bottled up by their feelings of potential or actual panic; they work at ridding themselves of their blocks, with the help of an efficient therapist; and then they quickly and easily find different kinds, and sometimes several kinds, of creative and productive outlets, and easily have a "ball," in their own inimitable ways, for the rest of their days.

Some—but hardly all! A great many other "successful" psy-chotherapy patients also rid themselves of their needless emotional difficulties, and live much less miserable existences, but still lead relatively dull, unfulfilled lives. They theoretically could find for themselves a better, more enjoyable existence, but they just don't—or, because of some remaining low frustration tolerance, won't.

Effective psychotherapy, therefore, often has two distinct parts: first, the basic and almost necessary part that helps people see exactly what they are doing to upset themselves and maintain their disturbances, and then to stop doing it; and second, a self-actualizing part that encourages them, and sometimes trains them, to fulfill themselves and enjoy themselves more. RET, as you can note throughout this book, specializes in the first of these two modes of psychotherapy, and its aim is to be as efficient in this respect as is possible, or at least feasible. But it also includes a second and more "self-actualizing" part, which consists of meth-ods of helping your patients to focus on and accentuate the good-ness of living so that, through positive as well as antinegative methodologies, they will enjoy themselves considerably more and leave themselves relatively little time and energy for self-inflicted pain. In this final chapter, we shall discuss this other, more self-actualizing side of RET, and show you what you can do to help your patients, or at least some of them, increase their creativity and delight.

A Philosophy of Long-range Hedonism

Like many other philosophies of life that have been espoused at various times in human history, RET is frankly hedonistic. It is sometimes falsely accused, in fact, of being an irresponsible, Epicurean, or Dionysian orientation, since it starts with the premise that humans wish to stay alive and be happy and that, since these are their basic goals, psychotherapy had better help them achieve these goals.

RET is prejudiced in favor of human happiness. But as I [A.E.] frequently tell my audiences when I speak to professional and lay groups throughout the world, Epicureanism posits the view that one had better "eat, drink, and be merry, for tomorrow you may die." True, but also true: "tomorrow you'll most probably live and have a hangover!" Epicureanism or short-range hedonism, therefore, has its distinct limitations. It rightly emphasizes pleasure or happiness at this moment, in the here-and-now. But it forgets that no one lives for a moment, and the Epicurean's future life—and many years of it!—may be somewhat grim and *un*happy if he or she only stresses immediate gratification.

Without encouraging ascetic or overdisciplined extremes, therefore, RET espouses long-range rather than short-range hedonism. Using it, you will therefore encourage your patients to fully accept their existence, to do their best to have a good time, to enjoy themselves, and to be quite unapologetic about normal pleasure seeking. In all probability, they will only live for about three-quarters of a century—and hardly forever! They'd consequently better take advantage of the one life they will ever have!

Long-range hedonism (alas and alack!) includes a good deal of discipline and hard work. For it is hard to refrain from too much eating and drinking today, in order to have a slim body and a clear mind tomorrow. And it is difficult to do rigorous exercises daily so that one can have maximum pleasure at sports, sex, and even relatively sedentary pursuits like painting or writing a book for a good many years to come. Difficult and hard, yes, but more difficult and harder if one does not force oneself to do certain onerous things now in order to maximize ones' enjoyments later.

If you can motivate your patients to be long-range rather than short-range hedonists, that will help them not only live longer but live better. For if they work—yes, w-o-r-k—at keeping themselves happier tomorrow as well as today, they will have greater incentive and greater likelihood of staying alive and seeking for new and more enjoyable experiences.

When people are motivated to fulfill themselves in the present and the future, they are not too likely to worry too much about death, and, to the degree that they are reasonably concerned about dying prematurely, they will probably take preventive measures to insure a longer life and more easily follow the medical prescriptions that are made for them. And they will tend to spend relatively little time inventing exaggerated worries about their health or about almost anything else!

Vital Absorbing Interest

Almost all humans, as noted in *A New Guide to Rational Living*, feel much better and lead a happier existence when they have some vital absorbing interest. This, again, is probably why some of the seemingly nutty religious creeds and crazy psychotherapies work wonders for some individuals, though the rest of us cannot figure out how they could do anyone any good. Their devotees not only devoutly subscribe to these views, which are rather constructive and far better than their earlier anxiety-creating and depressing outlooks, but they also become dedicated to *following* and *promoting* these creeds. And it is probably the zealously followed *life* they lead, rather than the validity of the creeds they follow, that takes them away from obsession with their own navels, and keeps them fairly happy.

Instructive in this connection is the testimony of P.D. Ouspensky, who for eight years studied with Georges Gurdjieff, one of the outstanding Westerners who have tried to translate the wisdom of the East into practical rules for Europeans and Americans to follow. As Ouspensky makes quite clear in his book, *In Search of the Miraculous*, Gurdjieff became quite an extremist toward the end of his life, and led his small band of followers into more and more bizarre pathways. He taught them to believe in angels and archangels; said that he could make himself invisible; held that everything (yes, *everything*) in the universe is alive and intelligent; claimed that no person could change himself or herself but had to become utterly dependent on and obedient to a leader or guru; invented physical exercises which he encouraged his followers to do for hours and literally for days at a time; thought that through astrology one could understand the essence of people; required the observance of all religious forms and ceremonies (when he had previously required nothing of the sort); and behaved personally in such a bizarre manner that Ouspensky got quite turned off to him and quit his group after eight years of intensive work with Gurdjieff. In spite of this extremism with his students, Gurdjieff seemed to hold their allegiance, to get most of them to devotedly follow his fanatical teachings, and many of them seemed to feel much better and to benefit from their devotion to his cause. As far as we can see, this was not because of the validity of the content of his teachings—many of which appear to have been as unbalanced as one could possibly make them—but because of their vital absorption in the rituals and the activity that he required of them.

We do not advocate, of course, that you encourage your own patients to become absorbed in some crackpot notions that will keep them vitally interested in ritualistic activity for the rest of their lives. This kind of preoccupation may well do more harm than good, especially in the long run. But many saner and wiser possibilities for vital absorption are available. For example, they can be greatly involved in creating and rearing a family for a good number of years; in raising funds for medical research; in writing stories, novels, or plays; in working for a political cause; or in pursuing a number of other complex activities. As long as they select projects that are fairly large, that require considerable energy, attention, and intelligence, and that last for a fairly long period of time, they will tend to focus on such interests, enjoy themselves participating in them, and distract themselves from a large number of potential anxieties and hostilities.

Social Interest. As Alfred Adler pointed out many years ago, although it is not absolutely necessary that people have strong social interest—for they can live happily, if they work at doing so, with a minimum of contact with others—it is usually highly desirable that they relate to other humans in general and to at least a few in particular. For you will find that your disturbed patients are frequently highly autistic, that is, abnormally centered in themselves, their own doings, and what others think of them. They may say that they have a strong desire to form intimate relationships with other people, but they are so into themselves, and so much in dire need of the approval or love of others, that they actually relate poorly, and wind up with no intimacies or an abortive series of social ties.

Not that social interest itself is a panacea for human disturbance; it isn't. For you may have patients who either become too absorbed in a single relationship, and are utterly dependent on the success of this relationship to feel good about themselves; and you may also have other patients who get absorbed in an intimate way with no one, because they are compulsively being the life of the party all the time, and flitting from one superficial group contact to another. Both these types of individuals may, in their own way, be socially involved, but not very happily or maturely. And the misery of both tends to stem from the same basic *must*urbatory philosophy, namely, "I *must* have this person (or those people) totally love me, and isn't it *horrible* if he/she (or they) don't!" This kind of obsession with *being* approved or loved can stand greatly in the way of one's *loving* or truly *relating* to others. Also, potential partners to whom these love slobs *have to* relate soon tend to discover their dire neediness, and to want to be a thousand miles away from them. So they, the love slobs, end up feeling alienated and lonely, and then, often, being even more desperate for others' approval.

You had better, therefore, not merely help your patients to relate sexually and nonsexually to other humans but to maintain their social interests on a wishing and preferring rather than on a dire need basis. To encourage them to find some person or group to devote themselves to, and to be absorbed in, is fine. But they need not put this individual or group on a pedestal significantly above themselves, and they do not *have to* maintain inalterably perfect relations with whomever they care for.

Your patients do not have to, moreover, fulfill themselves with one-to-one relationships. They can also devote themselves to a political organization, a health organization, an agency for the handicapped, a social organization, a group of underprivileged children, or a sports group. Such interests will often tend to be helpful to their community. But aside from their philanthropic aspect, they will often be of great benefit to the individual who devotes himself or herself to such social pursuits.

Health care itself can be something of a social interest, as well as a personal involvement. In the course of walking or participating in sports or gym activities people may easily meet and relate to others. And one of the most social of interests consists of helping with an antismoking, weight-reducing, or disease prevention or treatment campaign. This kind of social involvement can help keep your patients from worrying needlessly about their own health and can serve as a vitally absorbing interest that will encourage them to remain health-conscious and promote their own preventive programs.

Adventurousness and Experimentalism

As you help your patients accept the fact that they have a limited existence and will hardly live forever, you can also encourage them to work at making their days more adventurous. They can look for new things to do, overcome boring repetitiveness and low-level routines, learn more about what they really like and dislike, take exciting risks, and otherwise live more fully and put more of a premium on active living.

You can also help them to adopt a more experimental attitude toward life. For when they experiment with different ways of enjoying themselves, openmindedly try to discover more about what they really want and do not want to do, and try various alternative modes of existing rather than only the conventional ones that they were reared with, they thereby tend to discover more about themselves and are more likely to find absorbing pastimes and occupations.

When people are adventurous and experimental, they tend to have little time to make themselves anxious and despairing. They can, instead, spend more energy figuring out how to overcome their groundless fears. Thus, they can experiment with medically recommended activities, to see if any of them abet a less frightened approach to overcoming poor health.

Experimentation also implies a higher degree of risk taking. If your patients keep trying this kind of thinking or that plan of action, they will get into the habit of chancing certain inconveniences and possible failures, and will not hesitate to try sensible health-improving plans and projects, especially those that may at first seem unpleasant but will later lead to more satisfying results.

Acquiring Problem-solving Attitudes

If your patients try problem-solving approaches to their health difficulties, they will often tend to figure out novel and better solutions. If they explore new ways of reacting, they will view their health-related complications as interesting puzzles to be solved, will figure out ways of enjoying some of these hassles, and will tend to have better results.

If, for example, one of your middle-aged female patients is a hypochondriac, you can suggest a problem-solving attack on her health-related fears that may include reading books and articles on health, taking a good nutritional approach, learning about new methods of medical diagnosis, going for regular individual or group psychotherapy, or trying other new pathways. What are some of the alternatives she can explore? Which may produce better results? Which will prove less costly to her?

Problem solving can not only be efficient, but enjoyable. Why do so many people play bridge, chess, checkers, or therapist to others? Because they *like* the kinds of problem solving that are inherent in these pursuits. Similarly, you can help your patients *like* the kind of problem solving that helps them come up with answers to their own difficulties, and of those to whom they relate.

This is particularly true when you teach your patients RET. For if they really understand the A-B-C's of RET, and how to go on to D and Dispute their own irrational Beliefs (iB's), they will usually learn to enjoy doing this kind of discovering and unraveling of their irrationalities. Many of them will equally enjoy seeing how irrational their friends, relatives, and business or professional associates are, and how they can help them see and overcome their special irrational ideas. The senior author of this book [A.E] found, when bringing out one of the very first RET publications, *How to Live With a "Neurotic,"* that most intelligent people could learn how to handle their neurotic associates and, moreover, to help these people with some of their emotional problems—if they followed the RET procedures outlined in the book.

By the same token, you can help many of your patients enjoy the emotional problem solving that they do with the RET approach. You will probably find, as we do, that a number of them will even make a vital absorbing interest of RET, and use it continually with the people with whom they closely associate. This may have its limitations, since an enthusiast of RET may act somewhat obnoxiously, and turn others off. For the most part, however, it seems to have distinct advantages, and we have consistently found that if you teach your patients RET procedures, those who use it most often with others also tend to apply it well to themselves. The main point we are making here, however, is that a problem-solving approach to life can be both instructive and enjoyable. So if you help your patients acquire this kind of attitude, you may doubly or triply help them.

Work and Practice

As noted at the beginning of this chapter, you had better help your patients accept the fact that they are probably not going to become highly proficient at anything, including, ironically, enjoying themselves, without a great deal of work and practice. Everyone seems to admit this about pleasure-giving sports. Today, for example, millions of people become proficient at a sport like tennis mainly because they fully accept the reality that no matter how inherently talented they are and no matter how much they want to be a good player, only many months or years of effort and practice will make them even passably good.

The problem is that relatively few people accept this same dictum about proficiency at other kinds of pleasures. To do well at virtually anything, humans almost always have to keep working at it for a fairly long period of time. Then they may finally start enjoying it automatically or "spontaneously." But not at the beginning!

So, along with a philosophy of pleasure seeking, you had better help your patients also acquire an acceptance of the desirability of *working* at pleasure seeking. This philosophy of working for pleasure includes several important aspects for your patients to understand:

1. They had better work at overcoming their fears of certain pastimes, such as, say, sports, sex, painting, or fiction writing. Frequently, people refuse to pursue these kinds of enjoyments, even though they have dreamed about trying them for years, because they demand that they *must* do well if they did try them and that it would be *horrible* if they did poorly. Using the regular methods of RET outlined in this book, you can help your patients give up their *must*urbation and awfulizing about failing at various pleasurable pursuits, and encourage them to work at antiawfulizing procedures.

2. They can accept the fact that even pleasure frequently requires work. This is particularly true of activities like exercise, sports, painting, writing, and social activities. To get really adept at these kinds of involvements and to get to the point where they *flow* and one gets absorbed in them usually takes an initial, and sometimes prolonged, period of pushing and pushing oneself. One first laboriously and hesitatingly wields a tennis racket, paint brush, or chairperson's gavel. *Later* it becomes familiar and easy—but not for awhile!

3. They had better acknowledge and accept their own uniqueness and individuality. The mere fact that many or most people enjoy Bach or rock and roll does not mean that any one of your particular patients is in this large category. He or she may hate Bach and rock and roll, and thoroughly enjoy Gregorian chants or jazz.

For your patients to find what they truly prefer often requires a great deal of exploration and selectivity on their part. Only trial and error may, in this respect, win the day. One of my [A.E.] patients who said that she could not think of anything interesting to do in life finally, after persistent goading on my part, became devoted to painting children, which she had never previously tried because she said she "couldn't stand" their fidgeting around. One of my [E.A.] patients who could not engage in sports any more, because of a bad back, and said that he could not possibly think of anything else to enjoy, finally became almost obsessively preoccupied with popular songwriting. Both these individuals had to try several other interests, and definitely discard them, before they selectively discovered the one that really fit their own particular bents.

4. Becoming involved with a vital absorbing interest frequently requires a great deal of thought and experimentation. Some people, for example, would thoroughly enjoy breeding horses or dogs, but do not have the money or the space to do so. Others have to give up their main interest in life because they do not like the kind of people who are usually associated with it, are too old to get the required training for it, would have to devote more time to it than they can really afford, or have various other practical reasons. Your patients, therefore, had better select the involvements that are not merely possible but also feasible in their individual cases.

5. Many people block themselves from becoming vitally absorbed in some particular pursuit because they view it as "trivial," "unimportant," or "not contributing to human welfare." These individuals have preconceived notions of what kind of involvements they *should* (or their friends and associates *think* they should) have. You can help such people to fully accept the fact that they are here because they are here, and that they do not apologetically have to have any *special* reason for their existence. They are entitled to enjoy just about anything that they want—as long as they do not cause needless harm or interfere with other humans in the process. They can work, therefore, at unequivocally, unconditionally accepting their own enjoyments just *because* they enjoy them. And they can surrender any puritanical or self-sacrificing notions of doing things that they *should* or *must* do because these pursuits are "proper," "respectable," or "noble."

6. You can help some of your patients discover and maintain their interests in vocational or avocational endeavors that tend to be healthful rather than inimical to their lives and limbs. If they want to go skiing, and risk a broken leg in the process, that is their

prerogative—as long as they know what the dangers are. Even if they have certain diseases or ailments, such as diabetes or a bad back, they can still involve themselves in various sports or other participations that have dangerous elements for someone like them. But as a health care professional, you can certainly advise them of their limitations, and show them the advisability of placing some reasonable restrictions on themselves. People with paranoid tendencies had better watch how much marijuana they smoke. Those with heart ailments had better think carefully about entering running marathons. Many people can well be advised to avoid extremely cold, or, as the case may be, extremely sunny and hot temperatures.

On the other hand, some of your patients could well be encouraged to take up interests that would in all probability benefit their health, such as sports, outdoor activities, or certain sedentary preoccupations. Think over, in the cases of your individual patients, what kind of absorbing involvements would be better or worse for them, and see if you cannot sometimes help them to get with those that would be distinctly enjoyable as well as health-enhancing. This may require some work on both of your parts, but work and practice are often the essence of maximum enjoyment.

A Final Word

As a health professional, you often have a unique part to play in the uncovering and alleviating of emotional disturbance. For many of your patients will be prone to bring out their problems about themselves and the world to you first, long before they think of talking to a psychiatrist, psychologist, or social worker. Not a few of them, in fact, will see you instead of going for psychological help, because they would much rather construe their problems as physical than mental and would highly prefer to take a pill or undergo some medical procedure than to deal with their own self-created disturbances.

You, therefore, are the first to hear about innumerable emotional difficulties. You, moreover, can easily ascertain that many or most of your patients with physical problems also worry intensely about these problems and thereby, once they are ailing, upset themselves and contribute to the exacerbation of their diseases or disorders. If you look carefully at the thinking and emoting of your patients, you may well find that the majority of them, and not merely a small minority, are and for many years have been easily upsettable.

Too bad—but not *awful*! If you first use some of the RET principles on yourself, you will accept this unpleasant reality and learn to cope with it effectively. Do some antiawfulizing of your own; give up your notion that you *must* know everything possible about emotional disturbance and about psychotherapy and that you *have to* thoroughly cure all of your patients all of the time of anything, physical or mental, that ails them. No one, including you, can do this. Watch your own perfectionism!

In a nonperfectionistic manner, then, use the various methods of RET and cognitive-behavior therapy that are outlined in this book. You will not necessarily be the most outstanding therapist in the world, but you often can be a damned good one—if you persist.

Many of your patients, you will find, will listen to what you say, agree that they are acting irrationally, and even contract with you to do homework assignments that will help them give up their irrationalities, and feel and act better. Well, they may agree, but this does not mean that they will actually *do* anything to help themselves. Some will and some will not. Some will partially, and some will help themselves with amazing thoroughness. You won't win them all!

Nevertheless, just as you would usually do in regard to your patients' physical ailments that you are helping to treat, keep going! Don't discourage yourself; don't think that things are hopeless. Encourage your patients to understand the theory and practice of RET, and have them keep on working at it. Persuade them to experiment, to see for themselves and not merely accept on your word, that they largely create their own emotional problems and that they therefore can understand what they are doing and to a great extent can uncreate these same problems. Show them that they have nothing to lose by trying to accept themselves and to change their dysfunctional behavior. Get them to read and listen to some of the RET material, such as the books, articles, and recordings distributed by the Institute for Rational Living, 45 East 65 St., New York, N.Y. 10021, and listed in the back of this book.

Don't strive for miracles and do accept your own limitations. As a health professional, you have lots of important things to do in life and are probably quite busy. The psychotherapy you do will usually be relatively brief and often partial. And some of your patients will be very difficult customers, who have severe disturbances and will do little to work at minimizing them. If you run into problems with these individuals, don't hesitate to recommend a competent psychiatrist, psychologist, or other psychotherapist who has more time available for them than you have. Naturally, we suggest that you refer to an active-directive, rational-emotive, cognitive-behavior therapist. But a good one from many other schools may also be helpful.

None of your patients has to be extremely upset about virtually anything that may happen in his or her life. Through a combination of tranquilizing, antidepressant, or other drugs, when indicated, on the one hand, and solidly taught RET, on the other hand, you can help many of them to get this exceptionally important idea into their heads. If you do, they will usually be well on the way to helping themselves considerably.

Try it and see!

BIBLIOGRAPHY

BIBLIOGRAPHY

We have included in the following list of references the main books and articles we consulted in writing this volume, as well as useful materials in the general field of self-help and in rational-emotive therapy (RET) and cognitive behavior therapy (CBT). We have included suggestions for further reading and for recorded material. We have placed a check mark (√) before those items that are recommended for reading by professionals in the field of health and mental health and have placed an asterisk (*) before those items that are recommended for reading or for listening for self-help purposes. Many of the items with a check mark or an asterisk are published or distributed by the Institute for Rational Living, 45 East 65th Street, New York, N.Y. 10021. The Institute will continue to make available these and other materials on RET and on rational living, as well as to sponsor talks, seminars, workshops, and other presentations in the area of human growth. Those interested can send for its current list of publications and events.

Abrahms, Eliot. Practical diagnosis and drug treatments in rational-emotive therapy. Second National Conference on Rational-Emotive Therapy. New York: Institute for Rational Living, 1979.

Abrahms, Eliot. Rational-emotive therapy: an extension of individual psychology. Workshop presented at North American Society of Adlerian Psychology, Annual Convention, May, 1978.

Abrahms, Eliot, Abell, Richard, & Woldenberg, Lee. Modern techniques: transactional analysis, cognitive therapy, and feeling therapy. Course presented at American Psychiatric Association Annual Meeting, May, 1978.

Adler, Alfred. *Understanding human nature.* New York: Fawcett World, 1968.

Adler, Alfred. *What life should mean to you.* New York: Putnam, 1974.

Adler, Alfred. *Superiority and social interest.* Edited by H. L. Ansbacher & R. R. Ansbacher. Evanston, Ill.: Northwestern University Press, 1964.

Alberti, R. E., & Emmons, M. L. *Your perfect right.* San Luis Obispo, Ca.: Impact, 1973.

√Ansbacher, Heinz L., & Ansbacher, R. R. *The individual psychology of Alfred Adler.* New York: Harper & Row, 1970.

√Ard, Ben N., Jr. *Counseling and psychotherapy.* Palo Alto, Ca.: Science and Behavior Books, 1976.

Arnold, Magda. *Emotion and personality.* New York: Columbia University Press, 1960.

Assagioli, Roberto. *Psychosynthesis.* New York: Viking, 1971.

√Bandura, Albert. *Principles of behavior modification.* New York: Holt, 1969.

Bandura, Albert. *Aggression: a social learning analysis.* Englewood Cliffs, N.J.: Prentice-Hall, 1973.

√Bannister, D. & Mair, J. M. *The evaluation of personal constructs.* New York: Academic Press, 1968.

Barksdale, L. S. *Self-esteem.* Los Angeles: Barksdale Foundation, 1977.

Barlow, David H., Abel, Gene F., & Blanchard, Edward B. Gender identity change in a transsexual: an exorcism. *Archives of Sexual Behavior,* 1977, *6,* 387–395.

√Beck, Aaron T. *Cognitive therapy and the emotional disorders.* New York: International Universities Press, 1976.

*Bedford, Stewart. *Instant replay.* New York: Institute for Rational Living, 1974.

Berne, Eric. *Games people play.* New York: Grove Press, 1964.

Berne, Eric. *What do you say after you say Hello?* New York: Grove Press, 1973.

Bernheim, Hippolyte. *Suggestive therapeutics.* New York: London Book Company, 1947.

Binder, V., Binder, A., & Rimland, B. *Modern therapies.* Englewood Cliffs, N.J.: Prentice Hall, 1976.

*Blazier, Dan. *Poor me, poor marriage.* New York: Vantage, 1975.

Bourland, D. David, Jr. A linguistic note: writing in E-prime. *General Semantics Bulletin,* 1965–1966, *32–33,* 111–114.

Briggs, Kenneth A. Dr. Norman Vincent Peale still an apostle of cheer. *New York Times,* January 2, 1978.

Brown, Barry M. The use of induced imagery in psychotherapy. Unpublished manuscript, 1967.

Cadoret, R. J., & King, L. J. *Psychiatry in primary care.* St. Louis: Mosby, 1974.

Cautela, Joseph R. Treatment of compulsive behavior by covert sensitization. *Psychological Record,* 1966, *16,* 33–41.

Cole, J. O. & Stotsky, B. A. Improving psychiatric drug therapy: A matter of dosage and choice. *Geriatrics,* 1974, *29,* 74–78.

*Comfort, Alex. *The joy of sex.* New York: Crown, 1972.

*Comfort, Alex. *More joy.* New York: Crown, 1975.

Coué, Emile. *My method.* New York: Doubleday, Page, 1923.

*Danysh, J. *Stop without quitting.* San Francisco: International Society for General Semantics, 1974.

Dejerine, J. & Gaukler, E. *Psychoneurosis and psychotherapy*. Philadelphia: Lippincott, 1913.

Dewey, John. *Human nature and conduct*. New York: Modern Library, 1930.

√Dewey, John. *Quest for certainty*. New York: Putnam, 1960.

Dickinson, Robert Latou. *Human sex anatomy*. Baltimore: Williams & Wilkins, 1933.

√DiGiuseppe, R. A., Miller, N. J., & Trexler, L. D. A review of rational-emotive therapy outcome studies. *Counseling Psychologist*, 1977, 7(1), 64–72.

√Dreikurs, Rudolf. *Psychodynamics, psychotherapy and counseling*. Chicago: Alfred Adler Institute, 1974.

*Dyer, Wayne. *Your erroneous zones*. New York: Avon, 1977.

Ellis, Albert. *The American sexual tragedy*. New York: Twayne, 1954. (Rev. ed. New York: Lyle Stuart and Grove Press, 1962.)

*Ellis, Albert. *How to live with a "neurotic."* New York: Crown, 1957. (Rev. ed. New York: Crown, 1975.)

*Ellis, Albert. *Sex without guilt*. New York: Lyle Stuart, 1958. (Rev. ed. New York: Lyle Stuart; Hollywood: Wilshire Books, 1965.)

*Ellis, Albert, *The art and science of love*. New York: Lyle Stuart, 1960. (Rev. ed.: New York: Lyle Stuart; Bantam Books, 1969.)

√Ellis, Albert. *Reason and emotion in psychotherapy*. New York: Lyle Stuart, 1962. (Paperback ed.: New York: Citadel Press, 1977.)

√Ellis, Albert. *John Jones. Recorded Interview with a male homosexual*. Orlando, Fla.: American Academy of Psychotherapists, 1964.

*√Ellis, Albert. *Rational-emotive psychotherapy*. Tape recording. New York: Institute for Rational Living, 1970.

*√Ellis, Albert. *Theory and practice of rational-emotive therapy*. Tape recording. New York: Institute for Rational Living, 1971.

√Ellis, Albert. *Growth through reason*. Palo Alto, Ca.: Science and Behavior Books, 1971. (Paperback ed.: Hollywood: Wilshire Books, 1974.)

*Ellis, Albert. *Solving emotional problems*. Tape recording. New York: Institute for Rational Living, 1972.

*Ellis, Albert. *The sensuous person*. New York: Lyle Stuart and New American Library, 1972.

*√Ellis, Albert. *Executive leadership: a rational approach*. New York: Citadel Press, 1972.

√Ellis, Albert. *A demonstration with a woman fearful of expressing emotions*. Filmed demonstration. Washington, D.C.: American Personnel and Guidance Association, 1973.

√Ellis, Albert. *A demonstration with a young divorced woman*. Filmed demonstration. Washington, D.C.: American Personnel and Guidance Association, 1973.

√Ellis, Albert. *A demonstration with an elementary school child*. Filmed demonstration. Washington, D.C.: American Personnel and Guidance Association, 1973.

*√Ellis, Albert. *Humanistic psychotherapy: the rational-emotive approach.* New York: Julian Press and McGraw-Hill Paperbacks, 1973.

*Ellis, Albert. *How to stubbornly refuse to be ashamed of anything.* New York: Institute for Rational Living, 1973.

*Ellis, Albert. The no cop-out therapy. *Psychology Today,* 1973, 7(2), 56–62.

√Ellis, Albert. *Rational-emotive psychotherapy.* Filmed interview with Dr. Thomas Allen. Washington, D.C.: American Personnel and Guidance Association, 1973.

√Ellis, Albert. *Rational-emotive psychotherapy applied to groups.* Filmed interview with Dr. Thomas Allen. Washington, D.C.: American Personnel and Guidance Association, 1973.

√Ellis, Albert. *RET and marriage and family counseling.* Tape recording. New York: Institute for Rational Living, 1973.

*Ellis, Albert. *Twenty-five ways to stop downing yourself.* Tape recording. New York: Institute for Rational Living, 1973.

*Ellis, Albert. *Twenty-one ways to stop worrying.* Tape recording. New York: Institute for Rational Living, 1973.

√Ellis, Albert. *Cognitive-behavior therapy.* Tape recording. New York: Institute for Rational Living, 1974.

*Ellis, Albert. *Rational living in an irrational world.* New York: Institute for Rational Living, 1974.

√Ellis, Albert. *The theory and practice of rational-emotive therapy.* Video tape recording. New York: Institute for Rational Living, 1974.

*√Ellis, Albert. *Disputing irrational beliefs (DIBS).* New York: Institute for Rational Living, 1974.

*Ellis, Albert. *Conquering the dire need for love.* Tape recording. New York: Institute for Rational Living, 1975.

*√Ellis, Albert. *Sex and the liberated man.* New York: Lyle Stuart, 1976.

*Ellis, Albert. *Conquering low frustration tolerance.* Tape recording. New York: Institute for Rational Living, 1976.

*√Ellis, Albert. *Fun as psychotherapy.* Tape recording. New York: Institute for Rational Living, 1977.

*Ellis, Albert. *I'd like to stop but . . . Dealing with addictions.* Tape recording. New York: Institute for Rational Living, 1977.

*Ellis, Albert. *A garland of rational songs.* Songbook. New York: Institute for Rational Living, 1977.

*Ellis, Albert. *A garland of rational songs.* Tape recording. New York: Institute for Rational Living, 1977.

*√Ellis, Albert. *How to live with—and without—anger.* New York: Reader's Digest Press, 1977.

*√Ellis, Albert. *Rational self-help report.* New York: Institute for Rational Living, 1977.

*Ellis, Albert. *How to master your fear of flying.* New York: Institute for Rational Living, 1977.

Ellis, Albert. Rational-emotive therapy. In Virginia Binder, Arnold Binder, & Bernard Rimland. *Modern therapies*. Englewood Cliffs, N.J.: Prentice-Hall, 1976.

√Ellis, Albert. Rational-emotive therapy: research data that supports the clinical and personality hypotheses of RET and other modes of cognitive-behavior therapy. *Counseling Psychologist*, 1977, 7(1), 2–42.

√Ellis, Albert. Rejoinder: elegant and inelegant RET. *Counseling Psychologist*, 1977, 7(1), 73–82.

Ellis, Albert & Abarbanel, Albert. *The encyclopedia of sexual behavior*. New York: Hawthorn Books, 1961. (New York: Aronson, 1971.)

√Ellis, Albert & Abrahms, Eliot. *Dialogues on RET*. Tape recording. New York: Aronson, 1978.

√Ellis, Albert & Abrahms, Eliot. *Rational-emotive therapy in the treatment of severe mental disorders*. Tape recording series. New York: BMA Publications, 1978.

Ellis, Albert & Abrahms, Eliot. Uses of rational-emotive therapy by psychiatrists. Course presented at American Psychiatric Association Annual Meeting, May, 1978.

√Ellis, Albert. & Grieger, Russell. *Handbook of rational-emotive therapy*. New York: Springer, 1977.

√Ellis, A. & Gullo, J. M. *Murder and Assassination*. New York: Lyle Stuart, 1972.

*Ellis, Albert. & Harper, Robert A. *Creative marriage*. New York: Lyle Stuart, 1961. (Paperback, retitled: *A guide to successful marriage*. Hollywood: Wilshire Books, 1971.)

*√Ellis, Albert. & Harper, Robert A. *A new guide to rational living*. Englewood Cliffs, N.J.: Prentice-Hall, 1975. (Hollywood: Wilshire Books, 1975.)

*√Ellis, Albert & Knaus, William. *Overcoming procrastination*. New York: Institute for Rational Living, 1977.

*Ellis, Albert & Wholey, Dennis. *Rational-emotive psychotherapy*. Tape recorded interview. New York: Institute for Rational Living, 1970.

*Ellis, Albert, Wolfe, Janet L., & Moseley, Sandra. *How to prevent your child from becoming a neurotic adult*. New York: Crown, 1966. (Paperback edition, retitled: *How to raise an emotionally healthy, happy child*. Hollywood: Wilshire Books, 1972.)

Fay, Allen. The drug modality. In A. A. Lazarus (Ed.), *Multimodal behavior therapy*. New York: Springer, 1976.

Fay, Allen. *Making things better by making them worse*. New York: Hawthorn, 1978.

*Epictetus. *The works of Epictetus*. Boston: Little, Brown, 1890.

*Epictetus. *Enchiridion*. Indianapolis: Bobbs-Merrill, 1970.

Farrelly, F. & Brandsma, J. *Provocative therapy*. Millbrea, Ca.: Celestial Arts, 1974.

*Fensterheim, Herbert & Baer, Jean. *Don't say yes when you want to say no.* New York: Dell, 1975.

√Feshbach, Seymour. Dynamics and morality of violence and aggression. *American Psychologist,* 1971, *26,* 281–292.

√Frank, Jerome. D. *Persuasion and healing.* Rev. ed. Baltimore: Johns Hopkins University Press, 1973.

√Frankl, Viktor E. *Man's search for meaning.* New York: Washington Square Press, 1966.

Freud, Sigmund. *Standard edition of the complete psychological works of Sigmund Freud.* London: Hogarth, 1965.

√Friedman, Myles. *Rational behavior.* Columbia, S.C.: University of South Carolina Press, 1975.

Fromm, Erich. *The art of loving.* New York: Bantam, 1963.

*Garcia, Edward & Pellegrini, Nina. *Homer the homely hound dog.* New York: Institute for Rational Living, 1974.

√Glasser, William. Reality therapy. New York: Harper & Row, 1964.

√Goldfried, Marvin R. & Davison, Gerald C. *Clinical behavior therapy.* New York: Holt, 1976.

*Goodman, David & Maultsby, Maxie C., Jr. *Rational well-being through rational behavior training.* Springfield, Ill.: Charles C. Thomas, 1974.

Goodwin, F. K. & Ebert, M. H. Specific antimanic and antidepressant drugs. In Jarvik, M.E. (Ed.), *Psychopharmacology in the practice of medicine.* New York: Appleton, 1977.

Goodwin, F. K. Drug treatment of affective disorders: general principles. In Jarvik, M. E. (Ed.), *Psychopharmacology in the practice of medicine.* New York: Appleton, 1977.

*Greenburg, Dan. *How to make yourself miserable.* New York: Random House, 1966.

√Greenwald, Harold. *Active psychotherapies.* New York: Atherton, 1967.

√Greenwald, Harold. *Decision therapy.* San Diego: Edits, 1977.

*Grossack, Martin. *You are not alone.* Boston: Marlborough, 1974.

*Grossack, Martin. *Love, sex, and self-fulfillment.* New York: New American Library, 1978.

Group for the Advancement of Psychiatry. *Pharmacotherapy and psychotherapy: paradoxes, problems and progress.* New York: Mental Health Materials Center, 1975.

√Haley, Jay. *Problem solving therapy.* San Francisco: Jossey-Bass, 1976.

Harper, Robert A. *Psychoanalysis and psychotherapy: 36 systems.* Englewood Cliffs, N.J.: Prentice-Hall, 1959.

Harper, Robert A. *The new psychotherapies.* Engelwood Cliffs, N.J.: Prentice-Hall, 1975.

*√Harper, Robert A. & Ellis, Albert. *A tape-recorded interview.* Tape recording. Orlando, Fla.: American Academy of Psychotherapists, 1974.

√Hartman, William & Fithian, Marilyn A., *Treatment of sexual dysfunction.* Long Beach, Calif.: Center for Marital and Sexual Studies, 1972.

*Hauck, Paul A. *Overcoming depression.* Philadelphia: Westminster Press, 1972.

√Hauck, Paul A. *Reason in pastoral counseling.* Philadelphia: Westminster Press, 1972.

*Hauck, Paul A. *Overcoming frustration and anger.* Philadelphia: Westminster Press, 1974.

*Hauck, Paul A. *Overcoming worry and fear.* Philadelphia: Westminster Press, 1975.

*Hauck, Paul A. *The rational management of children.* 2nd ed. New York: Libra, 1976.

*√Hayakawa, S. I. *Language in action.* New York: Harcourt, Brace and World, 1965.

*Heiman, Julia, LoPiccolo, Leslie, & LoPiccolo, Joseph. *Becoming orgasmic: a sexual growth program for women.* Englewood Cliffs, N.J.: Prentice-Hall, 1976.

√Herzberg, Alexander. *Active psychotherapy.* New York: Grune & Stratton, 1945.

Hollister, L. E. Drugs for treating affective disorders. In Modell, W. (Ed.), *Drugs of choice.* Chapter 12. St. Louis: Mosby, 1978.

Homme, Lloyd. *How to use contingency contracting in the classroom.* Champaign, Ill.: Research Press, 1969.

√Horney, Karen. *Collected Writings.* New York: Norton, 1972.

Hudson, Liam. Quoted in Evans, Peter, A visit with Liam Hudson. *APA Monitor,* 1978, *9*(1), 6–7.

*Jacobsen, Edmund. *You must relax.* New York: Pocket Books, 1958.

Johnson, Wendell. *People in quandaries.* New York: Harper & Row, 1946.

Jung, C. G. *The practice of psychotherapy.* New York: Pantheon, 1954.

√Kaplan, Helen. S. *The new sex therapy.* New York: Brunner/Mazel, 1974.

√Kelly, George. *The psychology of personal constructs.* New York: Norton, 1954.

*Kiev, Ari. *A strategy for daily living.* New York: Free Press, 1973.

√Kinsey, Alfred C., Pomeroy, Wardell B., Martin, Clyde E., & Gebhard, Paul H. *Sexual behavior in the human female.* Philadelphia: Saunders, New York: Pocket Books, 1953.

Klein, D. F. The importance of diagnosis: an analysis and program. In Klein, D. F., & Davis, J. M. *Diagnosis and drug treatment of psychiatric disorders.* Baltimore: Williams and Wilkins, 1969.

Klerman, G. L., DiMascio, A., Weisman, M., et al. Treatment of depression by drugs and psychotherapy. *American Journal of Psychiatry,* 1974, *131,* 186–191.

√Knaus, William. *Rational-emotive education.* New York: Institute for Rational Living, 1974.

√Korzbyski, Alfred. *Science and sanity.* Lancaster, Pa.: Lancaster Press, 1933.

Krafft-Ebing, Richard von. *Psychopathia sexualis.* New York: Stein and Day, 1965.

*Kranzler, Gerald. *You can change how you feel.* Eugene, Ore.: Author, 1974.

Kurz, Paul, *Exuberance.* Buffalo: Prometheus Books, Hollywood: Wilshire Books, 1977.

√Lange, Arthur & Jakubowski, Patricia. *Responsible assertive behavior.* Champaign, Ill.: Research Press, 1976.

√Lazarus, Arnold A. *Behavior therapy and beyond.* New York: McGraw-Hill, 1971.

√Lazarus, Arnold A. *Multimodal behavior therapy.* New York: Springer, 1976.

*Lazarus, Arnold A. & Fay, Allen. *I can if I want to.* New York: Morrow, 1976.

*Lembo, John M. *Help yourself.* Niles, Ill.: Argus, 1974.

√Lembo, John M. *The counseling process: a rational behavioral approach.* New York: Libra, 1976.

*Lembo, John M. *How to cope with your fears and frustrations.* New York: Libra, 1977.

Liberman, R. P., King, L. W., DeRisi, W. J., & McCann, M. *Personal effectiveness.* Champaign, Ill: Research Press, 1977.

*Little, Bill L. *This will drive you sane.* Minneapolis: CompCare, 1977.

√Mahoney, M. J. *Cognition and behavior modification.* Cambridge, Mass. Ballinger, 1974.

Marks, I. M. The origins of phobic states. *American Journal of Psychotherapy,* 1972, *24,* 652–676.

*√Marcus Aurelius. *Meditations.* Boston: Little, Brown, 1890.

√Masters, William H. & Johnson, Virginia E. *Human sexual inadequacy.* Boston: Little, Brown, 1970.

*Maultsby, Maxie C., Jr. *Help yourself to happiness.* New York: Institute for Rational Living, 1975.

*Maultsby, Maxie C., Jr. Overcoming irrational fears. Tape recordings. Chicago: Human Development, 1973.

√Maultsby, Maxie C., Jr. & Ellis, Albert. *Technique for using rational-emotive imagery.* New York: Institute for Rational Living, 1974.

*Maultsby, Maxie C., Jr. & Hendricks, Allie. *Cartoon booklets.* Lexington, Kentucky: Rational Behavior Training Center, 1974.

√McCary, James Leslie. *Human sexuality.* 2nd ed. New York: Van Nostrand, 1973.

√Meichenbaum, Donald. *Cognitive behavior modification.* New York: Plenum, 1977.

Moreno, J. L. *Who shall survive?* Washington, D. C.: Nervous and Mental Disease Publishing Co., 1934.

√Morris, Kenneth T. & Kanitz, H. Mike. *Rational-emotive therapy.* Boston: Houghton Mifflin, 1975.

Newhorn, Paula. Profile: Albert Ellis. *Human Behavior,* 1978, *7*(1), 30–35.

Ouspensky, P. D. *In search of the miraculous.* New York: Harcourt, Brace & World, 1949.

Peale, Norman Vincent. *The power of positive thinking.* Greenwich, Conn.: Fawcett, 1962.

Perls, Frederick C. *Gestalt therapy verbatim.* Lafayette, Ca.: Real People Press, 1969.

√Phillips, E. Lakin. *Psychotherapy.* Englewood Cliffs, N.J. Prentice-Hall, 1956.

Premack, David. Reinforcement theory. In D. Levine (Ed.), *Nebraska Symposium on Motivation.* Lincoln Neb.: University of Nebraska Press, 1965.

√Raimy, Victor. *Misunderstandings of the self.* San Francisco: Jossey-Bass, 1975.

Reich, Wilhelm. *Character analysis.* New York: Orgone Institute Press, 1949.

Reichenbach, Hans. *The rise of scientific philosophy.* Berkeley: University of California Press, 1953.

Rickels, K. Drug treatment of anxiety. In Jarvik, M. E. (Ed.), *Psychopармacology in the practice of medicine.* New York: Appleton, 1977.

√Rimm, David C. & Masters, John C. *Behavior therapy.* New York: Academic Press, 1974.

Robie, W. F. *The art of love.* New York: Rational Life Press, 1925.

√Rogers, C. R. *On becoming a person.* Boston: Houghton Mifflin, 1961.

√Rokeach, Milton. *The nature of human values.* New York: Free Press, 1973.

*Russell, Bertrand. *The conquest of happiness.* New York: Bantam, 1968.

√Salter, Andrew. *Conditioned reflex therapy.* New York: Capricorn Books, 1949.

√Schiller, Patricia. *Creative approach to sex education and counseling.* New York: Association Press, 1973.

√Semans, J. H. Premature ejaculation. *Southern Medical Journal,* 1956, *49,* 353–358.

√Shelton, John L., & Ackerman, J. Mark. *Homework in counseling and psychotherapy.* Springfield, Ill.: Charles C. Thomas, 1974.

√Shibles, Warren. *Emotion.* Whitewater, Wisc.: Language Press, 1974.

Singer, Jerome L. *Imagery and daydream methods in psychotherapy and behavior modification.* New York: Academic Press, 1974.

√Skinner, B. F. *Beyond freedom and dignity.* New York: Knopf, 1971.

√Stampfl, Thomas & Levis, Donald. Phobic patients: treatment with the learning approach of implosive therapy. *Voices,* 1967, *3*(3), 23–27.

Sullivan, H. S. *Conceptions of modern psychiatry.* New York: Norton, 1953.

√Thorne, F. C. *Principles of personality counseling.* Brandon, Vt.: Journal of Clinical Psychology Press, 1950.

*Tillich, Paul. *The courage to be.* New York: Oxford, 1953.

√Tosi, Donald J. *Youth: toward personal growth, a rational-emotive approach.* Columbus, Oh.: Merrill, 1974.

Van de Velde, Th. *Ideal marriage*. New York: Covici-Friede, 1926.

√Watzlawack, Paul, Weakland, John, & Fisch, Richard. *Change*. New York: Norton, 1974.

*Weekes, Claire. *Hope and help for your nerves*. New York: Hawthorn, 1969.

*Weekes, Claire. *Peace from nervous suffering*. New York: Hawthorn, 1972.

Wiener, Daniel N. & Stieper, D. R. *Dimensions of psychotherapy*. Chicago: Aldine, 1965.

Wolberg, Lewis R. *The technique of psychotherapy*. 3rd ed. New York: Grune & Stratton, 1977.

*Wolfe, Janet L. *Rational-emotive therapy and women's problems*. Tape recording. New York: Institute for Rational Living, 1974.

Wolfe, Janet L., Aggression vs. assertiveness. *Practical Psychology for Physicians*. 1975, 2 (1), 44.

√Wolfe, Janet L. Rational-emotive therapy as an effective feminist therapy. *Rational Living*, 1976, *11*(1), 2–7. (Reprinted: Institute for Rational Living, 1976.)

√Wolfe, Janet L. & Brand, Eillen. *Twenty years of rational therapy*. New York: Institute for Rational Living, 1977.

√Wolfe, Janet L. & Fodor, Iris G. A cognitive-behavioral approach to modifying assertive behavior in women. *Counseling Psychologist*, 1975, *5*(4), 45–52.

√Wolfe, Janet L. & Fodor, Iris G. Modifying assertive behavior in women: a comparison of three approaches. *Behavior Therapy*, 1977, *8*, 567–574.

Wolpe, Joseph. *Psychotherapy by reciprocal inhibition*. Stanford, Ca.: Stanford University Press, 1958.

Wolpe, Joseph & Lazarus, Arnold. *Behavior therapy techniques*. New York: Pergamon, 1966.

√Wolpe, Joseph. *The practice of behavior therapy*. 2nd. ed. New York: Pergamon, 1973.

*Young, Howard S. *A rational counseling primer*. New York: Institute for Rational Living, 1974.

INDEXES

NAME INDEX

SUBJECT INDEX